ESSENTIALS
of CHRISTIAN
THEOLOGY

"I can think of few matters more important for today's church than the serious study of solid theological truths for life and ministry. And I know of no better volume to assist in that study than *Essentials of Christian Theology: Foundations of the Christian Faith*, edited by colleagues Dr. Michael Svigel and Dr. Nathan Holsteen. This tool is not just a resource but a reality. Read it. Learn it—then live it."

Mark M. Yarbrough, PhD, president, Dallas Theological Seminary

"This is an ideal introduction to theology for readers who aren't quite sure what it is, what it's for, or why it's necessary. *Essentials of Christian Theology* is just that: a guide to what every disciple needs to know about doctrine in order to know God, understand Scripture, avoid error, and live to God's glory in the ongoing drama of redemption."

Kevin J. Vanhoozer, research professor of systematic theology,
Trinity Evangelical Divinity School

"This is the perfect resource for laying a foundation of Christian theology. Whether you are looking for material to use for personal growth, needing a book to disciple someone through, or teaching a class on the basics of Christian theology, this is the ideal book for you. By keeping the content accessible and clear, and addressing theology with a broad enough approach to be useful across typical denominational lines, Holsteen and Svigel have written a fantastically practical and utterly essential work. This should be on every Christian's shelf."

Adam Griffin, lead pastor, Eastside Community Church, Dallas, Texas;
host, *The Family Discipleship Podcast*

"It is rare to find a theological book that is both profoundly deep and incredibly practical. This book is an absolute must-read for believers eager to grasp a richer understanding of God and the foundational doctrines of their faith. Dr. Holsteen and Dr. Svigel do not just explain the essential pillars of the Christian faith; they inspire readers to live them out confidently. This book is destined to be a staple in my ministry for many years to come."

Michelle Clifford, author, *Pursuit Women's Discipleship Program*;
executive leader and minister, Scottsdale Bible Church

"*Essentials of Christian Theology* frames foundational biblical doctrines in a way that draws the reader into participating in the biblical story of creation, fall, redemption, and restoration. The authors stress at every corner that theology is 'faith seeking understanding'—not understanding clouded by presuppositions and stacks of educational diplomas, but understanding from God's self-revelation of Himself to humanity. This work is a primer that encourages life transformation through consistent study and application of God's Word, and it would be a valued introductory resource for churches and the Opened Bible Academy."

Tina Brown, cofounder and president, Opened Bible Academy

"An accurate, engaging, and practical presentation of what God wants us all to know. It's as simple as that! Drs. Svigel and Holsteen do us a beautiful service in presenting the core of Christian belief in such an accessible way. Grounded in Scripture, Christian doctrine is presented with helpful analogies, memorable illustrations, and practical guidance for life. This book is a one-stop spot for anyone wanting to grasp the essential doctrines of the Christian faith."

Dr. Jonathan Murphy, senior pastor, Stonebriar Community Church, Frisco, Texas; professor of pastoral ministries, Dallas Theological Seminary; author, *The Story of God and Us*

"If you think theology is purely theoretical, impractical, and detrimental to a vibrant life of following Jesus, *and* you want to leave those misconceptions unchallenged, this book is not for you. Through a combination of careful biblical interpretation, historical analysis, pastoral sensibility, humility, and humor, *Essentials of Christian Theology* introduces readers to the core doctrines of the faith. Holsteen and Svigel effectively demonstrate that theology is not an end in itself, but a vital means toward the end of heeding the greatest commandments, to love God with our whole selves and our neighbors as ourselves."

Keith W. Plummer, PhD, dean of the School of Divinity, Cairn University

FOUNDATIONS OF THE CHRISTIAN FAITH

ESSENTIALS

OF CHRISTIAN

THEOLOGY

NATHAN D. HOLSTEEN AND **MICHAEL J. SVIGEL, EDS.**

BETHANYHOUSE

a division of Baker Publishing Group
Minneapolis, Minnesota

© 2025 by Nathan D. Holsteen and Michael J. Svigel

Published by Bethany House Publishers
Minneapolis, Minnesota
BethanyHouse.com

Bethany House Publishers is a division of
Baker Publishing Group, Grand Rapids, Michigan

Printed in the United States of America

ISBN 9780764245602 (paper)
ISBN 9780764245619 (casebound)
ISBN 9781493451227 (ebook)

Library of Congress Cataloging-in-Publication Control Number: 2025020426

The contents of this book are adapted from the 3-volume *Exploring Christian Theology* trilogy, edited by Nathan D. Holsteen and Michael J. Svigel, with editorial contributions from John Adair, Douglas K. Blount, J. Lanier Burns, Nathan D. Holsteen, J. Scott Horrell, Glenn R. Kreider, and Michael J. Svigel.

This abridged edition includes additional editing consultation by John Adair and Glenn R. Kreider.

Cover design by Peter Gloege, Look Design Studio

The authors are represented by The Steve Laube Agency.

We dedicate this volume to our many students over the decades, who have challenged us, motivated us, inspired us, and provoked us to contend earnestly for the faith once for all handed down to the saints.

CONTENTS

INTRODUCTION

Mastering the Essentials of Christian Theology

What comes to mind when you hear the word *theology*?

If your ideas are less than positive, you're not alone. For a lot of people, "theology" conjures up a host of negative images:

- stacks of thick books filled with boring facts
- balding old men arguing about Latin words
- churches dividing over minor doctrinal differences
- monotonous droning on irrelevant issues

In short, when some people hear "theology," they turn away, walk away, or even run away. Instead, what most people want is simple biblical teaching, clear practical application, and a personal relationship with God. They want down-to-earth principles, not sky-high theories. They want to *know* God, not just know *about* Him.

Yet the fact is we can't know the true God without knowing God truly. We can't experience real spiritual growth without solid spiritual truth. That's where good theology comes in. Theology, rightly understood, is thinking and talking about God, His works,

11

and His ways.[1] This means anyone who ponders God or utters a word about Him is "doing theology." It's unavoidable. In a sense, then, everyone is a theologian. They're just either a bad theologian or a good theologian.

But if the goal is *good* theology, how do you start? How do you begin to harvest in the fruitful field of God's bountiful revelation without getting caught in the tangled underbrush of mere opinions? How can you sort through countless contradictory theories to find the essential truths necessary for strengthening and living out your faith?

With *Essentials of Christian Theology*, our goal is to not only help you master the essentials, but establish a foundation upon which you can build your faith with confidence. This book differs from other mini-theologies in that it strives to present broad consensus, not a condensed systematic model of one teacher or tradition. This means any Bible-believing church can not only recommend it for personal study and edification, but also use it for discipleship, catechism, membership or leadership preparation—even formal or informal theological instruction.

After a brief survey of the Bible's creation-fall-redemption narrative in the prelude, each of the next six, easy-to-read chapters covers a pillar of Christian doctrine. These chapters emphasize what most—if not all—Christians agree on while introducing you to some areas of disagreement.

Each chapter also contains the following elements:

- **"In Short . . ."** provides brief surveys of each doctrine with points of unity and diversity.
- **"Passages to Ponder"** explains key Scriptures related to each doctrine.
- **"Realities to Remember"** presents the foundational truths for each doctrine.
- **"Errors to Avoid"** exposes false teachings associated with the doctrine.

- **"Lessons to Live"** explores practical implications and applications for each doctrine.
- **"Snapshot of History"** summarizes the history and development of each doctrine.

Once you've laid a foundation of essential Christian theology with this book, you'll be equipped to build on it with more detailed study. In the Conclusion, we even suggest some ways you can do that. But for now, set aside any negative notions about theology. Soon you'll see that it doesn't have to be boring, contentious, divisive, or irrelevant. In no time, you'll be informed and transformed, challenged and changed, educated and edified.

And all you have to do is turn the page.

Nathan D. Holsteen and Michael J. Svigel

General Editors

PRELUDE

The Biblical Drama in Three Acts

No one would attempt to put on a play, film a movie, or shoot a TV series episode without an outline, plot, story arc, and more. In fact, most productions would never get a producer's green light without first securing a competent writer, a stable script, a reliable director, and a cast compelling enough to bring it all to life. Before the first action can even begin, certain aspects must be firmly established.

Theology is the story behind the Bible, the "documentary" shot behind the scenes—watching as the Author conceives of the plot and characters, writes the Script, and then sets the story into motion, He himself stepping on stage at the right moment to take the leading role.

As we explore this great drama, we find that God's story flows much like a classic "hero cycle,"[1] with which authors throughout history have gripped audiences by tapping into universal experiences—elements common to most or all individuals and cultures:

- an experience of personal conflict between good and evil
- frustration with the present world
- anxieties about the future
- a sense of greater purpose and meaning
- the hope that someday things will be better

A Typical Hero Cycle

PARADISE
(Life)

REDEMPTION
(Ascent)

FALL
(Descent)

HELL
(Death)

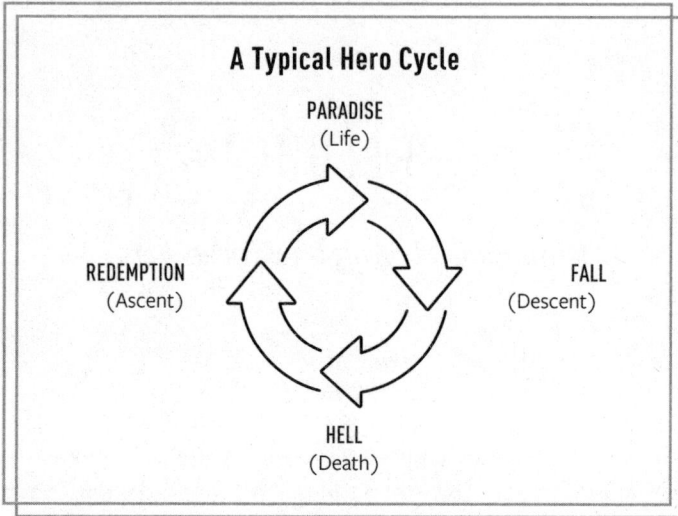

Our well-known stories of initiation, fall, struggle, testing, redemption, and ultimate victory put into words, portray on stage, or project on screen the unconscious realities we feel in our hearts. Our favorite movies or books are "favorites" because they touch on themes related to this cycle that resonate with our own lived experiences. They "speak" to us, inviting us to enter a larger story that transcends our lonely individualism and deteriorating world.[2]

Reminiscent of the hero cycle (with some astonishing twists), the chronicle of the classic Christian faith is a captivating account that can be summed up in three acts:

  I: Creation (Paradise)
 II: Fall (Descent), resulting in Hell (Death)
III: Redemption (Ascent), resulting in Restoration (Paradise)

God's Story: From the Garden to Glory

CREATION
(Paradise)

RESTORATION
(Paradise)

FALL
(Descent)

REDEMPTION
(Ascent)

HELL
(Death)

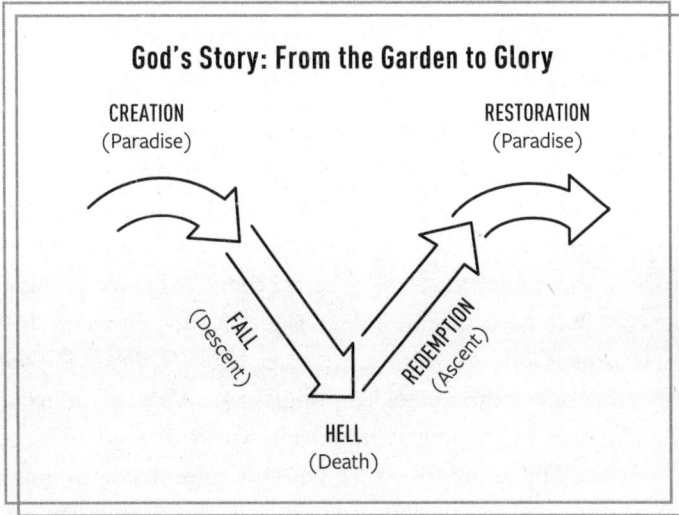

Act I: Creation

If a composer were to write a score for the Old Testament, what kind of musical motifs would they employ? Gentle harps and melodic strings? Majestic trumpets? Delightful woodwinds or pounding drums? Through whatever means, the theme would probably begin with a burst of symphonic grandeur, followed by a flourish of interwoven melodies signifying the creation of heaven and earth in glorious perfection.

As this bold overture resolved into a blissful ballad, however, a dark and ominous minor chord would slither into the melody, eventually turning the key from major to minor. Perhaps replacements would be sent in, like oboes and bassoons for flutes and piccolos, bass drums for xylophones, cellos and basses for violins and harps, and tubas for trumpets. We'd hear harsh, discordant notes.

Even so, amid this cacophony, hints of the original beauty, majesty, and power would occasionally break through, promising to reemerge and eventually—ultimately—triumph.

What in words is the theme of the Old Testament? *The tragic fall of a perfect creation followed by judgment and the promise of final redemption.*

Genesis 1–2 stunningly depicts the original creation of the heavens, the earth, all living things, and humankind. The story begins not with competing deities or an absolute nothingness, but with *God*: "In the beginning God created the heavens and the earth" (Genesis 1:1). God, through His eternal Son and Spirit, created everything that exists—whether things in heaven or things on earth, "things . . . visible and invisible" (Colossians 1:15–16).

The triune God is the Author, Producer, Director, and lead Actor in the story of creation and redemption. And as Master Storyteller, He has made himself known through His works of creation (Psalm 19:1–2) and His written Word (2 Timothy 3:16). He both shows and tells His power, His plan, and His purpose. Simply put, the great and mighty God is knowable and has made himself known:

> Long ago, at many times and in many ways, God spoke to our fathers by the prophets, but in these last days he has spoken to us by his Son, whom he appointed the heir of all things, through whom also he created the world. (Hebrews 1:1–2)

As the crowning work of His creation, God made humans, both male and female, and commissioned them as His co-regents with this mission: "Be fruitful and multiply and fill the earth and subdue it" (Genesis 1:28). God desired to share the stage of His production with these creatures He'd formed from earthly matter (Psalm 8:3–6). They were created in the "image of God"—that is, reflecting His glory and character and destined to rule as His representatives over creation (Genesis 1:26–30). As God's image-bearing envoys, humans were to work in the Paradise of Eden, cultivating it and ultimately extending its borders to cover the entire uncultivated earth (Genesis 2:7–25).

Act II: Fall

Alas, that state of innocence would not last. To test the first humans' trust and obedience, God permitted a devious foe to slither into the garden in the guise of a serpent (Genesis 3:1). We, the audience of the drama, now know the serpent was none other than Satan, the archnemesis of all that is good, holy, and true. That wicked being had once enjoyed an esteemed position in the presence of God, which he lost through pride and presumption (compare Isaiah 14:12–14). Then—as now—Satan wants nothing more than to see God's image-bearers follow his own fall into condemnation and death.

So with lying words that twisted God's truthful words, Satan, through the serpent, deceived the humans into disobeying God in the very Paradise where they'd enjoyed intimate fellowship with Him, their Creator (Genesis 3:1–6). As intelligent creatures given free will, those first two humans succumbed to temptation and turned their backs on God, forfeiting their role as His rulers over earth and falling victim to sin and death (Genesis 3:8–21).

From that day forward, Adam and Eve were plunged into an abiding curse—as were all their descendants, infecting every part of our lives and every part of our world. God said to Adam and through him to every human:

> Cursed is the ground because of you;
>> in pain you shall eat of it all the days of your life;
> thorns and thistles it shall bring forth for you;
>> and you shall eat the plants of the field.
> By the sweat of your face
>> you shall eat bread,
> till you return to the ground,
>> for out of it you were taken;
> for you are dust,
>> and to dust you shall return. (Genesis 3:17–19)

19

The blast wave of this disobedience resounds forward through all of human history, its devastating effects—murder, anarchy, destruction, and rebellion against God—illustrated in Genesis 4–11. Everyone today will admit that something is wrong with the world and the people in it. As the book of Ecclesiastes says, "Surely there is not a righteous man on earth who does good and never sins" (7:20) and "The hearts of the sons of men are full of evil and insanity is in their hearts throughout their lives" (9:3 NASB).

Thus, the first half of the story cycle is complete—from Paradise and life, through tragic fall, to an earthly state of living condemnation and then universal death.

Act III: Redemption

If we were to commission the same composer to score a New Testament sequel to the Old Testament part of the story, what kind of themes would we want? How does the continuation of the story in the New Testament relate to its beginnings in the Old?

The sequel's score would probably look like a mirror image of the initial themes. From darkness to light, from fall, judgment, and promises delayed to promises fulfilled, mercy and grace extended, and redemption realized. Discordant notes and chords would be replaced by a symphony of instruments and voices singing praises to our God and King. The nearly forgotten opening scenes of the prequel would be restored and then surpassed.

What, then, is the theme of the New Testament? *The long-awaited redemption of fallen humanity followed by the restoration and fulfillment of all God's promises and purposes.*

God did not abandon humankind to hopelessness. Already in Genesis 3, after the fall of Adam and Eve, He pledged that the offspring of the woman would bruise the serpent's head, ultimately destroying sin and evil (Genesis 3:15). He then advanced His plan of redemption through the calling of Abraham (Genesis 12), to whom He promised that a particular offspring would mediate blessings to the world (Genesis 13:15; Galatians 3:15–16). After this promise passed from Abraham through Isaac and Jacob to the tribe of Judah, it then narrowed to the dynasty of King David (Isaiah 9:2, 6–7).

The redemption plan continued to be revealed throughout the Old Testament Scriptures. Despite human failures—even of those to whom He'd given amazing guarantees of His presence and love— God remained faithful to His promises, ultimately sending the promised Offspring—His own divine Son (Luke 1:31–33; John 3:16).

As the plot unfolded, though, God's narrative took a world-shaking turn. Instead of following the cycle's upward path—the Hero passes through various trials, endures setbacks, and overcomes failures while pressing on toward His reward—God's Chosen One *retraced the descent*, surrendering His life to the executioner. The only being in human history who deserved never-ending life with God voluntarily suffered a brutal death (Philippians 2:5–8). Yet even this ironic fate had been foretold in the prophecies of Isaiah (Isaiah 53:4–6). Every twist and turn of the plot had been scripted centuries earlier.

Nevertheless, for God's matchless Hero, death was not the end.

Against all expectations, including those of His despairing followers, Jesus of Nazareth was raised from the grave and stepped out of the tomb more than alive—He was *glorified*. Having died in a mortal body susceptible to sickness, pain, and death, He was raised in a physical but immortal body incapable of illness, impervious to hurt, and overflowing with eternal life.

Furthermore, through Jesus Christ, God began writing history's final chapter. Those people who became united with Christ by placing their faith in Him could now partake of His glory too—sharing the Hero's reward and surpassing even the original purpose for humankind God had established ages ago in Eden.

The Hero's victorious reentrance into the halls of heaven opened a new chapter in God's unfolding drama. After the resurrected Savior's ascension, and prior to His future return as Judge and King, God sent His Spirit to stir the hearts of His former enemies and call them to His cause. Countless converts from every nation, tribe, people, and language have been and still are flocking to His side (Revelation 7:9–10). Through spiritual union with their King, this kingdom-in-the-making also experiences a shared spiritual communion in the church.

Through this spiritual-physical community of the life-giving Spirit, centered on Jesus Christ's person and work and focused on the glory of God the Father, members of Christ's body grow in faith, hope, and love. Together they become more and more like Jesus their King, the Spirit working in them to carry out the Father's redemptive mission in this still-fallen world (Ephesians 2:10; Philippians 2:12–13; Matthew 28:19–20).

This brings us to the climax of the Act of Redemption: the future restoration of the original creation. In the beginning, humans were expelled from Eden, unable to experience immortality in a Paradise free from suffering, frustration, fear, and death. At the present time God, through Christ and by the Spirit, is calling to himself a people who will participate in His drama's final chapter. When Jesus returns and renews all things, creation's groaning will be turned to glory as the entire earth is transformed into a new, even better Eden, and all those who've been united with Christ will be made like Him (Romans 8:18–25; 1 John 3:2; Revelation 21:3–4).

Thus, between Genesis and Revelation—from the Garden to Glory—God's unparalleled story unfolds. Every person and event moves history and humanity *forward* toward a final goal: restoration. God's grand narrative of creation, fall, and redemption truly satisfies our restless longings for purpose and meaning. It also fulfills our heart's desire for love in meaningful relationships.

The good news about God's story is that anyone can become a part of it. Jesus of Nazareth is truly God in the flesh, He truly died and was raised from death, and He truly offers a new identity and new future for all who trust in Him alone for salvation. And those who embrace by faith the Hero of this story will have a share in the restoration of all things (Revelation 21:5–7).

ONE

A Firm Foundation— God's Revealed Truth

You have searched the holy scriptures, which are true, which were given by the Holy Spirit; you know that nothing unrighteous or counterfeit is written in them.[1]

—Clement of Rome (c. 95)

So, the first point is that we treat Scripture with the same reverence we do God, because it is from God alone, and unmixed with anything human.[2]

—John Calvin (c. 1560)

In Short . . .

As we begin the profoundly important task of exploring the foundations of the Christian faith, we concern ourselves with deep mysteries. In fact, Paul calls them "the deep things of God" (1 Corinthians 2:10 NIV). Happily for us, though, discerning the essentials of Christian theology doesn't depend on our own wits or merely human understanding (Proverbs 3:5). God has given us a ready and reliable guide to lead us to the truth we seek. His very Spirit, whom Jesus called "the Spirit of truth" (John 14:17), guides us and opens our eyes to the truth.

This doesn't mean we shelve our minds, shift into neutral, and simply coast to the theological finish line. Christ called His followers to love God with our whole being (Matthew 22:37–40), which includes our minds. If left to our own feeble devices, though, we couldn't begin to fathom God's mysteries. But He hasn't left us alone; Jesus promised He and the Father would send the Spirit to "teach [us] all things" (John 14:26) and "guide [us] into all the truth" (16:13).

God Is Knowable . . . and Has Made Himself Known

In doing theology, we don't need to worry about our inadequacies. Our hope of success rests in God's willingness to make himself known to those who seek Him (Hebrews 11:6). And He has done so in a number of ways!

First, He's made himself known—that is, revealed himself—in His creation (Romans 1:19–20). And David said the heavens themselves testify to God's glory (Psalm 19:1). Tragically, what God has revealed in creation has become obscure to us. By the fog of sinful thoughts and actions, people have become blinded to what God has made known in creation.

Even though our sin has blinded us to what creation makes evident about God—"his eternal power and divine nature" (Romans 1:20)—God nonetheless has revealed himself to people throughout history by other means: angels, miracles, divine manifestations, the words of His prophets, and His written Word, the Bible. And all these, we are told, are given to fix our gaze on God's ultimate embodiment of revelation and truth, the God-Man, Jesus Christ.

The Inspired Word of God

Though the Bible comes to us over a period of centuries and across numerous cultural contexts, the human writers who penned those texts were moved by the Holy Spirit so that they wrote God's words, not merely their own (2 Peter 1:19–21). Thus, each biblical text has two authors: the divine author and the human author. The Bible's source, then, is simultaneously human and divine.

When describing the Bible as "inspired," we Christians don't mean the authors God chose were merely mentally inspired. Rather, we mean Scripture's *very words* are God's words. And in maintaining "verbal plenary inspiration," we affirm that *each and every word* of the Bible is inspired. A succinct basis for this doctrine is found in Paul's declaration to his understudy Timothy: "All Scripture is breathed out by God" (2 Timothy 3:16).

This means whatever the Bible affirms, God affirms. God can't speak falsely, so the Bible can't speak falsely. This teaching, called the "inerrancy" of Scripture, has been the overwhelming view of the Christian church throughout its history.

INERRANCY INFERRED FROM INSPIRATION

1. God speaks truthfully. (Numbers 23:19; Psalm 31:5; Isaiah 65:16; Titus 1:2; Hebrews 6:18)

2. Therefore, God's words are true. (Psalm 119:160; John 17:17)

3. God spoke His words through Scripture. (Acts 1:16; Romans 1:2)

4. Scripture is the written Word of God. (John 10:35; 2 Peter 1:19 [compare Romans 16:26])

5. Therefore, Scripture is true.

Faith Seeking Understanding

Our culture, obsessed with the scientific method, would have us believe that reason must precede faith. Not so! As Hebrews 11:3 says, "By faith we understand that the universe was created by the word of God." Don't miss this: *We don't reason our way into belief; rather, by faith, we understand.* It's by faith that we're able to perceive the truth and attain accurate understanding.

Christian thinkers throughout history have called this approach to theology "faith seeking understanding." To some this seems counterintuitive. We might think theologians would start with the best of human reason—philosophy, science, history, experience. In that view, only when we have enough evidence do we embrace something as true.

But what God has made known about himself, His works, and His ways—that is, His revelation—becomes clear only in a context of belief. *Faith comes before understanding.* Yes, in the context of faith and with a commitment to faith, we draw on reason, philosophy, science, history, and experience as means to better *understand* and *explain* revelation. But the engine that drives the train is faith, which ultimately is fueled by God himself (Romans 10:17; Ephesians 2:8).

If this point still seems strange, don't despair. It'll become clearer as we proceed—exploring the essentials of Christian theology not by means of reason seeking faith but by faith seeking understanding. In due course, Scripture will resolve this dilemma

---

Basic Method of Christian Theology

NOT

Understanding $\Longrightarrow$ Faith

BUT

Faith $\Longrightarrow$ Understanding

---

as we trust in the Lord with all our heart, leaning not on our own understanding (Proverbs 3:5–6).

Passages to Ponder

To open God's Word and explore His world with a view toward better understanding our Lord, we need to begin with some fundamental truths for comprehending God's revelation. As if constructing a building to weather the winds and erosion of time, we begin by laying a firm foundation of content, the Christian faith "once for all delivered to the saints" (Jude 3). Certain basic doctrines—the essentials of Christian theology—render that foundation immovable and the lives we build on that foundation unshakable.

The following passages form that firm foundation on which we can rest deeper doctrinal exploration—faith seeking understanding. They'll also provide the standard for practical Christian living.

(1) Psalm 19:1–6; Romans 1:19–20—God Speaks Through Creation

We've all had the experience of hearing a recorded song for only the first time yet instantly recognizing who's singing—the source. Whether the distinctive voice of Bob Dylan, the harmony of the Eagles, or the rhythm of Fats Domino, the details and patterns of the artistic creation point toward or even reveal the identity of its creator.

Similarly, creation points us to the One who created the heavens and the earth (Genesis 1:1): "The heavens declare the glory of God, and the sky above proclaims his handiwork" (Psalm 19:1). This psalm personifies this revelation as if it were speaking to us mortals without taking a breath: "Day to day pours out speech, and night to night reveals knowledge . . . Their voice goes out through all the earth, and their words to the end of the world" (19:2, 4).

Of course, God didn't write "Seek Me!" in the sky. We can't connect the dots of the stars and get the name "Jesus." The psalmist's point is that God's revelation in creation is as clear as if it had come to us by actual speech. God's fingerprints are all over His handiwork, revealing His glory. At least for those of us who know God personally and have experienced His salvation in Jesus Christ, Psalm 19 means we can dive deeper into our knowledge of God, His works, and His ways through what's been known by His work of creation.

This leads us to Romans 1, in what may be the apostle Paul's exposition of Psalm 19. There Paul addresses the question of salvation as it relates to God's revelation through creation. He first declares his confidence in the gospel, "the power of God for salvation to everyone who believes" (Romans 1:16). In short, the gospel alone—that is, the person and work of Jesus Christ revealed to us through Scripture—is the means of salvation. There's no other way for anyone to be saved, for in the gospel, "the righteousness of God is revealed from faith for faith" (1:17). Salvation is by grace alone through faith in Christ alone (Ephesians 2:8–9).

Yet most people have never embraced this light-giving gospel, so they're still in darkness even with regard to God's revelation in creation. Even though "what can be known about God is plain to them" (Romans 1:19) through the things God created—including His unseen attributes, limitless power, and divine nature—sin has clouded the minds of unbelievers. What should be clear to the eyes of faith became cloudy in faithlessness.

The problem isn't insufficient divine revelation. Rather, humans have responded to the knowledge of God that comes by means of creation by suppressing the truth (Romans 1:18), failing to honor God or thank Him (1:21), and trading the truth of God for lies and false gods (1:23, 25). Because of this, God allowed humans to go their own way and to experience the consequences of their faithlessness and sin (1:24, 26, 28, 29–31).

God's revelation in creation, then, is clear and plain. But on our own, none of us recognize Him, respond in worship, or submit to

Him (Romans 3:23). The general consensus of the Christian faith, with only a few exceptions, has been that God's revelation in creation (Proverbs 19:1–6; Romans 1:19–20) is not sufficient in itself to provide salvation (1 Corinthians 2:6–14). But when perceived through the eyes of faith, creation is seen for what it actually is: an awesome revelation of God, His works, and His ways. In a balanced approach to faith seeking understanding, God's revelation through creation and His revelation through Scripture—both centered on His revelation in Jesus Christ—should complement, not compete with, each other.

(2) Hebrews 1:1–2—God Spoke Through His Prophets . . . and Then Through His Son

Everyone knows you get a better deal if you cut out the middleman, right? But then why did God use "middlemen"—the prophets—to speak to His people? Isn't God capable of speaking for himself? Why would He risk His message being muddled or misunderstood by mediocre and messy middlemen?

One glance at Israel's encounter with God at Mount Sinai will give us an idea. When they beheld God's glorious revelation, they

---

PASSAGES TO MASTER AND MEMORIZE

Deuteronomy 31:26	2 Thessalonians 2:15
Joshua 1:8	2 Timothy 3:16–17
Psalm 19:1–2	Hebrews 1:1–2
John 17:17	2 Peter 1:20–21
Romans 1:19–20	2 Peter 3:15–16
1 Corinthians 2:13	

Note: Not all these passages are discussed in the text, but they'll all help you master the doctrines of God's Self-Revelation and Scripture.

---

were terrified! They begged Moses to speak to them for God and speak to God for them (Exodus 20:18–19). Moses was just one in a long line of divinely appointed mediators between God and His people, a line that would culminate in the coming of an ultimate Mediator (Deuteronomy 18:15–18; 1 Timothy 2:5).

Regardless of whether Christians believe God can or does reveal things through prophet-like figures after the early church, all agree that the scriptural canon is closed. That is, Scripture is our sole final authority in all matters of faith and practice. No new revelations would ever contradict the biblical prophets or fail to point us to Jesus Christ.

The writer of the letter to the Hebrews expressed it this way: "Long ago, at many times and in many ways, God spoke to our fathers by the prophets" (1:1). Over a long period of time, from Moses to Malachi, God spoke through human beings, some of whom wrote books that are part of the canon (such as Samuel, Isaiah, and Jeremiah) while others spoke but didn't leave a written record of God's words (such as Elijah and Elisha). Either way, God communicated His will to people through the prophets He appointed.

Sometimes God spoke through visions and dreams, sometimes with powerful and spectacular signs, and sometimes in a quiet voice—once even through a donkey (Numbers 22:21–39)! God's prophets pointed forward in anticipation of the greatest Prophet (Deuteronomy 18:15), who would be God's own Son, Jesus Christ. Again, formerly, God's mediators were those He raised up from among His people: "Long ago, at many times and in many ways, God spoke to our fathers by the prophets" (Hebrews 1:1). But now, finally, "in these last days he has spoken to us by his Son" (1:1–2).

Jesus, the Word, is the ultimate revelation of God (John 1:1; Hebrews 1:2). He's the Creator of the world (Hebrews 1:2; Genesis 1:1), the "radiance of the glory of God," "the exact imprint of his nature" who "upholds the universe by the word of his power" (Hebrews 1:3). He isn't a creature or inferior to God; He *is* God (John 1:1–2), and He's the ultimate mediator between God and humanity (1 Timothy 2:5). When He finished His work on the cross, in anticipation of His return to the earth to renew it (Revelation 21), "he sat down at the right hand of the Majesty on high" (Hebrews 1:3). He was and is and ever will be superior to all.

Jesus wrote none of the Scriptures, but He's the subject of both the Old Testament (John 5; Luke 24) and the New Testament—"the testimony of Jesus is the spirit of prophecy" (Revelation 19:10). He promised the disciples in the upper room, "When the Helper comes, whom I will send to you from the Father, the Spirit of truth, who proceeds from the Father, he will bear witness about me. And you also will bear witness, because you have been with me from the beginning" (John 15:26–27). He also guaranteed, "He will teach you all things and bring to your remembrance all that I have said to you" (John 14:26).

TWO OLD TESTAMENT TESTS OF A FALSE PROPHET

Failed Prophecies

If you say in your heart, "How may we know the word that the LORD has not spoken?"—when a prophet speaks in the name of the LORD, if the word does not come to pass or come true, that is a word that the LORD has not spoken; the prophet has spoken it presumptuously. You need not be afraid of him. (Deuteronomy 18:21–22)

False Theology

If a prophet or a dreamer of dreams arises among you and gives you a sign or a wonder, and the sign or wonder that he tells you comes to pass, and if he says, "Let us go after other gods," which you have not known, "and let us serve them," you shall not listen to the words of that prophet or that dreamer of dreams. (Deuteronomy 13:1–3)

(3) 2 Timothy 3:16–17; 2 Peter 1:19–20—All Scripture Is Inspired by God

Open your hand and hold it in front of your mouth as close as you can get it and still be able to speak. Then read the following words aloud: "All Scripture is inspired by God and profitable for teaching, for reproof, for correction, for training in righteousness" (2 Timothy 3:16 NASB). What did you feel? Even if you whispered, you felt your breath on your hand. In a literal sense, you "breathed out" the words from this page, bringing them to life.

The doctrine of Scripture's *inspiration* is derived from the language of 2 Timothy 3:16. In all the New Testament, the word *God-breathed* (often translated "inspired") appears only here. Yet the concept is found throughout Scripture. When prophets spoke for God, their words were from God, by means of God's Spirit, and this is what *God-breathed* means—carried by the Spirit, the very "breath" of God. Written down by human authors, they are nevertheless the words of God.

This doesn't mean the Scriptures were *dictated* by God, as if He whispered every word into the authors' ears, which they then recorded like a secretary takes dictation. Nevertheless, the Scriptures are the result of a process by which God used the human authors' experiences, word choices, and intentions to accomplish His will.

This quality applies to both the whole and the parts. *All* Scripture is God-breathed because *every* Scripture is God-breathed (compare Matthew 5:18–20; John 10:35). Since the parts are from God, the whole is likewise from God. Because all Scripture is God-breathed, it's true in all it affirms. Even when it reports falsehoods,

> "God superintended the human authors of the Bible so that they composed and recorded without error His message to mankind in the words of their original writings."[3]
>
> Charles C. Ryrie (1999)

like the words of the serpent in Genesis 3:4 or the utterances of the fool in Psalm 14:1, it does so truthfully, though not affirming those false statements.

Paul lists the kinds of things God's inspired Word accomplishes: It's profitable "for teaching, for reproof, for correction, and for training in righteousness" (2 Timothy 3:16 NASB). In this context, Paul lists two purposes for the Scriptures: (1) They're "able to make you wise for salvation through faith in Christ Jesus" (3:15), and (2) they produce people of God who are "complete, equipped for every good work" (3:17). This is sometimes referred to as the doctrine of the "sufficiency of Scripture." The Bible is sufficient for the purposes for which it was written: to provide saving knowledge of Jesus Christ and everything necessary to live a God-honoring life.

This brings us to a second key passage regarding the inspiration of Scripture—2 Peter 1:19–20. On the heels of urging his readers to persevere in faithfulness, Peter underscores the reliability of the message delivered by all of Jesus' apostles. Their message, Peter says, wasn't a clever invention (1:16). Instead, they relayed events they saw themselves, such as the display of glory on the Mount of Transfiguration. On that day, Peter, James, and John experienced a supernatural validation, hearing a voice from heaven confirming that Jesus is God's beloved Son (1:17–18), the long-expected Messiah. Through this event, Peter says, the message of the Old Testament prophets was confirmed (1:19).

In this context, Peter sheds light on the nature of prophecy: "No prophecy of Scripture came about by the prophet's own interpretation of things" (1:20 NIV). That is, God's prophets didn't conjure messages and portray them as being from God. These never came via human will or impulse. Instead, men "spoke from God as they were carried along by the Holy Spirit" (1:21). The term translated "carried along" is used both for the voice Peter heard on the holy mountain ("We ourselves heard this very voice *borne* from heaven," 1:18, emphasis added) and for the way the Spirit uses prophets to deliver God's intended message ("Men

Paul **doesn't** say "All **prophets** were inspired by God," then they wrote the best they knew how.

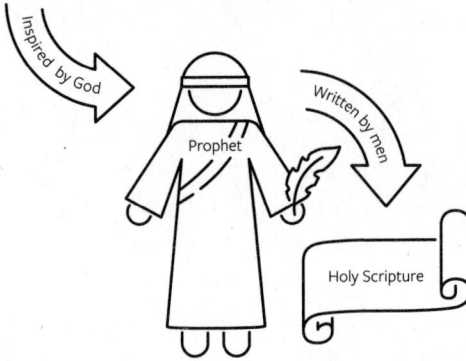

Inspired by God

Prophet

Written by men

Holy Scripture

Paul **does** say "All **Scripture** is inspired by God," written by means of Spirit-guided men.

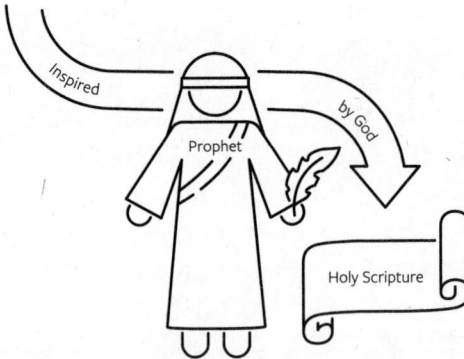

Inspired

by God

Prophet

Holy Scripture

Paul **doesn't** say "Prophets had good ideas and wrote them down in what we call Scripture."

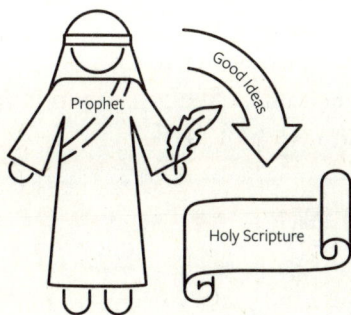

Prophet

Good Ideas

Holy Scripture

Paul **does** say "Prophets spoke [or wrote] messages from God as they were carried along by the Spirit."

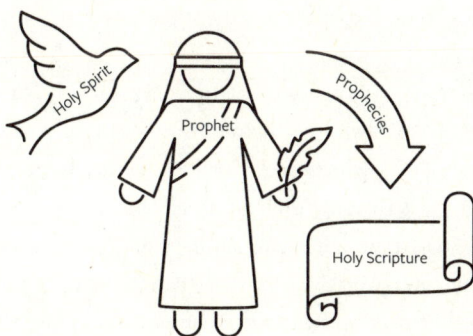

Holy Spirit

Prophet

Prophecies

Holy Scripture

spoke from God as they were carried along [*borne*] by the Holy Spirit," 1:21).

In the same way God's message to us on the mountain was made clear (carried by a supernatural voice), God's message to you is made clear (delivered through men who were carried by His Spirit in the process of crafting that prophetic message).

Together, in 2 Timothy 3:16–17 and 2 Peter 1:19–20, Paul and Peter present us with important truths regarding Scripture. The Bible is inspired, inerrant, and sufficient. Scripture is true because God's words are true (John 17:17).

(4) John 17:17—God's Word Is True

Since at least the 1970s, the saying "Pobody's nerfect!" has been a lighthearted way to acknowledge that everything that frail, fallen people touch has flaws. We're all fallible, imperfect humans, and despite our best intentions, we get it wrong. So to some, the notion that Scripture, written by people who are fallen, frail, and fallible, could nevertheless be without error in all it affirms seems absurd. In fact, for the last few centuries, some scholars have worked hard to find evidence that the Bible isn't really special, that it's the product of human imaginations, and that it may be *inspiring* but not *inspired*. Thus, like all human endeavors, they conclude that it must contain errors, because, after all, "pobody's nerfect!"

But this isn't the classic Christian view. Rather, for two thousand years, Christians have affirmed what's come to be known as the "inerrancy" of Scripture. According to theologian Paul Feinberg, "inerrancy is the view that when all the facts become known, they will demonstrate that the Bible in its original autographs and correctly interpreted is entirely true and never false in all it affirms, whether that relates to doctrine or ethics or to the social, physical, or life sciences."[4]

John 17 is a famous passage that buttresses the doctrine of inerrancy. In that chapter, sometimes called Jesus' High Priestly

Prayer, the Lord prays for His disciples. He asks the Father to make them holy, to "set them apart," to sanctify them. But this isn't just a generic, plain-vanilla kind of sanctification. Jesus asks the Father to "sanctify [His disciples] in the truth; your word [that is, the word of the Father] is truth" (17:17). When Jesus says this, He has in mind the written Word of God we now call the Old Testament. Jews in general (and Jesus exemplifies it here) believed that the Law, the Prophets, and the Writings—as the texts were known to many—came from God, and they considered this collection of writings "God's Word."

This statement, while simple, has profound implications. It demonstrates Jesus' own attitude toward Scripture. And Jesus' own attitude toward Scripture is a thorn in the side of all who would wish to deny either the truthfulness or the authority of Scripture. It's difficult to claim you follow Jesus and then say you're unwilling to adopt His own attitude toward the truthfulness and authority of Scripture. It almost sounds like you're saying "I follow Jesus, but I know better than Jesus on this topic." That, in a nutshell, is spiritually arrogant.

At the same time, this claim of the truthfulness of Scripture raises a number of important questions. What do we do, for example, with the observation that the transmission of the New Testament from the earliest manuscripts until today is littered with evidence of unintentional (and some intentional) changes made by those tasked with making copies of the Bible?

For this reason (and for a number of other reasons like it), Christians offer clarifications about what the doctrine of inerrancy does *not* mean. The following list, adapted from Paul Feinberg's discussion of qualifications concerning the doctrine of inerrancy, has become a standard understanding among Bible-believing Christians.[5]

1. Inerrancy does not demand strict adherence to the rules of grammar.
2. Inerrancy does not exclude the use of either figures of speech or literary genre.

3. Inerrancy does not demand historical or semantic precision.

4. Inerrancy does not demand the technical or observational language of modern science.

5. Inerrancy does not require verbal exactness in the citation of the Old Testament by the New.

6. Inerrancy does not demand that the sayings of Jesus contain the exact words of Jesus, only the exact voice.

7. Inerrancy does not guarantee the exhaustive comprehensiveness of any single account or of combined accounts where those are involved.

8. Inerrancy does not demand the infallibility of non-inspired sources used by biblical writers.

The bottom line: Jesus' own attitude toward Scripture is captured in the simple statement "Your word is truth."

(5) 1 Corinthians 2:10–13—Words Taught by the Spirit

Our view of Scripture is in line with the church's historic teaching when we affirm three facts about the Bible's inspiration: (1) God is the source, (2) the very words are the product, and (3) the Holy Spirit is the agent. But how does the Spirit work through the human authors of Scripture to relay God's message through inspired words? In his first letter to the Corinthians, Paul answers this question.

In chapter 2 of 1 Corinthians, Paul defends his authority as a genuine, God-sent apostle. In this defense, he explains that the content of his teaching didn't come from his own personal imagination. He didn't just dream up the gospel. Instead, the message—containing the "depths of God" and the "thoughts of God" (2:10–11)—was revealed to the apostles by the Holy Spirit. These can come only from the Spirit of God.

This brings Paul to his summary of the whole situation: The apostles, he says, impart the thoughts of God in "words not

Paul **doesn't** say "We speak words taught to us by human wisdom."

Prophet

Early to bed, early to rise, makes men healthy, wealthy, and wise.

Paul **does** say "We speak words taught us by the Spirit, expressing spiritual things in spiritual words."

Holy Spirit

Prophet

Spiritual things

Spiritual words

I make known to you, brethren, the gospel which I preached to you...

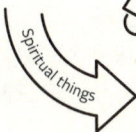

taught by human wisdom but taught by the Spirit" (2:13). The *very words* came from the Holy Spirit. Notice that in this passage, Paul carefully distinguishes between the thoughts of God (which is the content of his teaching) and spiritual words taught by the Holy Spirit (which is the form of his teaching). The apostolic doctrine, according to Paul, involves God's thoughts—"interpreting spiritual truths to those who are spiritual" (2:13) in words taught by the Holy Spirit himself.

To put it another way, apostolic teaching is from God due to the revealing and teaching work of the Holy Spirit. That teaching ministry extends even to the very words that express the thoughts of God. As one scholar puts it, "Inspiration is a supernatural influence of the Holy Spirit upon divinely chosen agents in consequence of which their writings become trustworthy and authoritative."[6]

The upshot of all this is significant for our understanding of what Scripture is. Since the apostles' message is conveyed in words taught by the Holy Spirit, the church of Jesus Christ has always held to the inspiration of Scripture and therefore its truthfulness in all it affirms. That is, because the very words of Scripture are taught by the Spirit through the apostles (1 Corinthians 2:10–13), God's Word is without error.

(6) Deuteronomy 31:24–26—Birth of the Old Testament Canon

Jesus, Peter, and Paul all affirmed the inspiration and truthfulness of the Old Testament. But how did those particular books find their way into the Bible? That important question wasn't immediately or completely settled in the early church. It took time to reach a consensus on which ones were *inspired* and thus absolutely authoritative and which ones were merely *inspiring* and thus helpful for personal reading.

The history of the growth, development, and final form of the Old Testament spans almost two thousand years, from the time of Moses (c. 1500 BC) all the way toward the beginning of the church's medieval period (c. AD 500). Much of this history is shrouded in mystery. Though we have no direct records of when or by whom these writings were collected, we *do* have the final result of that process.

Nevertheless, Deuteronomy gives us a glimpse of the original canon and how it was to function among God's people. The passage and its historical and biblical context also yield hints about the future development of the canon Paul would later describe as "God-breathed" (2 Timothy 3:16).

Near the end of Moses' life, he "finished writing the words of this law in a book to the very end" (Deuteronomy 31:24)—that is, he completed Genesis, Exodus, Leviticus, Numbers, and Deuteronomy. Explaining why he wrote them and how they were to function, verses 25 and 26 say, "Moses commanded the Levites who carried the ark of the covenant of the LORD, 'Take this Book of the Law and put it by the side of the ark of the covenant of the LORD your God, that it may be there for a witness against you.'"

Immediately after their writing, these books were to start functioning as a canon—the standard against which God's people measure all their beliefs and practices. Significantly, the first biblical canon was placed beside the ark of the covenant, a representation of God's presence among His people. The implication was clear: When you read these words, you're hearing from God himself, because these books, though written by Moses, are God's Word.

This passage reveals the fundamental reason for a believing community to accept a writing as canonical, that is, authoritative: the prophetic authority of the writer. Since Moses' authority as God's prophet was unquestioned, his writings were received as from the mouth of God. No wonder, then, that at the time of Joshua, we see the Old Testament functioning the way Moses had prescribed in Deuteronomy 31 (Joshua 1:8). And Joshua's obedience to the command written in Deuteronomy 27:2–8 demonstrates that the people had immediately received the five books of Moses as the binding canon to be believed and obeyed (Joshua 8:30–35).

The original five books included a promise that future God-sent prophets would have the same authority as Moses (Deuteronomy 18:15–19). When an authentic, God-called prophet arose, his written and spoken words were to be accepted as instantly "canonical"—authoritative for belief and practice. Because God himself was speaking through true prophets, His people were to embrace their words and their writings as God-inspired.

So from the beginning, revelation in the form of canonical writings was tied to the prophetic office or to the special gift of prophesying demonstrated in those like Joshua, Samuel, David, Isaiah, Jeremiah, Ezekiel, and Daniel, as well as others among God's people. Presumably, the long line of faithful saints was also responsible for receiving and passing on the inspired writings from the past.

The people's instant recognition of the authority of the first scriptural canon (Deuteronomy 31:24–26) shows that its prophetic quality would be the foundation of future canonical writings. The answer, then, to the question *How did those Old Testament books find their way into the Bible?* is that they were written throughout history by proven prophets of God whose writings were received by the community of the faithful as the very words of God.

(7) 2 Peter 3:15–16—Rise of the New Testament Canon

In the previous passage we considered, we saw that the Old Testament writings were received by God's people as authoritative because they were written by God-ordained prophets. For the New Testament writings, the story is more or less the same.

Inspired writings were recognized by the original recipients as they were written and received (2 Thessalonians 2:15). This was due to the already recognized authority of genuine apostles and prophets, gifted and given by Jesus Christ to the church (Ephesians 2:20; 4:11). Very early in the apostolic period, churches began copying, sharing, collecting, and using the writings of Jesus' apostles and prophets as standards alongside the Old Testament Scriptures.

In 2 Peter 3, Peter told the churches to whom he was writing that Paul had written to them "according to the wisdom given him" (3:15)—that is, divine wisdom from the Holy Spirit (see 1 Corinthians 2:12–13), indicating that Paul wrote the same way "in all his letters" (2 Peter 3:16). Peter was evidently aware of a collection of Paul's writings already in wide circulation. In this context, Peter equated Paul's authoritative writings with Old Testament Scriptures by saying that those who misinterpret Paul's writings "twist [them] to their own destruction, as they do the other Scriptures" (3:16). The term translated "other" (the Greek *loipos*) refers to the remaining members of the same category. Thus, around AD 65 Peter had already placed Paul's writings in the same category of the canonical Old Testament Scriptures.

Just as the Old Testament writings were completed by the end of the age of Old Testament prophets, the end of the apostolic era saw the end of the writing of inspired New Testament books. Because the inspired, inerrant writing of the New Testament was tied to the apostolic and prophetic offices (Ephesians 2:20), the passing of the age of apostles and prophets would mark the end of the canon. It would have closed with the last work authored or sanctioned by an apostle, presumably the book of Revelation, which most Christians believe John wrote near the close of the first century.

Realities to Remember

Common sense tells us you don't have a cheeseburger without a burger and cheese. Now, you can have all sorts of extra stuff—bacon, ketchup, pickles, onions, lettuce, and even jalapeños. But without the essential ingredients of meat and cheese, you can't call it a "cheeseburger."

The same is true in the Christian faith. Without certain essential truths, you can't call it "Christian." Some of the following "realities to remember" surfaced earlier in this chapter, and some will come up again. But they're so foundational to the study of God's revealed truth that they bear highlighting.

1. God is knowable and has made himself known.

From Adam and Eve onward, God has directly entered the history of this world. He called Abraham and blessed him for his faith. He appeared to Moses and through him set the Hebrews free from Egyptian bondage. He parted the Red Sea to rescue the helpless and destroy one of the most powerful armies on earth. According to His wise plan, God visited some of the strangest, most unlikely people: the fearless Deborah, the hesitant Gideon, the man-boy Samson, the tenaciously loyal Ruth, the young shepherd David.

Besides revealing himself personally and providentially to people throughout history, God also gave us His inspired Word through some of those very same people. God didn't simply parachute a book out of heaven. Rather, through His Holy Spirit, He guided human authors to articulate the truth using their own personalities and words, infallibly superintending the entire process (2 Peter 1:19–21). Even Job's questioning, Habakkuk's complaining, and David's pleas for rescue came to us as *God's* Word. In His act of inspiring Scripture, we see God in our world, at close range, speaking even through human struggles. The infinitely personal God of the Bible is not aloof—too important for covenants, too majestic for fellowship with people of simple faith.

Our God loves to draw near to His people. He made us for himself. He fashioned us in a way that we would be able to know Him. Not exhaustively, not perfectly, yet really and truly *know* Him. He's at once the sovereign Lord God over all creation, who comes to us and speaks in a still, small voice, in our times of prayer, in our moments of need.

2. God reveals himself through various means.

Scripture testifies that God reveals himself through various means—divine appearances, visions, dreams, and His own acts in human history. Beyond this, God reveals himself in all creation (Romans 1:19–20). He has revealed himself in the person and work of Jesus Christ (John 1:14) and by His inspired Word, messages in the form of language (2 Timothy 3:16).

According to Scripture, God has revealed himself in messages that came directly from Him, and one example is the Ten Commandments (see Exodus 20). Yet most of the time, His written revelation comes through chosen human agents. The Old Testament prophets spoke from God, and they also spoke *for* God whenever He gave them a message for His people.

Now, there's a potential for abuse in an arrangement like this. What keeps someone—anyone—from claiming they have a message from the Lord that we must believe and obey? Because of this potential danger, God put principles in place so His people could have confidence in His revelation when it occurs through human agency. That confidence starts with the principle of *authenticated messengers*. God uses only authenticated messengers when revealing himself through people. So, for example, the Old Testament Scriptures were written by prophets authenticated both by Moses and the *supernatural validation* that God placed on each of them.

For example, they made detailed predictions that came to pass or performed astonishing miracles only God could do. Likewise, the Lord's apostles were authenticated both by Jesus himself and by supernatural attestation of their authority. We see evidence of this principle in Hebrews 2:4: "God also bore witness by signs and wonders and various miracles and by gifts of the Holy Spirit distributed according to his will."

All of this leads us to affirm that the Scriptures, which stand by divine authentication, are the most objectively verifiable form of divine revelation. Christians are united in the conviction that the whole Bible is God's true Word, the measure and framework for all claims to revelation. Sufficient, authoritative, and inerrant for our knowledge of God, His Word invites us to know Him personally.

3. Scripture is true in all it affirms.

None of us would choose to do business with someone who's either intentionally deceitful or notoriously incompetent. We all prefer straight shooters whose expertise we can trust. The same is true when it comes to our authority for life—both eternal life and daily living. By God's gracious provision, we have such a straight shooter, because Scripture is true in all it affirms.

This basic tenet has far-reaching consequences. Affirming the truthfulness and trustworthiness of Scripture gives us assurance to take each faithful step in life. Unfortunately, you'll encounter both pastors and teachers who have backed away from embracing the classic Christian doctrine of biblical inerrancy. They fear the doctrine could be (or even has been) proven untrue. On the contrary, all Christians of every generation since the founding of the church through the Protestant reformation have embraced the complete truthfulness of Scripture.[7]

Scripture identifies itself as the truth of God. The vast majority of orthodox, protestant, Bible-believing Christians throughout history have accepted this as an unalterable article of faith. We should remember that, and we should seek involvement in churches and ministries that hold this principle dear.

> "They are the words of the Lord, and it is not permitted to doubt or hesitate."[8]
>
> Bernard of Clairvaux (c. 1150)

4. Jesus Christ is the center and goal of Scripture.

For over a hundred years, the doctrinal statement of Dallas Theological Seminary has affirmed that "all the Scriptures center about the Lord Jesus Christ in His person and work in His first and second coming, and hence that no portion, even of the Old Testament, is properly read or understood until it leads to Him."[9] Not only is it the common statement of biblical and historical Christian teaching (Luke 24:27, 44), but it's also a reality to remember as Christ-followers strive to keep Christ at the center of Scripture, theology, and life.

Acts 11:26 records the first use of the term *Christian*, and most scholars believe it was created by the populace of Antioch as a term of disparagement. But soon followers of Christ accepted this term and began to use it to describe themselves. They saw themselves as "followers of Christ," and perhaps that's the best way we can understand our identity. We are those who follow Christ and give Him first place in all things—even in the way we read Scripture.

The centrality of Christ as the center and goal of Scripture seems to be slipping in a lot of churches today. Instead of seeking to have Scripture point us to the person and work of the Lord Jesus, the awesomeness of God, and the transforming power of His Spirit, we too often use the Bible to answer questions it was never meant to answer: "How can I have my best, most successful life now?" or "How can I feel better about me?" or "What does this say about me, my feelings, my welfare . . . my *self*?"

The Bible isn't primarily a self-help manual, or a book of financial advice, marriage pointers, or frame-worthy inspirational sayings. It's about the eternal, divine Son of God. He revealed the Father's will, became incarnate in true humanity to die for our sins, and rose from the dead. He works through the Spirit and God's written Word to accomplish His will in us, in His church. He will return to transform all creation under His perfect rule. The person and work of Jesus Christ is the center and goal of Scripture.

5. The goal of theology is transformation, not just information.

For all the naysaying about "doctrine" in some modern churches, the word simply means "teaching." Jesus himself is the supreme Teacher, whose doctrine astonished His hearers (Matthew 7:28; 22:33; Mark 1:22; 11:18; Luke 4:32). Not surprisingly, several New Testament letters to churches begin with deep doctrine—teaching about God intertwined with rejoicing and wonder (see, for example, Romans 1–11 and Ephesians 1–3). Sound doctrine establishes the foundation upon which we should build a God-honoring life. The apostles repeatedly exhorted leaders to believe and defend "sound doctrine" (1 Timothy 4:16; Titus 1:9; 2:1).

Good theology functions as a series of road signs that help lead us on the way to a joyful relationship with the living God. Yes, we can become enamored with the intellectual greatness of the subject. This leads some believers to conclude that theology is not only unnecessary but may even get in the way of our personal relationship with God. And true, sometimes those who know the most about theology seem to be unconcerned about the fruit of the Spirit, the salvation of the lost, and loving their neighbors. Sometimes full heads don't translate into overflowing hearts. The road signs fascinated and distracted them from where they were supposed to go.

That's why it's vital to remember that the goal of theology is *transformation*, not merely *information*.

Errors to Avoid

To a ship or submarine navigating international waters during World War II, few things were as hazardous as naval mines floating just below the surface of the water. Just a tap would blast a hole in its hull, sending the unsuspecting vessel plunging into the dark abyss. Christians too encounter errors that deny the truth of God's Word and so wield the risk of plunging us into spiritual ruin.

Error 1: Failing to Teach the Whole Truth

In his farewell address to the elders of the Ephesian church, Paul made a significant point in defending his ministry: "I did not shrink from declaring to you the whole counsel of God" (Acts 20:27). We too ought to seek out churches, teachers, and friends who teach God's "whole counsel."

False teachers today fail to teach the whole truth in various ways. Some suggest we really only need to focus on the words of Jesus (not those of Paul or Peter or John). Or they focus almost exclusively on the New Testament and all but reject the Old Testament. They develop a sort of "canon within a canon," setting parts of God's Word on a figurative second shelf and focusing all their attention on portions they select. Others excise or ignore doctrines they don't like, such as sexual purity, gluttony, salvation exclusively through Christ, gender differences, and even miracles that sound too "mythical."

Beware of preachers, teachers, pastors, or professors who fail to teach the whole counsel of God.

Error 2: Downgrading Scripture

Some preachers and teachers today suggest that the Bible isn't really God's Word but rather a "good book." Even if culturally acceptable, that belief massacres Scripture's claims for itself. As Jesus said to God the Father, "Your word is truth" (John 17:17).

Others say, "The Bible isn't God's Word per se, but it *becomes* God's Word for us when we choose to live it." This may be even more subtle than the previous example, but it's no less destructive. If the Bible isn't unconditionally God's Word, we humans will find ways to exempt ourselves from its teaching. Unfortunately, we're so gifted at finding ways to justify our own selfishness and wrongdoing that a small, subtle distinction such as this is all we need. If Scripture *becomes* God's Word only when some other factor or ingredient is mixed in, then our obedience to it becomes even easier to debate and eventually avoid.

Still others downgrade the Word's authority by equalizing it with other authorities: church dogmas, legalistic traditions, cultural expectations, and even the priority of personal pleasure. How often have we fled the blunt demands of true discipleship because it would challenge us or get in the way of our personal comfort? "I know the Bible says that, but . . ." is a sign that we're mixing imperfections into the purity of the truth.

Error 3: Hearing Without Heeding

Over and over again the Bible demonstrates that we humans have a problem listening to messages from God. The Old Testament prophets delivered His messages, and the people didn't listen (Isaiah 6:8–10). The prophets vividly declared God's plans for the people of Israel, but though they heard, they didn't heed.

Take the ministry of the prophet Ezekiel as an example. Commanded by God, Ezekiel began baking barley cakes over a fire of cow dung as a testimony that the people of Judah would be forced to do this during the coming siege of Jerusalem (Ezekiel 4:12–15). Though they heard, they didn't heed. Then with a sword Ezekiel shaved off his hair and beard and used the hair to teach the people a lesson about the impending siege (5:1–17). Again, they didn't heed the warning. The result? Judgment.

And consider this true story about a Christian police officer heavily involved in an AWANA program—a program where year after year, week after week, church kids hear Christian truth and earn prizes and awards for Scripture memorization. Even as they study the Bible and work through their AWANA workbooks throughout the week, these kids are steeped in the Word.

One year that police officer busted a young man who had gotten himself deep into criminal activities—drug dealing, violence, and all sorts of destructive behavior. After acquiring a search warrant to go through the young man's home, the cop was brokenhearted at what he found in his bedroom. All along his bookshelves, like perfect soldiers standing at attention, were year after year of AWANA achievement awards.

He memorized all the verses. He got all the awards. But he never let the Word touch his heart.

Today we face a similar danger. Even when we recognize the Bible as God's true Word, we can find ourselves hearing without heeding. When we hear it, we ought to listen in rapt attention and stand ready to do anything that needs to be done to ensure that we actually *do* what God's Word commands.

We face a similar danger in our approach to Scripture. We can know the Bible inside and out, memorize all the best Bible verses, and purchase all the best commentaries, yet utterly miss out on the lifestyle that *ought* to result. We can teach all the right truths, and then live a lie. The simple fact is this: We who hear God's Word must be the first to heed God's Word. We'll make mistakes, for we all stumble in many ways (James 3:2). But of all people, Christians ought to be the ones who follow Christ!

Error 4: Self-Centered Reading

Some people read Scripture in self-serving, self-affirming, and self-centered ways. They use the Bible as a means to an end—and that end is always their own benefit. They wield the Bible as if it were a weapon to bludgeon their opponents, of which they have many. Their biblical knowledge feeds their pride, promotes their own opinions, and always seems to prove them right and everyone else wrong.

This can also happen in less pompous and obvious ways. We open the pages to Scripture wanting to be affirmed, not corrected. We want God's Word to agree with our opinions, our decisions, even our politics. Instead of letting Scripture point out our flaws and failings, we want it to make us feel better about ourselves.

This error also shows up when we gather for Bible study and ask, "What does this passage mean to you?" Now, most times, the real question being asked is "How do you think this passage challenges you?" or "How can you apply its meaning to your life?" But it's worth remembering that we don't *create* the meaning of Scripture; the meaning of God's Word is from God. We *respond* to its truth. And that means letting the Bible say what it says, not what we want it to say.

When we read the Bible, even when we read it *alone*, we should never read it in *isolation*. Every false teacher who ever lived became one by *not* engaging God's Word with the accountability of others—in a supportive community of believers, with the goal of growing together and exhorting one another to stay true to the faith "once for all delivered to the saints" (Jude 3). False teachers and errant followers sprout from the soil of individualistic, separatist, and isolationist approaches to faith and practice.

Error 5: Doctrine-Free Discipleship

Many things in life simply must go together. Meat and potatoes. Bert and Ernie. C-3PO and R2-D2. Salt and pepper.

Likewise, doctrine and discipleship must always go together. To put it another way, discipleship without doctrine is dangerous. Remember, "doctrine" simply means "teaching" and refers to the teachings of right beliefs and right living.

Discipleship programs abound in today's churches. And that's a good thing! Jesus made disciples, and the disciples made disciples. As a matter of fact, Jesus' command immortalized in what we call "The Great Commission" affirms that this is what we should be doing as well: "Go therefore and make disciples of all nations!" (Matthew 28:19).

But in our discipleship, sometimes we lose sight of the fact that doctrine is the basis of discipleship. It's not enough to make people who believe a simple gospel message about how Jesus died for their sins and rose from the dead. Discipleship certainly starts with that, but it doesn't end there. Rather, Jesus himself instructed us how disciples are to be made: "Make disciples of all nations, baptizing them in the name of the Father and the Son and the Holy Spirit, teaching them to observe all that I have commanded you" (Matthew 28:19–20).

We need to *teach*. What do we teach? The truth of the Father, Son, and Holy Spirit for starters. As we'll see in chapter 2, the doctrines of the triune God and the person of Christ are the foundation of the Christian faith. But upon that foundation we are to teach right living, living in a way that follows Jesus' example.

Simply put, "doctrine-free discipleship" just won't do. We are to make disciples who *know* the teachings of Scripture, and because they know the teachings of Scripture, they *obey* the teachings of Scripture.

Lessons to Live

Regarding Scripture, we ought to practice a number of other things as well—things that could spell the difference between spiritual vitality and spiritual failure.

Lesson 1: Heed Scripture as from the mouth of God.

For many basketball fans—young and old, men and women—nothing compares to the excitement of the NCAA Division's March Madness, which culminates in the tournament that crowns the year's national champion. But the tournament is much more exciting now than it was before the 1986–87 season. That year included a brand-new (to the college game) factor: the three-point shot.

The "trey" has made the Madness even madder. For instance, a team with less depth can sometimes ride the coattails of a hot marksman to a string of upset victories. In fact, that very season the Providence Friars did just that, relying on the accurate shooting of guard Billy Donovan to advance all the way to the Final Four.

When we consider the doctrine of Scripture, we should think of another three points: (1) God is the source of inspiration, (2) God's very words are the product of inspiration, and (3) the Holy Spirit is the agent of inspiration. Accepting Scripture as inspired by God and viewing inspiration through this reliable set of lenses involves an important lesson to live. Namely, we must heed Scripture as from God's mouth. It's *His* message and therefore is of paramount importance. His Word, as His message, carries His authority. We submit to the authority of Scripture because that authority is God's.

Finally, this submission to Scripture's authority gives shape to the very geography of Christianity. Scripture itself describes the practical consequences of its inspired status. Because Scripture is inspired, it's profitable "for teaching, for reproof, for correction, and for training in righteousness" (2 Timothy 3:16). Because Scripture is inspired, we heed it as from the mouth of God, and we align ourselves with its teaching as we grow in Christ.

Lesson 2: Be taught to be stable.

Is the Bible difficult to understand? Well, yes and no.

Some truths are so clear and obvious that if the Bible were in 3D they'd jump off the page and grab your nose. For example, God created all things, Jesus died for our sins and rose from the dead, and in the end, God wins.

Not everything is so clear, though. In fact, some elements are flat-out difficult to grasp. Not impossible, but difficult. Again, the apostle Peter said as much when he wrote concerning Paul's writings, "Some things [are] hard to understand, which the untaught and unstable distort, as they do also the rest of the Scriptures, to their own destruction" (2 Peter 3:16 NASB).

Furthermore, some of these things, handled in the wrong way, can be truly hazardous. How do we avoid being like those Scripture twisters who destroy themselves and others? Well, Peter said their problem was they were "untaught" and "unstable." The Greek word translated "untaught" is the literal opposite of "discipled." In the ancient world, a disciple was an apprentice who learned from a teacher over the course of several years. Thus, one way to be a Scripture twister is to be *untaught*, that is, *not* taught by someone who's been trained.

The implication is clear: Only those who have been trained can be expected to weave together what God has revealed into a unified whole centered on Christ and faithfully representing the overall pattern of truth. Paul called this skill "rightly handling the word of truth" (2 Timothy 2:15).

We need to be careful about how we read Scripture. To be *only* self-taught is to be untaught. For example, have you ever been advised to not consult commentaries until you've come up with your own personal interpretation? In light of Peter's serious warning, such exhortations encourage Christians to go on being self-taught (in other words, "untaught").

Again, this in no way means we should stop reading on our own. But once more, we should never read our Bibles *in isolation*. Taking initiative to read and study Scripture is right. Rejecting training under qualified teachers and shunning accountability to other believers as we do so is wrong.

What, then, are we to do to handle the Bible rightly? To understand it accurately? Peter's words include the answer: *Be taught in order to be stable*. How? That's simple: by submitting to the teaching of the Holy Spirit as He works through His gifted teachers within the Spirit-indwelled community. This corporate model of how we're to be taught and made stable through the working of Christ's body is most clearly expressed in Ephesians 4:11–16 (NASB):

> He gave some as apostles, and some as prophets, and some as evangelists, and some as pastors and teachers, for the equipping of the saints for the work of service, to the building up of the body

of Christ; until we all attain to the unity of the faith, and of the knowledge of the Son of God, to a mature man, to the measure of the stature which belongs to the fullness of Christ. As a result, we are no longer to be children, tossed here and there by waves and carried about by every wind of doctrine, by the trickery of men, by craftiness in deceitful scheming; but speaking the truth in love, we are to grow up in all aspects into Him who is the head, even Christ, from whom the whole body, being fitted and held together by what every joint supplies, according to the proper working of each individual part, causes the growth of the body for the building up of itself in love.

Did you catch all these ingredients? Learning under teachers . . . being fitted together . . . each individual playing a part . . . growing from childhood to adulthood . . . attaining the unity of the faith. Instead of throwing out our study Bibles, we ought to let them fill gaps in our knowledge. Instead of making commentaries our last-ditch effort, we should learn from godly scholars. Rather than reinventing the wheel or seeking out the latest fad, we should explore the rich heritage of Christians who have come before us. And rather than leaning on our own personal understanding, we ought to glean what we can from the insights of other believers around us.

If we want to avoid becoming Scripture twisters, we need to balance our personal reading with community study under skilled teachers. Only in the context of a Bible-believing community with guidance from qualified leaders will we become taught and stable, "rightly handling the word of truth" (2 Timothy 2:15).

Lesson 3: Be a doer, not merely a hearer.

Without doubt, you've received one (or more likely, hundreds) of those emails touting a breakthrough dietary supplement. For only $49.99, we're told, we can get a bottle of *very special stuff* that will change our lives for the better in ways we can scarcely imagine. *Everything* will be better.

As it turns out, the link in the email leads to a suspicious website that transmits malware or infects your computer with a virus. Talk about disappointment! The only "life change" involved in that guarantee is the frustration and misery of dealing with computer problems!

A promise in Scripture is exactly the opposite. It's a promise that absolutely *will* change your life for the better, a promise that will never let you down. It's found in James 1:22–25:

> Be doers of the word, and not hearers only, deceiving yourselves. For if anyone is a hearer of the word and not a doer, he is like a man who looks intently at his natural face in a mirror. For he looks at himself and goes away and at once forgets what he was like. But the one who looks into the perfect law, the law of liberty, and perseveres, being no hearer who forgets but a doer who acts, he will be blessed in his doing.

This passage gives us one of our central lessons to live when it comes to the doctrine of Scripture: *Be a doer, not merely a hearer.* Being a doer means God will bless you in your doing.

Frederick W. Robertson, a British preacher who memorized the entire New Testament—*in Greek*—reminds us of the danger of being only a hearer:

> It is perilous to separate thinking rightly from acting. He is already half false who speculates on truth, and does not do it. Truth is given, not to be contemplated, but to be done. Life is an action, not a thought. And the penalty paid by him who speculates on truth, is that by degrees the very truth he holds becomes to him a falsehood.[10]

So be a doer, not just a hearer. This doesn't mean life will be problem-free. But it does mean God will bless you in your doing.

You'll be on the path of obedience He desires for His children, and His blessing will be seen in and through your obedience.

Lesson 4: Maintain a balanced diet of truth sources.

Some of us are old enough to remember when throwing together what experts described as a healthy meal was much easier than it is today. We had it down to just four "food groups": grains, meats, dairy, and fruits/vegetables. We knew that to have a balanced diet, we shouldn't have too much of one group or too little of another. If we turned our noses up at our turnip greens, our mommy could always point at the fourth group as a model of balance. We knew balance was the key, achieved through moderation and variety.

The same is true of the Christian walk. Believe it or not, a believer can overdose on just one aspect of an otherwise well-balanced faith. Too much Bible study alone can lead to overconfidence in one's own personal reading and a headful of trivia that fails to move from the head to the heart to the hands. Too much academic theology can produce a dogmatic know-it-all with a lot of *passion* but no *com*passion. Too much exposure to practical how-to manuals can create shallow pragmatists tossed about by every trendy tide or blown around by every idiosyncratic interpretational fad. These disciplines—all good and necessary—need to be pursued together, without our embracing one and neglecting the others.

Further, to keep these three "food groups" (Scripture, theology, and practical living) in proper balance, believers also need historical perspective. Knowing the history of interpretation will help us balance our own reading. Grasping the course of doctrinal development, controversy, and consensus will balance our own doctrinal confession. And learning how believers of the past lived their faith in a variety of unique cultural contexts can inform us as we try to live ours in the twenty-first century.

Like a four-legged table, a complete and balanced faith draws on biblical, theological, practical, and historical sources. These stabilizing elements of knowledge and wisdom must be applied with moderation and variety, neither overindulging in one or two nor ignoring the input of another.

As we seek to be diligent students of Scripture, we need to recognize that God's Word itself points us outside itself to other sources of truth—not to supplant but to *supplement* His inspired, verbal revelation. We're to ponder God's creation (Psalm 19:1–2; Romans 1:20), even learning life lessons from an ant (Proverbs 6:6)! Because a right understanding of the Bible corresponds with reality, established truths from other sources—like science, experience, theology, philosophy, and history—will necessarily correlate, creating a clearer picture of reality and our own place in it.

We must never surrender our Bibles as the inspired source of truth. Even so, we must also balance our Christian life with other truth sources. Remember, everything in the Bible is true, but not every truth is in the Bible.

Lesson 5: Seek understanding in the context of faith.

Some have understood the classic definition of theology—"faith seeking understanding"—to mean we seek to understand Scripture with an *attitude* of faith (believing). While that's a good attitude to have, it's not the whole picture. This definition also refers to the *content* of faith, as in "the faith which was once for all handed down to the saints" (Jude 3 NASB). While the Bible is our starting point, our foundation for theology, students of Scripture must read the Bible in light of the central doctrines that defined the faith even before the church had the complete Scriptures. Read Scripture in light of all Scripture, but also do theology in light of good theology.

But if reading the Bible is how we arrive at good theology, can good theology help us better read the Bible? Or is that kind of like being your own parent? Or chasing your own tail?

The answer is that the content of "the faith" isn't *everything* in the Bible or *everything* Christians can discover through Scripture, history, reason, and experience. Rather, "the faith" refers to the central tenets or essentials of Christian theology. So seeking understanding in the context of "the faith" means starting out with the core (fundamental) doctrines or foundational truths that make Christianity what it is. A firm grasp of these teachings will prevent a person from ignorantly or arrogantly reading the Bible in a way that contradicts the faith and leads to destruction. At the very least, it will keep the student of Scripture from getting completely lost.

While the Christian faith has always been characterized by diversity of opinions in nonessentials, it's also been known for unity on the essentials of orthodoxy, those things that have been believed everywhere, always, and by all. Some of the foundational doctrines that constitute this "faith," to which all true Christians must adhere even before they begin seeking understanding in Scripture, include such vital doctrines as the triune God as Creator and Redeemer, the fall and resulting lostness of humanity, the full divinity and humanity of Christ, Christ's atoning death and resurrection, salvation by grace through faith, the inspiration and authority of Scripture, and the ultimate judgment of humanity and restoration associated with Christ's future return.

If you want to better understand God's revelation—that is, be a better theologian—then focus on and firm up the content of the faith once for all delivered to the saints. Keep the main things in the middle and the secondary matters in the margins.

Lesson 6: Nurture the character of a virtuous theologian.

Bible? *Check*. Commentaries? *Check*. Church history books? *Check*. Bible study software? *Check*. Ministry experience?

Check. Theological references? *Check.* Character and virtue? *Uhhhh . . .*

We can focus on good tools—the ones necessary for doing good theology—and try to follow solid methods to get the best answers to our questions but still find that something vital is missing. Tools and skills are great, but without the necessary spiritual virtues, we'll never be genuinely good students of theology.

So how do we become virtuous theologians doing virtuous theology? Consider these four simple couplets that sum up how:

Do theology with humility and prayer. Prayer admits our inability and our humble dependence on God's enabling (1 Corinthians 2:14; Ephesians 1:17–19; Jude 20). The virtuous theologian begins on their knees.

Do theology with faith and obedience. A disposition of responsive belief is presupposed in the pursuit of truth (Hebrews 11:3, 6; 2 Timothy 3:16–17; John 14:21). The virtuous theologian seeks *trans*formation, not merely *in*formation.

Do theology with diligence and discipline. God enables understanding, faith, and obedience, yet this enabling leads to active participation (1 Timothy 4:13–15; 2 Timothy 2:15; 3:15; 2 Peter 3:16). The virtuous theologian braces for long, hard labor.

Do theology with caution and discernment. In our human weakness we can deceive, be deceived, and deceive ourselves (Jeremiah 17:9; Philippians 1:9; 1 Thessalonians 5:21; 1 John 4:1). The virtuous theologian proceeds with care.

Snapshot of History

Throughout the four periods of church history—the Patristic (100–500), Medieval (500–1500), Protestant (1500–1700), and Modern (1700–Present)—the doctrine of Scripture developed in various ways. The following chart summarizes the major developments related to Scripture in these four periods.[11]

Patristic Period (100–500)	Medieval Period (500–1500)	Protestant Period (1500–1700)	Modern Period (1700–Present)
• New Testament apostles and prophets recognized as authoritative (c. 100).	• Latin Vulgate becomes the standard version of the Bible in the Western church.	• Reformers respond to Catholic Church with the doctrine of *Sola Scriptura*— Scripture alone as the final authority in matters of faith, not councils and popes.	• The rise of historical-critical methods of studying texts leads many to challenge the authority of Scripture.
• Church fathers interpret Scripture in light of Christ's person and work (100–500).	• Greek Old and New Testaments become the standard versions of the Eastern Orthodox churches.	• The Bible translated into several popular languages from the original Hebrew and Greek languages.	• In liberal circles, "natural theology," resting on human reason, morality, experience, or feeling, replaces traditional biblical theology, leading to a reaction of classic orthodox doctrines.
• The "Muratorian Canon" describes the New Testament books accepted and rejected by the Church of Rome (c. 175).	• Interpretation of Scripture increasingly viewed as the domain of official teachers, especially the pope.	• Protestants reassert the literal and Christ-centered interpretation of Scripture.	
• Apologists draw on insights of philosophy to aid in explanation and defense of Christianity (c. 150–300).	• Scholars attempt to understand the faith by use of philosophy and church fathers in addition to Scripture.	• Roman Catholics officially add the Apocrypha to the canon at the Council of Trent (1545–1563).	• The Modernist-Fundamentalist controversy regarding the inerrancy of Scripture and the place of classic orthodoxy leads to a split in mainline denominations and the birth of new denominations and independent churches (1850–1950).
• Church fathers combat heresies that added or removed parts of the Bible or misinterpreted the Bible (c. 150–400).	• Scripture thought to contain multiple layers of meaning beyond the literal.	• Protestant confessions officially list the 66 Old and New Testament books, rejecting the Apocrypha as inspired and authoritative.	
• Churches achieve stable agreement regarding the Old and New Testament canons, though questions about the Apocrypha endure.	• Uncertainty persists regarding the canonical status of the Apocrypha.	• Scripture becomes the primary basis for reforming the church's doctrine and practice.	• Inspiration and inerrancy of Scripture defended and articulated in light of increasing doubts and attacks by modern critics (1900–Present).
• Inspiration and inerrancy of Scripture assumed.	• Renaissance leads to rediscovery of long-lost texts.	• Inspiration and inerrancy of Scripture assumed.	
	• Inspiration and inerrancy of Scripture assumed.		

TWO

God in Three Persons—
The Trinity: Father, Son,
and Holy Spirit

We believe in one God, the Father Almighty, maker of heaven and earth and of all things visible and invisible. And in one Lord Jesus Christ, the only begotten Son of God, begotten of his Father before all worlds, Light of Light, very God of very God, begotten not made, being of one substance with the Father, by whom all things were made. . . . And [we believe] in the Holy Ghost, the Lord and Giver-of-Life, who proceedeth from the Father, who with the Father and the Son together is worshiped and glorified.[1]

—The Constantinopolitan Creed (381)

There is one only and true God, but in the unity of the Godhead there are three coeternal and coequal Persons, the same in substance but distinct in subsistence.[2]

—Benjamin B. Warfield (1930)

63

In Short . . .

It seems like our media-and-meme-maddened world is engineered to keep us from pondering the profound questions of life:

- Why am I here?
- What's my purpose in life?
- Is there anything beyond this world?
- How can I be sure?

Let's face it. Often the most meaningful matters of life are nudged out by the trivial here and now. A lot of noisy, worldly worry draws our attention. There's always another short video queued up in our feed, another text message awaiting our reply, another episode ready to start before the one we just watched even finishes the credits, or a song some algorithm thinks we'll love, eager to coax us to hum along.

Yet the weighty questions never really go away. In those rare moments of calm, the ultimate questions return:

- Why is there something instead of nothing?
- Is there a God?
- If God is real, who is He?
- Or is there more than one god? Three? A million? None?

Answering the Ultimate Questions

People who call themselves *agnostics* (meaning "not knowing") find no certain and satisfying answers to the big questions. For *atheists* ("no god"), somehow convinced there is no God, the answers are more certain but no more settling. For those who buy into *pantheism* ("all god"), the answer to the ultimate question is "God is everything, and everything is God. You're God. I'm God. That dirt, the stars—all God!"

Last, we have the *theists*, who believe in at least one personal god. And if there's a god, then there's more to this world than meets the eye. There must be meaning in life beyond the noise, the bright lights, the big city, even beyond the stars.

But not all theisms are created equal.

According to Islam, Allah is a transcendent, solitary being who remains aloof. He makes no covenants or promises. He's not interested in personal relationships. Humans exist to submit to Allah, and not much else matters.

In polytheism, the gods are just like us, only bigger—more powerful, more voracious, more dangerous. As in a cosmic soap opera played out behind the scenes, they bicker over relationships, jostle for power, ravish mortals, and generally make a titanic mess of things.

In Judaism, God gives imperatives to follow, traditions to keep, and stories to tell. He commands and corrects. He creates, orders, prescribes, and judges. He also picks one special people for himself and has them do all sorts of things other people think are a little strange. But ultimately G–d, as He is revealed and known through Judaism, is not inherently relational.

Meeting Your Maker

Distinct from agnosticism, atheism, pantheism, and all other forms of theism, the Christian faith answers the ultimate questions about God and the universe in a way that's completely unique. We find that the one and only true God exists in three eternal, equal, fully divine persons: Father, Son, and Spirit—the "Trinity." The Father sends His Spirit to act in creation, revelation, and redemption. And He sent His Son, the Lord Jesus Christ, to enter the suffering that resulted from humankind's tragic fall. He offers forgiveness, reconciliation, and an intimate spiritual relationship with himself—from the Father, through the Son, and by the Holy Spirit.

Theology, in its basic sense, is thinking and speaking about God, His works, and His ways. Theology draws on the various means He's chosen to reveal himself—through creation, through Scripture, and especially through the person of Jesus Christ. And we know God through these means by the eye-opening work of the Holy Spirit.

As Christians throughout history and around the world have thought and spoken about God—as they've done theology— they've affirmed various doctrines (that is, "teachings") in response to His revelation. No doctrine has occupied Christians across time more than the theology of Father, Son, and Spirit—the Trinity. We can learn much from the countless believers who have gone before us.

Formulating the Trinity

Though the word *Trinity* doesn't appear in the Bible (but neither does the word *Bible*), the Trinity is a biblical doctrine. Scripture affirms the following basic truths that together constitute the classic doctrine of the Trinity—one God in three persons. So simple are these biblical assertions that even a child could learn them:

- There is one God (Deuteronomy 6:4).
- The Father is God (John 6:27).
- The Son is God (John 1:1).
- The Spirit is God (Acts 5:3–4).
- The Father is not the Son (John 20:17).
- The Son is not the Spirit (John 14:16).
- The Spirit is not the Father (John 14:26).
- There is one God, not three gods (1 Corinthians 8:6).

Incidentally, for nearly twenty centuries Christians have referred to the Father, Son, and Spirit as "persons" (not "people,"

"In the divine nature there subsist three Persons, Father, Son, and Holy Ghost; and that these three are one God, being distinct from one another by relations alone."[3]

Thomas Aquinas (c. 1260)

"personalities," or "individuals"). We've described them as "distinct" (not "separate") from one another. And we refer to them as "members" (not "parts") of the Trinity. This core truth of the Christian faith summarizes the Bible's teaching concerning Father, Son, and Holy Spirit: three distinct persons in one divine essence.

For centuries, the relationships of the Father, Son, and Holy Spirit have been summarized by the "Shield of the Trinity" (see the following illustration), reminding Christians that though the Father, Son, and Spirit are all properly called "God," they are distinct from one another in their eternal relationships.

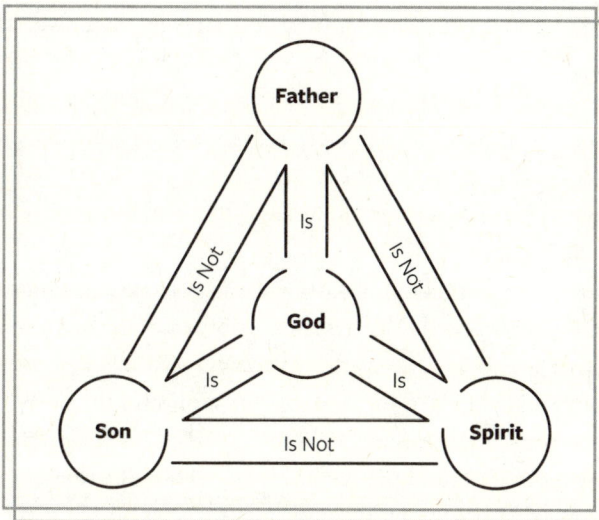

Embracing the Incarnation

The heart and soul of the gospel message itself is the person of Jesus Christ. Scripture demonstrates Him to be all that God is as God (but not the same person as the Father or the Spirit) and all that we are as human (but without sin). Jesus is the God-Man.

Amid gruesome persecution, the early Christians of the first three centuries sealed their faith in the God-Man with their blood. And since those early centuries, millions of believers have also suffered for their identification with the Father, Son, and Spirit through Christian baptism—most recently in Asia, North Africa, and the Middle East.

Today as much as ever, to confess Jesus Christ as the Son of God can carry grave consequences. But if we're not called to die for Him, we're nevertheless called to live for Him. Because Jesus is much more than a moral teacher, mighty miracle worker, wise sage, or proven prophet, He deserves our allegiance, love, and worship. He is fully human and fully divine—two complete natures in one unique person.

Living by the Spirit

Last (but certainly not least), Christians live by the power of the Spirit. In fact, without the Spirit, we couldn't truly worship the Father (John 4:23–24). The Spirit spoke through the prophets in the Holy Scriptures (2 Peter 1:21), and that same Spirit teaches us concerning the saving truths about God (John 16:13). Not only that, but He also dwells in believers to help them live a life pleasing to God (Galatians 5:16–25).

Thus, everything God has done for us—from creation to salvation—is from the Father, through the Son, and by the Spirit. And we relate to God in faith in obedience by the Spirit, through the Son, and to the Father. And for this we praise the one God in three persons, Father, Son, and Holy Spirit, "for from Him and through Him and to Him are all things. To Him be the glory forever. Amen" (Romans 11:36 NASB).

Passages to Ponder

While we can't speak *exhaustively* of the divine Being, we can speak *sufficiently* about who God is because God has chosen to reveal himself to us. And while He reveals himself in many ways in creation and history, the words of Scripture provide a sure foundation, for they were given "to give you the wisdom that leads to salvation" (2 Timothy 3:15 NASB). Throughout history, God's people have pondered key passages in their thinking about the divine. But even when we've mastered these sections of Holy Scripture, we'll still be novices in the infinite mysteries of God.

(1) Genesis 1:1–3—In the Beginning . . . God

The Bible's opening words set the stage for everything that follows. "In the beginning, God created the heavens and the earth" (Genesis 1:1) proclaims the existence of the supremely intelligent Designer. God is not an impersonal cosmic force (as in pantheism). Nor is the world an accident in a purposeless universe (as in atheism). Earth is not a trillion-to-one lottery jackpot. Rather, the Creator is personal and intentional.

Genesis 1 then describes the orderly, rhythmic process of creation. For nearly two thousand years, Christians have debated about how, when, and in what manner the days of creation occurred. What's clear, though, is that God fills the void, brings order to chaos, brings life from non-life, and does all this in a way that is "good" (Genesis 1).

Ultimately, God brought everything into being "out of nothing" (the Latin *ex nihilo*). We can't prove this by observation or reason. Rather, "by faith we understand that the universe was created by the word of God, so that what is seen was not made out of things that are visible" (Hebrews 11:3).

(2) Exodus 3:13–15; 20:7—What's in a Name?

In an epic scene from Exodus 3, Moses encountered the one true God in the strangest circumstance. While tending sheep in the wilderness, he happened upon a burning bush unconsumed by the flames. Then, we're told, "the angel of the LORD appeared to him in a flame of fire" (Exodus 3:2). Many commentators, both ancient and modern, view this title "Angel of the Lord" as a reference not to a created angelic being but to a Christophany—a manifestation of the preincarnate Son of God. The Hebrew word translated "angel" means "messenger." In any case, the voice from the flame announced, "I am the God of your father, the God of Abraham, the God of Isaac, and the God of Jacob" (3:6).

In the dialogue that followed, God revealed His name to Moses so Moses could tell the Israelites who sent him: "'I AM WHO I AM.' And he said, 'Say this to the people of Israel, "I AM has sent me to you"'" (Exodus 3:14). Here we come to the most sacred revelation of the entire Old Testament: God's personal name, *YHWH*, related to the Hebrews' word for "to be" or "to exist"—that is, I AM. Those four Hebrew letters, *YHWH*, that make up the name are often simply rendered "LORD" in English-language Bibles.

PASSAGES TO MASTER AND MEMORIZE

Genesis 1:1–3	Matthew 28:19
Genesis 1:26–27	John 1:1–3, 14, 18
Exodus 3:14	John 14:16–17; 15:26
Exodus 20:7	Ephesians 1:3, 13
Deuteronomy 6:4	Philippians 2:6–11
Psalm 139:7–10	Colossians 1:15–19
Isaiah 6:3	1 John 4:13–16

Note: Not all these passages are discussed in the text, but they'll all help you master the doctrine of the Trinity.

Whereas another name for God, *Elohim*, normally denotes the concept of Sovereign Creator, *YHWH* designates God's personal name, especially in His personal relationship with His people. The self-existent One—the God who always and ever simply *is*—has chosen for himself a people by whom He wants to be known.

But God has revealed himself to us with other names and titles besides *YHWH*, and they play an important role in developing our understanding of God. While they don't tell us everything about Him, God's names, like the individual brushstrokes of a complex painting, culminate in a beautiful picture that helps us better know and relate to Him.

Three basic principles carry us further along in understanding the God of the Christian faith: the divine names (1) reveal God's person, (2) represent God's presence, and (3) thus are sacred.

THE DIVINE NAMES . . .

REVEAL GOD'S PERSON

Disclose His Character
Couple His Functions With His Identity
Unfold in Progressive Revelation

REPRESENT GOD'S PRESENCE

Serve as Figures of Speech for His Person
Sometimes Represent His Personal Will
Invoke His Presence and Authority

AND THUS ARE SACRED

Are to Be Safeguarded as Revelatory Instruments
Are Not to Be Blasphemed or Taken Lightly or in Jest
Signify That We Must Approach Oaths With Caution

El and *Elohim* exalt God as the all-powerful One. *YHWH* points toward the timeless "I AM," who joined with His people in personal covenant relationship. Scripture reveals names of exaltation: *El Olam,* "the Everlasting God" (Genesis 21:33; Isaiah 40:28); *El Elyon,* "God Most High" (Genesis 14:17–22; Deuteronomy 32:8; Psalm 78:35); and *El Shaddai,* "God Almighty" (Genesis 17:1–3). The Greek *pantokrator* means "the Almighty" (Revelation 1:8; 4:8; 11:17; 16:7), and "LORD of Hosts" indicates His command of vast heavenly armies (1 Samuel 1:3,11; Psalm 24:10; Isaiah 1:9).

Divine names often couple God's identity with His activities. The Lord is "the Judge of all the earth" (Genesis 18:25); "the Rock [Protector] of Israel" (Genesis 49:24 NIV); the good "Shepherd" (Psalm 23:1); the "Redeemer" (Isaiah 44:6); "Husband" (Isaiah 54:5); "Savior" (Isaiah 63:8); and "King of kings and Lord of lords" (1 Timothy 6:15; compare Revelation 19:16). Together, dozens of colorful divine titles form a brilliant portrait of our God, of His attributes and of His acts.

In what many call "the Lord's Prayer," Jesus taught His disciples how to pray: "Our Father in heaven, hallowed be your name" (Matthew 6:9). The term *hallowed* means to "make holy," "set apart," "honor," "revere." We are to "make holy" God's name in the world. Just before this prayer, Jesus issued a stern warning about making frivolous oaths, "swearing falsely," before God or man (Matthew 5:33–37). Because God's names reveal His person and represent His presence, they are sacred. We are to hallow the divine names, guard them in our own lives, and defend them against misuse as best we can.

(3) Deuteronomy 6:4—God the One and Only

Repeated in evening and morning prayers by faithful Jews even today, the Shema is the John 3:16 of the Old Testament: "Hear, O Israel [Hebrew: *Shema Yisrael*]: The LORD our God, the LORD is one. You shall love the LORD your God with all your heart and with all your soul and with all your might" (Deuteronomy 6:4–5). Earlier, Deuteronomy 4:39 made it clear that only one God exists, not many gods: "The LORD is God in heaven above and on the earth beneath; there is no other." Any other so-called "gods" have no turf in the cosmos. The God of Israel is the Creator, the Sovereign, the one and only *true God*.

Yet if God is "one," how can Christians believe the Father is God, the Son is God, and the Spirit is God? Isn't that three gods? No. The Hebrew term for *one* (*ehad*) can denote a composite unity—that is, a one-in-many. For example, Adam and Eve become "one [*ehad*] flesh" in their marriage (Genesis 2:24). Notably, another Hebrew word, *yahid*, means "only one, solitary," and this term is never used of God. In other words, the Old Testament's insistence on God's unity emphasizes His uniqueness: He's the *one true* God. It doesn't rule out God's triunity. The New Testament's further revelation maintains the Hebrew insistence on monotheism, but not "single-person" monotheism as in Islam or Unitarianism.

The fact is the Old Testament's word usage points toward divine unity in plurality. Many have taken God's declaration "Let us make man in our image" (Genesis 1:26; compare Isaiah 44:24) as suggesting a mysterious unity within the Godhead. The "Spirit" of *YHWH*, the Holy Spirit, acts and speaks as God by giving life, order, and beauty to creation, yet the Spirit is also distinct from God (Isaiah 40:13–14; 63:10; Nehemiah 9:20). What's more, we've seen the "Angel of YHWH" speaking and acting directly as God (Exodus 3:2). Again, in exalted language, the messianic "Son of David" is declared to be "God" (Psalm 45:6–7; 110:1—in Hebrew, *Adonai*), "Mighty God" (Isaiah 9:6), and possibly even the YHWH "whom they have pierced" (Zechariah 12:10).

Let's be clear. The Old Testament alone doesn't clearly lead to the doctrine of the Holy Trinity—Father, Son, and Spirit, the same in essence but distinct in personhood. Nevertheless, it never

73

rules out a concept of "plurality in unity," and more than that, it contains all the pieces for the clearer revelation of Jesus Christ in the New Testament.

(4) Psalm 139—The Perfections of God

Christians often categorize God's divine attributes into two categories: *communicable* and *incommunicable*. *Communicable* attributes address who God is in His personal character: good, faithful, holy, righteous, just, wise, and loving. These are called "communicable" because we humans can exhibit them in our own lives by the power of the Holy Spirit working in us—though we do so partially and imperfectly. Only God himself displays these perfections to the utmost.

The *incommunicable* attributes indicate that these perfections separate God from all creatures. The term doesn't mean we can't talk about such attributes, but we can't truly participate in them, even imperfectly. God alone can be described as self-existent, simple, one, self-sufficient, eternal, immutable, impassable, free, infinite, omniscient, omnipresent, omnipotent, and immanent.[4]

So God's *incommunicable* attributes are those that are His alone, those that distinguish Him from all of creation. God's *communicable* attributes are characteristics with which we can relate and participate. We can't become all-present or all-powerful, but because God made us in His image and likeness (Genesis 1:26–27), we can grow in love, holiness, righteousness, and mercy.

(5) Ephesians 1:3–14—God the Father

It might surprise you to learn that the title "Father" for God in the Old Testament is especially rare. But the New Testament describes God as "Father" more than 250 times! Perhaps at the time of the Old Testament, God wanted to reveal himself in a way that clearly distinguished Him from the various fertility gods and "just-like-us-but-bigger" concepts in the ancient Near East. But in the New Testament, God reveals himself with language that indicates not only His fatherly relationship with all humanity but His distinction from God the Son and God the Holy Spirit—one God in three persons.

One of the most powerfully Trinitarian and worshipful texts in Scripture is Ephesians 1:3–14. There Paul sets forth a majestic panorama of how Father, Son, and Spirit work together in salvation. "Praise be to the God and Father of our Lord Jesus Christ," he says, "who has blessed us in the heavenly realms with every spiritual blessing in Christ" (1:3 NIV). In love, the Father, as the gracious Designer, "predestined us for adoption to sonship" (1:5) through His beloved Son in whom "we have redemption through his blood, the forgiveness of sins" (1:7). When made sons and daughters in Christ, we're sealed by the Holy Spirit, "who is a deposit guaranteeing our inheritance" (1:14).

The persons of the Godhead work together to secure the believer's salvation, and they powerfully move toward the culmination of God's saving purpose in the world. The Father, Son, and Holy Spirit act in harmony with distinct but inseparable functions in the plan of salvation.

In light of the rarity of "father" language in the Old Testament, it's hard to miss the repeated use of God the Father—distinct from the Son and Spirit—in this passage. Note the language: "the God and Father of our Lord Jesus Christ" (Ephesians 1:3), "the glorious Father" (1:17 NIV), the "one God and Father of all, who is over all and through all and in all" (4:6). James describes God as "the Father of lights" (James 1:17). Jesus famously teaches us to pray to "our Father in heaven" (Matthew 6:9).

But John's Gospel most solidifies the Christian's language of God as "Father," using the title 122 times, about half the whole New Testament's uses of "Father." To God the Father are especially ascribed the roles of Creator (Acts 17:24–29), sovereign ruler (1 Timothy 6:15–16), holy judge (2 Peter 3:7), compassionate reconciler (2 Corinthians 5:18–19), and the one to whom all things return (1 Corinthians 15:24–26). The other persons of the Trinity share in these works as well, so the classic Christian understanding of the relationship of the persons of the Trinity has been that all things are *from* the Father, *through* the Son, and *by* the Holy Spirit.

(6) John 1:1–18—God the Son, in the Flesh

Central to all Christian confession is that Jesus Christ is the eternal Son of God, God incarnate. The word *incarnate* means "in the flesh," and the incarnation of God the Son means the second person of the Trinity took on full humanity, including a body of flesh like us—but without sin. Thus, Jesus of Nazareth is the "God-Man."

Chief among several passages that assert the full deity and full humanity of Christ, John's prologue in John 1 most directly and explicitly establishes that Jesus is the eternal God who took on true humanity. Thus, Jesus is fully God. Just as Genesis 1:1 recounts the creation of heaven and earth, John 1:1 picks up the same language to speak of the condition before anything existed except God himself: "In the beginning was the Word, and the Word was *with* God, and the Word *was* God" (emphasis added).

Though the title *Logos* (translated "Word" from the Greek) as the Son of God is used only a few times, it's a word heavy with both Hebrew and Greek connotations. In the Old Testament, the Hebrew equivalent, *dabar*, is God's Word that goes forth to do His bidding, to create, to bring life, even to judge. The "Word" sometimes even seems to have appeared in tangible form (Genesis 15:1, 4–5; Jeremiah 1:4–5, 7, 9). Also, at the time John wrote his Gospel, the Greeks regarded the Logos as the divine organizing principle of the universe, that which brings all else into existence. *Logos*, then, was a term pregnant with potential meaning to the original readers.

Because Jesus is God the Son incarnate, He's rightly addressed as God or described in terms that make clear His unity with the Father and essential divinity throughout the New Testament (John 8:58; 10:30; 17:5; 20:28; Acts 20:28; Romans 9:5; Colossians 2:9; Hebrews 1:3). Both the Father and the Son are Lord, Mighty God (Isaiah 9:6; 10:21), King of kings and Lord of lords (1 Timothy 6:15; Revelation 19:16), and Alpha and Omega (Revelation 1:8; 22:13). For this reason, the earliest church worshipped Jesus as truly God. Still, the Bible equally asserts that there are not two gods, or many gods, but one true God (Isaiah 43:10–11; James 2:19).

Twice in John 1:1–2 the text states that before anything, the Logos already was *with* God. This implies not only nearness but personal fellowship. And most decisively the Logos *was* God—like Father, like Son. These two words—*with* and *was*—establish both unity and distinction between Father and Son, preventing us from the two errors of (1) separating the two into different gods, and (2) collapsing the two into one person with different names. Thus, the Father and the Son are distinct persons. God the Father and God the Son, each fully God by nature, abide in extraordinary personal unity.

John 1:14 says, "The Word [not the Father] became flesh and dwelt among us, and we have seen his glory, glory as of the only Son from the Father, full of grace and truth." And John ends his prologue with pristine clarity regarding both: "No one has ever seen God, but the one and only Son, who is himself God and is in closest relationship with the Father, has made him known" (1:18 NIV).

Finally, John 1:3 makes it clear that everything was created through the Son. To those who argue that the Son was God's first creation or that the Word was *a* god but not absolute deity, John 1:3 makes this impossible: "All things were made through him, and without him was not any thing made that was made." If the Son were a created being, then He would have had to cre-ate himself, for nothing was created apart from Him. As John's prologue necessarily excludes the Son as a created being, He must be coeternal with the Father—both are equally God.

(7) Colossians 1:15–19; Philippians 2:6–11—The Son Before, In, and Above Creation

Plenty of funny stories remind us that ideas can get mangled when communicated from one language to another. So it is with certain biblical words, like *firstborn* in Colossians 1: "The Son is the image of the invisible God, the firstborn over all creation" (1:15 NIV). This term can mean either a parent's eldest child, the literal "firstborn" (Luke 2:7), or the chief heir of a father's legacy, preeminent in rank, the metaphorical "firstborn" (Psalm 88; compare Deuteronomy 21:15–17).

The context of Colossians 1:15–19 requires that we understand the Son as the "firstborn" heir over all creation, "so that in everything he might have the supremacy" (Colossians 1:18 NIV). Colossians also describes Jesus as the living image of God in whom dwells "all the fullness of deity" (Colossians 2:9)—that is, He is full deity incarnate. He is the one through whom all things were created—heavenly, earthly, visible, and invisible (1:16–17). Therefore, He himself could not be a created being.

Similar to the prologue of John's Gospel (1:3) and that of the letter to the Hebrews (1:2), Paul ascribes to the Son what no Jew

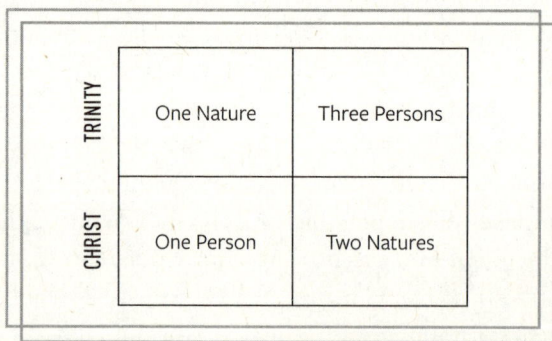

	One Nature	Three Persons
TRINITY		
CHRIST	One Person	Two Natures

would ever say of anyone other than the great "I AM": The Son is the Origin, Sustainer, and Ruler of all creation. He is absolute God.

This leads us to another central passage on the deity and humanity of Christ, what many Christians believe to have been an early hymn of worship: Philippians 2:5–11. To strengthen his exhortation to unity through humility, Paul appeals to the belief in Christ's deity and incarnation as a model to follow (2:5–7). The humility of the Son is the preeminent example for us. If Jesus, "who, being in very nature God" (2:6 NIV) did not flaunt His divine attributes—and He had every right to do so—then how dare we selfishly pursue our own way? Rather, God the Son "made himself nothing by taking the very nature of a servant, being made in human likeness" (2:7 NIV). And "being found in appearance as a man, he humbled himself by becoming obedient to death—even death on a cross!" (2:8 NIV). God the Son doubly humbled himself, first in becoming human, second in suffering the most shameful, torturous death known in that day. And for this work of redemption, He was crowned with glory in the bodily resurrection (2:9–11).

From this powerful passage comes the Greek term *kenosis*, the divine Son's "self-emptying" to assume a human nature. What does it mean that Christ "emptied" himself? First, Paul couldn't have meant that Jesus gave up His deity. Think about it: If Jesus were not God, then Paul's example would make no sense. And even after His incarnation, Jesus was ascribed as both human and divine.

So in what sense did the Son empty himself? Certainly not some of His divine attributes, because then He wouldn't have the "whole fullness of deity" in bodily form (Colossians 2:9). The *kenosis* (or "emptying") of Christ, then, refers to the Son of God's voluntary humiliation involved in *adding* a fully human (and therefore finite) nature to His divine, infinite nature and submitting to the suffering and death inherent in that act.

When it comes to statements concerning the incarnate God-Man, we're neither to reduce His humanity merely to the physical body (that is, He's not just "God in a bod"), nor are we to separate the two natures of Jesus Christ, such that we posit two persons occupying the same space (as a demon might possess a human person). Nor should we confuse and mix the two natures like red and blue paint mixed to become a new color: purple.

Rather, the fifth-century Council of Chalcedon (AD 451) rightly affirmed that Jesus Christ is both fully God and fully human in one person. His two natures can neither be separated nor confused. Indeed, the eternal Son assumed a human nature not only in His earthly sojourn but also for all eternity as Messiah, Lamb, our God and Brother. Yet in assuming a human nature forever, the Son of God still isn't limited by that nature.

(8) John 14–17—The Holy Spirit Is God

Hours before the cross, Jesus prepared His disciples for the unimaginable events ahead in what is arguably the deepest revelation of the Gospels, the Upper Room Discourse. This is the epicenter of Trinitarian revelation. Jesus boldly asserted His oneness with the Father: "Whoever has seen me has seen the Father" (John 14:9). The Father and the Son are one in Godhood and yet distinct in personhood: "I am in the Father and the Father is in me" (14:10–11).

But rather than asserting a two-person, "binitarian" doctrine of God, Jesus promised One like himself, "another Helper," to be with believers forever: "the Spirit of truth" (14:16–17). Of course, the Spirit isn't a "new" member of the Trinity. His activity is evident in the Old Testament (Genesis 1:2; Psalm 51:11; Isaiah 63:11) and throughout the Gospels themselves (Matthew 1:18; Mark 3:29; Luke 1:41). Specifically, Jesus said God would send the Spirit into the world in a new way—to empower the lives of those who trust in the Son.

We shouldn't imagine God the Spirit as an impersonal force or power. Rather, the Holy Spirit "will teach you all things and bring to your remembrance all that I have said to you" (John 14:26). The Spirit convicts the world of sin, righteousness, and judgment (16:8–11). In fact, "when the Spirit of truth comes, he will guide you into all the truth . . . and he will declare to you the things that are to come" (16:12–13). Teaching, reminding, convicting, guiding, and glorifying are not the works of an impersonal force. He also intercedes for believers (Romans 8:27), knows the deepest things of God (1 Corinthians 2:13), and can be grieved, lied to, and insulted (Ephesians 4:30; Acts 5:3, 9; Hebrews 10:29; compare Isaiah 63:10).

The Spirit also speaks and instructs (Acts 8:29; 13:2), gives spiritual gifts to the church according to His will (1 Corinthians 12:11), and "helps us in our weakness" (Romans 8:26). All these activities manifest a personal third member of the Trinity who shines forth intelligence, will, and emotion.

It's hardly surprising, then, that all the divine attributes belonging to the Father and the Son are also ascribed to the Spirit (Isaiah 40:12; Genesis 6:3; 2 Timothy 3:16; Luke 1:35; John 3:5–7; Romans 8:1–16). In 2 Corinthians 3:17–18, Paul writes, "Now the Lord is the Spirit, and where the Spirit of the Lord is, there is freedom . . . this comes from the Lord who is the Spirit." And Peter equates lying to the Spirit with lying to God (Acts 5:3–4).

The Spirit of truth is none other than the "other Helper," one like the Son sent from the Father (John 14:16). At the Son's request, the Father sent "the Helper, the Holy Spirit" to advance His ministry in the world by teaching the disciples "all things" (14:26). John 15:26 takes us one step further: "When the Helper comes, whom I will send to you from the Father, the Spirit of truth, who proceeds from the Father, he will bear witness about me."

The breathtaking truth is that God the Spirit lives in and among all of us who have trusted in Jesus Christ as God's Son and our Savior. The Holy Spirit is God in us. We don't become God, of course. Rather, the Spirit indwells us by God's wondrous grace. The Spirit's effective, vital presence regenerates and seals us for God (John 3:5–8; Ephesians 1:13), functioning in the believer much as the Lord Jesus Christ functioned in the lives of the disciples. God the Spirit carries on God the Son's work as Guide, Counselor, Advocate, Mentor, Challenger, Lord . . . and God.

TEN WAYS GOD CAN BE "PRESENT"

1. TRANSCENDENTLY present to himself outside of creation.	John 17:5
2. EXALTEDLY present on the throne of heaven amid angels and saints.	Job 1:6; Isaiah 6:1–3; Daniel 7:9–10; Revelation 4–5
3. PERCEIVABLY present in specific places such as the Holy of Holies, Mount Zion, and the Holy Land.	Numbers 10:33–35; 2 Samuel 6:2; Psalm 26:8; 46:5; 48:1–3; Joel 3:16–17
4. VISIBLY present through theophanies (e.g., the burning bush, *shekinah* glory).	Exodus 3:2–5; 33:18–34:7; Numbers 12:5–8; 1 Kings 8:10
5. PERSONALLY present through the incarnation.	John 1:14, 18; Acts 7:56; Colossians 2:9; Hebrews 1:3; Revelation 5:7; 22:1–4
6. CORPORATELY present in the church.	Matthew 18:20; 1 Corinthians 3:16–17; Ephesians 2:12–22; 2 Peter 2:5
7. INTIMATELY present by indwelling individual believers.	John 14:23; Romans 8:9, 11; 1 Corinthians 6:19
8. EFFECTIVELY present in filling and empowering believers.	Acts 7:55; compare 4:8, 31; 10:44–45; Colossians 1:17
9. IMMANENTLY present by sustaining all created things with His power.	Psalm 19:1–6; Isaiah 40:25–26
10. GLORIOUSLY present among His people in the new heavens and new earth.	Revelation 21:1–4

(9) Matthew 28:19—In the Name of the Father, Son, and Spirit

The "baptismal formula" at the end of Matthew's Gospel stands as the template for historic Trinitarian development: "Go therefore and make disciples of all nations, baptizing them in the name of the Father and of the Son and of the Holy Spirit" (28:19). For a Jew such as Jesus (and the writer, Matthew) to include three distinct persons in the singular "name" (likely meaning the sacred name of God) would be tantamount to blasphemy—*were it not absolutely true!*

The Father's inclusion wouldn't have surprised anyone. All knew the Father was fully God. And by the close of Jesus' earthly ministry, He had more than proven His identity as God the Son.

Having been vindicated in His earthly mission by His miracles and miraculous bodily resurrection, Jesus now exercises "all authority in heaven and on earth" (28:18). Thus, the second person, "the Son," under the one name (28:19) likely didn't surprise any of the disciples.

But the baptismal formula's third person, "the Holy Spirit," might have caught them a little off guard, at least until they thought about it for a minute. Remember, the Spirit was God-in-action in the Old Testament. And the Spirit came upon the Virgin Mary to conceive "God with us" (Matthew 1:18–23). John the Baptist proclaimed that the Messiah would baptize with the Holy Spirit (3:11), and God's Spirit descended "like a dove" at Jesus' baptism (3:16). Later, Jesus sent forth the disciples two by two, promising them that the Spirit would speak through them (10:20). Now, as the resurrected Christ readied himself to ascend into heaven, He declared that another should also be understood as sharing in the sacred name. If the divine Being includes the Father and the Son, then the Spirit is also a distinct divine person in the Godhead.

So we baptize in the name of the Father, and of the Son, and of the Holy Spirit. We pray and worship in the name of the Father, and of the Son, and of the Holy Spirit. We trust and obey the Father, Son, and Spirit. In fact, all things come from the Father, through the Son, and by the Spirit. And all glory, honor, power, and strength return to the Father, through the Son, and by the Holy Spirit. This is the one true God—God in three persons, the blessed Trinity.

Realities to Remember

When it comes to theology, some topics are weightier than others. Without question, the weightiest subject is the Trinity—Father, Son, and Spirit. As such, attention to the truth about God carries great consequences. The central issues are often matters of salvation and damnation—Christianity and anti-Christianity. Failing to face these foundational claims of faith can injure or destroy the soul.

To prevent doctrinal disaster before it happens, step back to remember some realities about the one true God: Father, Son, and Holy Spirit.

1. God is both infinite and personal.

The ancient deities of the Greeks and Romans, Canaanites, Egyptians, Assyrians, Babylonians, Persians, Hindus, and all tribal religions appear as petty human projections compared to the one true God. None of them are transcendent. All of them are stuck in the same timeline we are.

As the ultimate reality, the true God is infinite. He stands above and beyond all creation. He doesn't live in temples, He's not served by people, and He "gives everyone life and breath and everything else" (Acts 17:25 NIV). Because of Him we creatures "live and move and have our being" (17:28 NIV). Nothing is behind God—not space, not time, not chance, not even laws of logic. The Almighty is "the blessed and only Ruler, the King of kings and Lord of lords, who alone is immortal and who lives in unapproachable light, whom no one has seen or can see" (1 Timothy 6:15–16 NIV).

Finite beings have no access to the infinite God unless He stoops down to make himself known in ways we can grasp. How astonishing that the God who spun out the unthinkably immense universe still reveals himself upon the particle of dust that is our planet! He's outside of and effortlessly sustains all creation, yet He determines to come to us and make himself known.

So while God is transcendent, He reveals himself as vividly, radically personal. Just as no words can capture the complexity of a human person, we cannot fathom the depths of divine personhood. Yet still God gives us His Word, the Bible, which describes and informs us as to the richness of God as personal, indeed the tripersonal being. Beyond all creation exists the infinite God in relationship as Father, Son, and Holy Spirit. And He has invited us into personal fellowship with the triune life.

2. Evidence and arguments point to God's existence.

God created everything to reflect His mystery and glory. Historic Christian faith maintains that all things except sin and evil point toward the Creator. Yet "in the beginning, God created the heavens and the earth," and "it was very good" (Genesis 1:1, 31).

CLASSIC ARGUMENTS FOR GOD'S EXISTENCE

The Cosmological Argument (Psalm 102:25; Hebrews 3:4): Effects observed in the world require a sufficient cause. Motion requires an original unmoved Mover; subordinate temporal effects require a superordinate atemporal Cause; contingent beings require the existence of a necessary Being. God is the sufficient Cause.

The Teleological Argument (Psalm 19:1–6; 94:9–10): Complex order and design in the universe require an intelligent Designer. Such order could not have occurred by chance. The Designer must be of sufficient intelligence to order with purpose. God is the intelligent Designer.

The Anthropological Argument (Psalm 8:3–8): The appearance of mind, emotion, and will in humans is most reasonably the result of a superior intelligent, feeling, and willing Being. The alternative—that mind, emotion, and will were the result of unthinking, unfeeling, random causes—is less plausible. God is the superior intelligent, feeling, and willing Being.

The Moral Argument (Proverbs 28:1; Romans 2:14–16): Moral awareness is found generally among individuals and cultures. The sense of moral obligation affects people so radically as to produce either obedience or guilt. The presence of an absolute moral obligation implies the existence of an absolute moral Lawgiver. God is the absolute moral Lawgiver.

The Aesthetic Argument (Psalm 19:1–4; 27:4): Capacity for the admiration of beauty, even when the object of beauty has no practical value, is universal. Particular estimations of beauty can be subjective, yet the idea of beauty is universal. The existence of beauty must be accounted for by a ground and giver of beauty. God is the Ground and Giver of beauty.

The Pragmatic Argument: Belief in God has practical personal and social benefits. Belief in God can have positive psychological effects on human well-being. Belief in God can aid in overcoming addiction and healing relationships. Belief in God can motivate philanthropic acts that benefit humanity. Belief in God is better than disbelief in God.

Christian theology has offered various evidences for God's existence based on observation of and reflection upon His creation. These and other arguments from God's revelation in creation remain as strong as ever. They're not absolute proofs—if one considers proof to be the irrefutable conclusion of empirical evidence or necessary logic. Rather, natural evidence evokes humility and faith in a Creator.

Here are a couple of thoughts on the arguments for God's existence:

First, *God doesn't exist because the arguments are true; the arguments are true because God exists*. This is an important distinction, for God is not a logical conclusion. God is the logical cause; the universe is the effect.

Second, *we need to consider "the buoy effect" of unbelief*. Just as a buoy floating atop a body of water rises and falls with the tide, if unbelievers don't want to see the truth and believe, they'll stubbornly float on a perceived ocean of evidence to avoid believing in God. When even smart, credentialed people examine the universe and find no trace of God, it's not because the arguments are riddled with flaws; it's because people (all of us) are. Apart from the work of God's Spirit, who opens eyes, minds, and wills to see the truth, spiritually blinded people will refuse to acknowledge God as the Creator of all things.

3. Jesus Christ—God incarnate—is the ultimate revelation of God.

What an amazing reality that God the Son came into the world and took on a human nature to live among us. The Son was sent into the world, yet He is its Creator (John 1:3; Colossians 1:16–17; Hebrews 1:2). He is God, with all the attributes of God the Father, yet He's distinct from the Father. From the beginning, the Word was already with God and was God (John 1:1–2). Hebrews 1:3 says, "The Son is the radiance of God's glory and the exact representation of his being, sustaining all things by his powerful word" (NIV). And John 1:18 tells us, "No one has ever seen God, but the one and only Son, who is himself God and is in closest relationship with the Father, has made him known" (NIV).

The Son, incarnate in Jesus, is as fully God as the Father. Like Father, like Son. And the Father and the Son love each other— volitionally, rejoicingly, fully.

In the classical language of the Nicene-Constantinopolitan Creed, the eternal Son of God is "God from God, Light from Light, true God from true God."[5] Christians for centuries have used the language of "eternal begottenness" or "eternal generation" to summarize the teaching of Scripture that the Son is eternally the Son of the Father, and the Father is eternally the Father of the Son. This technical language has served to distinguish the Son from the Father not only in name but also in terms of eternal relationship. That eternal Son of God became incarnate for us and our salvation.

Isaiah 9:6–7 foretold the coming Messiah would be "born" as the heir of David's throne, yet He would also be known as "Mighty God." Micah 5:2 prophesied that the one born in Bethlehem would yet have His origins "from ancient times" (NIV). The New Testament too sets before us all Jesus as a human being *and* as God the Son (John 1:1, 14; Philippians 2:6–11). The Chalcedonian Definition (AD 451) articulates that Christ's two natures coexist in the one person, truly God and truly human. The Son took on a human nature in the incarnation, and those two natures, though distinct, cannot be mixed or separated. Using the Greek word *hypostasis*, meaning "person," theologians for centuries have used the term *hypostatic union* to describe the unity of natures in one person.

4. The Spirit is fully, distinctly, and personally God.

Some Christians today think if they don't *feel* or *sense* the Spirit's presence and continually experience His power, then the Spirit has left them. But the Spirit functions as far more than God's power in moments of elation and spiritual victory. In one sense, everything

God does in our lives is by the Spirit, even in solace and quiet, in struggle against temptation, in the discipline of prayer, in studying Scripture, and in witnessing to an unbeliever.

All the divine attributes are displayed not only in the Father and the Son but also in the Spirit. The Spirit—true God from true God—reveals himself in Scripture as intelligent (Romans 8:27; 1 Corinthians 2:10–13), exercising personal will (Acts 8:29; 13:2; 15:28; 1 Corinthians 12:11), and manifesting emotions (Ephesians 4:30; Hebrews 10:29). The Spirit is "*another* Helper" (John 14:16, emphasis added), one *like* the Son but distinct from the Son who with the Father sends the Spirit forth (15:26).

In certain activities of God, the work of the Spirit is emphasized. Thus, the Son and the Spirit in Scripture bear witness that the Spirit himself is personally and distinctly God. As the Father sent the Son, empowered by the Spirit, so the Father sends the Spirit, mediated by the Son. Jesus ascended to the Father, but the new Comforter would be everywhere present, representing and carrying on Jesus' ministry. The Spirit would lead, counsel, teach, defend, convict, and empower believers in the church. So the Spirit manifests all that is God by nature, and His activities reflect all that God does.

5. The Holy Trinity is truth we can believe and trust.

The Trinity may be defined as the one true God who eternally exists as three persons—Father, Son, and Holy Spirit—equal in nature, equal in glory, and distinct in relations. God is one, even as all three persons of the Trinity share this absolute Godness or Godhead. Several primary observations remind us of vital realities to remember about our triune God.

First, the Son and Spirit have been with the Father from before the beginning of creation. There was never a "time" when the Father was without the Son or the Son and Father were without the Spirit. They have coexisted (that is, "existed together") for all eternity.

Second, each divine person testifies of the others. The Spirit reveals and glorifies the Son and the Father; the Son and the Father announce and promise the Spirit; the Father proclaims, "This is my beloved Son" (Matthew 3:17) and sends the Spirit.

Third, each person reflects self-rendering love toward the others. There is an "otherness" in the love between them even as God's collective glory is the purpose of all creation. God is love, eternally among the persons of the Trinity as well as temporally in relationship with creation.

Fourth, each member of the Trinity indwells the others without confusion of the persons. Jesus' declaring "I am in the Father and the Father is in me" (John 14:10–11) immediately clarifies personal distinctions: "I am going to the Father" (14:12) "that the Father may be glorified in the Son" (14:13).

The doctrine of the Trinity gives wondrous consistency in the reading of God's Word from creation in Genesis 1:1–3 to the exalted, divine titles of Jesus Christ in Revelation 22:13. The biblical revelation is compelling for Trinitarian faith. At the same time, the early church's creedal formulations recognized the limitations of human understanding. The infinite personal God stands beyond us, even as we seek to express faithfully what He has revealed of who He is.

Errors to Avoid

As we explore the essential truths of the Christian faith regarding God the Father, God the Son, and God the Holy Spirit, we need to be keenly aware of common pitfalls, dangers, and downright damnable doctrines. Biblical savvy will help you reject doctrinal hucksters and avoid history's theological dead-end alleys. Doctrinal discernment helps you avoid churches and denominations that speak a sweet-sounding dialect masking an insidious, non-Christian concept of the Father, the Son, and/or the Spirit.

Error 1: Kidnapped and Tortured Verses

Most false teachers "love" the Bible. They read it, study it, quote it, and teach it. But they also misunderstand, twist, torture, and misapply it (2 Peter 3:16). One of the oldest tricks is to rip a verse out of context and make it mean something that was never intended. Like a kidnapper snatching a helpless victim from his family and placing him where he doesn't belong, heretics take Scripture out of context, adapting it to fit their own ideas.

For example, on first take, one might think Paul's description of Jesus as "the firstborn of all creation" (Colossians 1:15) teaches that the Son was the first created being (as taught by fourth-century Arians and today's Jehovah's Witnesses). But when we learn the original context, we see that Paul was using the Greek *prototokos* ("firstborn") in the same sense as for the promised Davidic King: "I will make him the firstborn, the highest of the kings of the earth" (Psalm 89:27). The context of Colossians 1 itself shows that Paul intended "firstborn of all creation" to be taken in the sense of "*over* all creation," as his whole point is that "in everything he [Jesus] might be preeminent" (1:18).

Proverbs 8:22–25, when taken out of context and applied to Jesus, can sound like He was God's first work of creation. But the original context makes clear that the writer is talking of God's *wisdom* personified (8:1, 12).

In John 14:28, Jesus says, "The Father is greater than I." Here, though, He refers to His submission to the Father during His incarnation, when He humbled himself, taking on the form and role of a servant during His earthly ministry (Philippians 2:6–8; see also Hebrews 2:9).

In Revelation 3:14, another favorite "victim" of wrong interpretation, Jesus is called the "beginning of the creation of God." Yet the Greek term *arche*, translated "beginning," can also mean "source" or "supreme authority," and the whole context of the message to the Laodiceans is Christ's supremacy over all things (see also Revelation 1:5).

So when a teacher quotes scriptural snippets to support bad theology, *beware.* We need to rescue these verses from their abductors, place them back into their own (contextual) homes, and let the Bible say what it really says.

Error 2: Single-Attribute Exaggeration

Through the centuries the church has defended the doctrine of God's *simplicity*, meaning God is not composed of individual parts as humans are. God is not the sum of separate attributes (such as "God is love" in 1 John 4:8) as a child's Lego construction is the sum of the colorful plastic bricks. God isn't made up of pieces of characteristics and virtues; He's a single perfect whole.

Too often, popular conceptions of God reject some of His attributes and embrace others. For instance, sometimes people pit divine attributes against each other: God's kindness versus God's severity, His justice against His grace, His anger toward sin against His unconditional love. God doesn't have mood swings, attitude adjustments, or personality developments like humans do. The Father isn't grumpy, the Son isn't friendly, and the Spirit isn't touchy-feely. In God—Father, Son, and Spirit—is absolute wholeness of perfections and harmony in His actions.

We make a grave error when we emphasize or exaggerate our favorite attributes of God and downplay or displace (or even reject) those that make us uncomfortable. Several centuries ago, Puritan theology heavily stressed God's holiness and justice; contemporary popular theology pushes God's love, mercy, and grace. Yet both the Old and New Testaments assert all these divine attributes. We must resist theology that distorts and deforms by using one attribute to trump or reinterpret another.

> "In the unity of the Godhead there be three persons, of one substance, power, and eternity: God the Father, God the Son, and God the Holy Ghost."[6]
>
> Westminster Confession (1646)

Error 3: Holy Triplets (aka "Tritheism")

The church has always strived to maintain three truths in tension: the unity, diversity, and equality of Father, Son, and Spirit. When one of these truths is let go, error ensues. When belief in unity is eased while maintaining equality and distinction, the result is tritheism: three gods joined at the hip—so distinct they're separate, so equal they're like three identical siblings! Throughout its history the church has taken great care to reject any such notion. One thing is clear in the Old and New Testaments—there's only *one* God.

The three persons of the Trinity *are* distinct (not separate), and they each freely delight in, glorify, and love one another. But some so-called "Christian" traditions have fallen into tritheism. For example, the Church of Jesus Christ of Latter-day Saints (often called "Mormonism" and founded by Joseph Smith, who died in 1844) teaches that the Father, Son, and Spirit are three separate, finite gods born at different times: "Many men say there is one God; the Father, the Son and the Holy Ghost are only one God: I say that is a strange God anyhow—three in one and one in three!"[7] In fact, Mormonism moves beyond tritheism into polytheism, holding that there are galaxies of gods, the father god being only one. He himself had a father, who had a father, who had a father, and so on.

While Mormons may claim to be Christians and even affirm some of the language of monotheism and even the Trinity, dig a little deeper and you'll find their faith has abandoned the orthodox emphasis on the unity of God.

Error 4: One Person, Three Names (aka "Modalism")

Denying the *diversity* of the three persons results in modalism—the false teaching that Father, Son, and Holy Spirit are merely three names, titles, or roles of a single divine person. For instance, in the same way a man may be "husband" to his wife, "father" to his children, and "co-worker" to his colleagues, modalists say God can sometimes act like Father, sometimes like Son, and sometimes like Spirit.

But John 14–17 reveals that Father, Son, and Spirit are distinct persons, not the same person. "Father," "Son," and "Spirit" are not masks worn by God at different times for different roles. The Father is always Father of the Son. The Son is always Son of the Father. The Spirit is always Spirit of the Father.

In the twentieth century, a movement known as Oneness Pentecostalism, or Jesus-Only Christianity, attempted to popularize the idea that God is one person with three roles, manifestations, or names. In 1913, after hearing a message on Acts 2:38 and baptism in "Jesus' name" at a camp meeting in California, a minister named John G. Scheppe spent the night in prayer. He then ran through the camp telling other attendees about a revelation from God's Spirit: Father, Son, and Spirit really were all just one person.[8]

From that misguided spark a flame erupted that almost destroyed the newly formed Assemblies of God (AG) denomination. In 1916 the AG voted to defend the classic view on God's triune nature and Trinitarian baptism. Those who clung to the modalistic position soon formed their own breakoffs, the largest of which is the United Pentecostal Church International (UPCI).

But Oneness Pentecostalism wasn't really new. In the third century, false teachers such as Praxeus, Noetus, and Sabellius were already spreading this heresy. They said personal manifestations of God as "Father," "Son," and "Spirit" were just temporary "modes" of God's relationship to the world. Likewise, Jesus-Only Pentecostals deny genuine relationships between Father, Son, and Spirit:

93

Supposedly, God is manifest as the Father in creation, appears as the Son for our redemption, and is revealed as the Spirit in regeneration and in the church today. In short, they say the Father *is* the Son *is* the Spirit.[9]

Beware of those who deny distinctions between Father, Son, and Spirit. Though modalism has been rejected as unbiblical all along, several popular Oneness evangelists, writers, and musicians push their subtle heresy among unsuspecting Christians untrained to know the difference.

Error 5: Junior God and His Pet Birdy (aka "Subordinationism" or "Arianism")

In the beginning was the Word, and the Word was with God, and the Word was a god.

A god?

That faulty translation of John 1:1, found in the Jehovah's Witnesses' theologically twisted *New World Translation of the Holy Scriptures*, reminds us that the ancient heresy of Arianism is alive and well. What was Arianism? Arius of Alexandria (AD 256–336) claimed Jesus Christ was the highest of all created beings, similar but not equal in nature to God the Father. In Arius's view, the Son was only *a* god, a kind of "junior god." He was created out of nothing to be the greatest creature in the universe but not truly divine. And what about the Spirit? Well, maybe He's just an angelic being, or it's merely God's impersonal active force. This heresy, so nasty it gets a six-syllable word (sub–or–di–na–tion–ism), denies the essential equality of Father, Son, and Spirit.

One final note: The error of "subordinationism" shouldn't be confused with the Son's and the Spirit's functional submission or "subordination" to the Father in their earthly ministries. That's the biblical and orthodox teaching—the Father did send the Son (John 5:23) and the Spirit (Galatians 4:6) into the world. But this voluntary submission and ordered working in the work of creation, revelation, and redemption doesn't mean the Son and Spirit

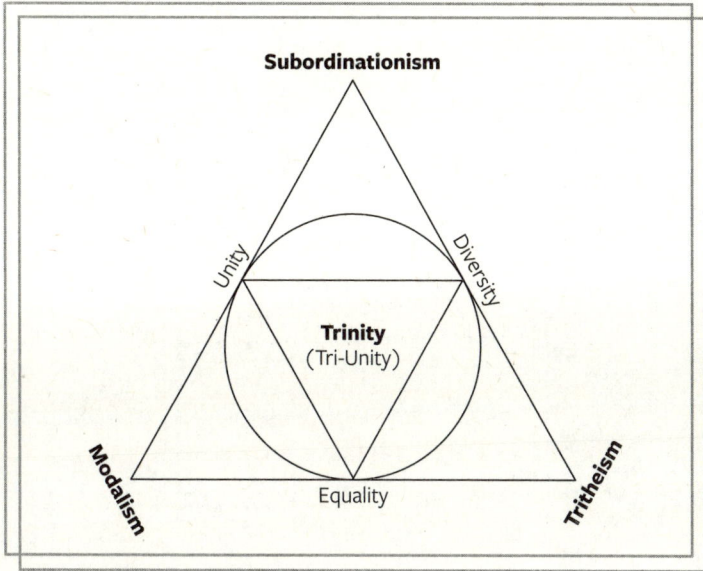

are "junior gods" of a different nature than the Father any more than workers' submission to the authority of their bosses at work implies they're less human.

Jesus is not a mini-god. Nor is the white "dove" of the Spirit the Father's inferior pet—an active force or a lesser being who does God's bidding. The Father is God, the Son is God, the Spirit is God, and these three are one God, not three.

Error 6: Driving Christology into a Ditch

A car's driver is constantly making minor, imperceptible course corrections. Skilled drivers aren't even aware they're doing so; it just comes with years of experience. But watch sometime. A tiny tug to the right or a subtle pull to the left, and the car seems to hold a straight, steady line. Why? Because of all the constant little corrections. If any driver takes their hands off the wheel for long, the vehicle will be heading for a ditch (or worse).

```
. . . without confusion

without separation                                    . . . without mixture

              ONE AND ONLY CHRIST—SON,
              LORD, ONLY-BEGOTTEN—
              IN TWO NATURES . . .

. . . without division
```

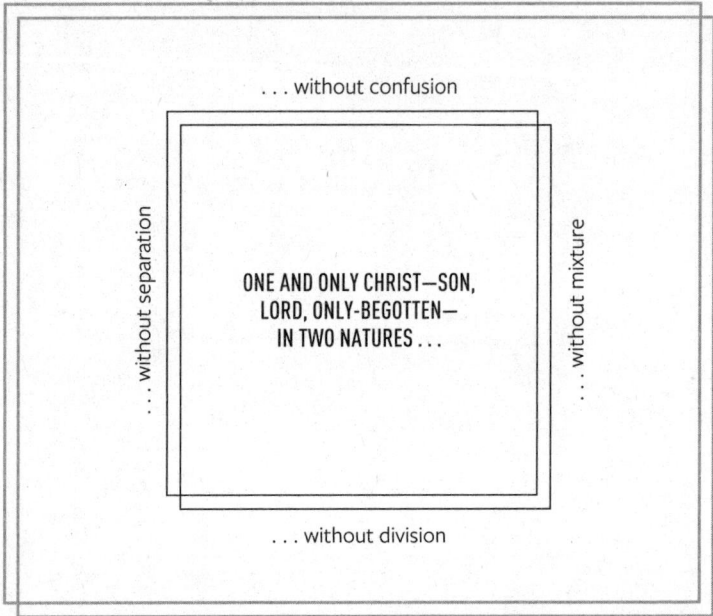

Similarly, consider the orthodox view of Christ's divine and human natures: If we fail to maintain these in tension, the result will be theological disaster. But we'll be able to hold a straight and narrow course if we keep both hands on the steering wheel of the Chalcedonian Definition from AD 451. That council, beautifully and succinctly summing up the Bible's teaching and four centuries of Christian thought and reflection, declared that Jesus is all that is God and all that is human—simultaneously. As Paul wrote, "in Christ all the fullness of the Deity lives in bodily form" (Colossians 2:9 NIV).

Chalcedon affirms that Jesus Christ has two complete natures in one unique person. It also avoids careening into two ugly ditches: (1) separating the two natures into two persons (aka the heresy of "Nestorianism"), and (2) mixing the two natures into one new nature (aka the heresy of "Eutychianism"). The Chalcedonian Definition used specific, well-crafted language to keep future orthodox believers from driving Christology into a ditch: Jesus has two complete natures without division or separation (avoiding Nestorianism) and without confusion or mixture (avoiding Eutychianism).

Error 7: God or Man, but Not the God-Man

Against non-Christian religions and secularism, Christianity generally has been quick to defend the full deity of Christ. Whether in pagan Rome, in the face of Islam, amid Genghis Khan's brutal regime, or under atheistic dictators such as Stalin or Mao, believers were willing to die for the confession that Jesus is Lord and God. Because nonbelievers attack this crucial doctrine, Christian apologists, evangelists, and teachers rightly stress the Savior's full deity.

But an over-emphasis on Christ's deity can actually lead to error if we fail to just as passionately embrace His humanity. In some long-standing Christian traditions, the exaltation of Jesus' deity practically excluded Him from being our human example: "You know, Jesus is God, so He couldn't really have been tempted. Or suffered. Not like me. He doesn't quite understand me. Not really. I'll talk to Mary instead. She's His mother—she's really human, filled with grace. She'll talk to her Son for me, and He'd never deny His mother."

From a desire to exalt the glory of Christ's deity grew a pragmatic theology that gradually filled the sky with mediators between humanity and the triune God. Mary became Blessed Ever-Virgin Mary, Mother of Christ and so Mother of Christ's body, the church—indeed, Queen of heaven. Peter and the apostles, martyrs, and saints became the human conduits to heaven.

While some people tilt far too much toward the divine nature in their view of Christ, others tilt far too much toward the human. Two centuries of liberal theology have produced hundreds of books on the life of Jesus in which His deity is denied. The so-called "Historical Jesus" portrayed by these critical scholars is only a man, a "great moral teacher," an itinerant rabbi, a peasant prophet, a charlatan wonder-worker, a wild-eyed apocalyptic, a political revolutionary, or a cynic sage.

That man of Nazareth, that "great man" but not the God-Man, who foolishly got himself killed, is remembered for all those engaging conversations and that brutal martyrdom. And agenda-driven, special interest theologies present Jesus as "one of them": cultural agitator, social belligerent, political rebel, armed revolutionary, communist, individualistic libertarian, and so on.

Beware of honoring others before Jesus Christ as our human example. Beware of replacing our Great High Priest with mediators whom God's Word never reveals as such. Beware of a broken Christology that places one of His natures above the other. Jesus Christ, the God-Man, is our Brother, Perfect Example, High Priest, Complete Substitute, Risen Lord, Coming Messiah, Everlasting Savior, and Holy God, who with the Father and the Spirit should be worshipped and glorified forever and ever.

Amen.

Lessons to Live

When seeking a driver's license, we study state laws to pass a written test. But getting the facts correct on a multiple-choice exam at the Department of Motor Vehicles doesn't qualify us to take a carload of friends onto the interstate. *Knowing* must be integrated with *doing*.

The same is true about God. We can know *about* God without really *knowing* God. But if we *know* God, we truly live our lives in keeping with that relationship. You see, when we learn about God, far more is at stake than avoiding a traffic ticket or getting in a fender bender. God exists as the Reason for everything else. He's the Architect, Maker, and Sustainer of all life, all existence. At every instant our lives are contingent on the Creator's good will. We exist because God is gracious rather than selfish. These realities demand our full worship and obedience.

So where do we start in living out the truth about the triune God?

Lesson 1: Knowing God encourages us to learn more of God.

Nearly two hundred times the New Testament says belief, faith, and trust are needed for salvation. Believing on the Lord Jesus is the only requirement for being made right with our Maker (John 3:14–18; Romans 5:1–2; Ephesians 2:8–9).

But that belief is just the beginning of a Christian life. That faith drives us to learn more about God—to understand as much of Him as we can, to "get" as much of Him as we can. By now it should be clear that this includes wrestling with God's self-revelation as

---

THE GOSPEL IN TRINITARIAN PERSPECTIVE

1. The God who created the universe—Father, Son, and Holy Spirit—also created us in His image (Genesis 1:26–27). We are persons in community because God is tripersonal and made us relational beings. Had our first parents never sinned, they'd have grown in their relationship with God and with each other in unending immortal life.
2. Although we're made to be in relationship with the triune God, we have turned away (Romans 3:23). On our own, we are all guilty and rightly under God's judgment. No one is without sin; sin severed relationship with the Supreme Judge.
3. Because God is triune, He can do something no other "god" could. First, the Father sent the Son into our world as the incarnate God-Man (John 3:16). Jesus showed us who God is and what we humans are meant to be. He bore the punishment for our sins on the cross. Then He rose from the grave to defeat death and seal our salvation.
4. Finally, by the work of His Spirit, God calls us to believe in Jesus (John 20:31). Through faith in Jesus, we're made right with God. Then God the Spirit enters our lives and makes us daughters and sons of God (3:5–8). We receive the gift of eternal life and experience wondrous relationship with the Father, the Son, and the Spirit—the relationship for which we were originally created.

---

the One who subsists in three persons. It should drive us to devour Scripture, looking for clues as to the nature and work of Jesus as the God-Man. We should scout out evidence for the Spirit's role in the plan of salvation and in our lives as believers today. We should seek new understanding of the Father's relationships with the Son and the Spirit—and with us.

Here again it helps to look at the gospel from a Trinitarian perspective. Yes, the Christ-centered good news can be summarized in short statements (Romans 1:1–3; 1 Corinthians 15:1–5). But if we step back and look at the whole of God's revelation through this lens, we see Father, Son, and Spirit united in their work to save us.

Lesson 2: In light of the Trinity, be all you were meant to be.

Genesis declares that male and female are created *in God's image* (1:26–27). What could be more staggering than to comprehend that our existence as finite persons reflects what God is like as Father, Son, and Spirit? In Scripture, the Father, the Son, and the Spirit each thinks, speaks, wills, loves, and relates to the others. Scripture shows that our own personhood in community finds its root in our Creator: We think, speak, will, love, and relate to others.

For the Christian, our self—our personhood—finds its essence and reason for being in the tripersonal God. We have a reason for reason. Truth exists outside us and beyond a cultural consensus. Language itself has meaning because we've been created with the capacity for communication. We make real choices that influence not only our own lives but also those of others around us. Life has moment-by-moment importance, and we bear the consequences of our actions both in this life and the one to come.

Because Jesus reveals all the "fullness of deity" (Colossians 2:9) in the fullness of humanity, when we see Him joyful, angry, compassionate, sad to the point of weeping, and with deep struggles of the soul, we realize that our own emotions are dense with meaning as well. This is intrinsic to what we are as humans. When we care for others, love our spouses, take care of our children, have candid friendships and authentic fellowship with others—all this stands truly related to the God of the Bible. It loudly shouts what is meant to be in our human lives, our lives as finite beings created in God's image, created for fellowship and communion with one another.

We fully experience what it means to be human, individually and communally, only when we trust in the lavishly personal God: the Father of life; the Son as the way, the truth, and the life; and the Spirit of life.

Lesson 3: Learn to parent from the perfect Father.

Both male and female were made in the divine image (Genesis 1:26–27), so in our understanding, the Godhead exists beyond gender. God is neither male nor female, but we address Him as Father and Son with masculine pronouns as this is the language of Scripture and tradition. And the Father is exemplary of what fathers should be in this world. He is the archetypal father, the true father to those betrayed and abused by "dads."

Even when images of our earthly father flash repulsive, or when there's no "dad" picture on the mantel at all, still our Lord replaces the absent and the shameful. He is our heavenly Father, the "Father of the fatherless" (Psalm 68:5). That role isn't exclusively that of God the Father; the Son too is deemed "Mighty God, Everlasting Father" (Isaiah 9:6) as ruler and benefactor of His kingdom.

Like other shared functions in the Trinity, God's fatherhood also has implications for mothers. Scripture employs feminine analogies of God (Deuteronomy 32:11–12; Psalm 22:9–10; Isaiah 66:13). And to all believers, Paul exhorts, "Be imitators of God, as beloved children. And walk in love, as Christ loved us and gave himself up for us, a fragrant offering and sacrifice to God" (Ephesians 5:1–2). God's character, the example for every believer, is especially appropriate for parents in regard to their children.

As the Father is profoundly good, so parents should be full of His goodness, integrity, and purity. As He loves the Son, so parents should love their kids. As God is eternally wise, parents should call on His wisdom in orienting and instructing their families. As God is infinitely creative, so parents can model creativity for their offspring. As God disciplines His children, so parents are to guide and correct, firmly but not harshly (see Hebrews 12:6–10). As the Father deserves our respect, so parents ought to act in such a way that earns respect, not in pride but in dignity. And as the Father is self-giving toward creation, so parents should be characterized by generosity and self-sacrifice toward each other, their children, and others.

God's fatherhood is perfect; human parenthood is not. Our humility before God recognizes that we're fallen. We aren't self-sufficient. We don't know all things, and we often make mistakes. We need grace. Nevertheless, God's perfect fatherhood helps shape what parents, as imitators of Him, should seek.

Lesson 4: Follow Jesus, Our Lord and Brother.

Jesus declared, "Whoever would save his life will lose it, but whoever loses his life for my sake will save it" (Luke 9:24). The New Testament presents a remarkable window into the relationships of Father, Son, and Spirit. The Father gives all things to the Son. The Spirit doesn't glorify himself but glorifies the Father and the Son. And the Son gives all things back to the Father (1 Corinthians 15:28). God as Trinity is the self-giving God of infinite love and sharing.

Think about it. God displays His character through the incarnation, ministry, and death of the Son (Hebrews 1:2–4). The beauty of the Son seen in Jesus' faithfulness and sacrifice reveals the nature of the triune God. We see the Father and the Spirit in the Son's work. Before the cross, we were not God's friends but His enemies (Romans 5:8–10). Yet simultaneously, at the cross, God's glorious love and grace break forth and radiate into the world. God is revealed as both the Just *and* the Justifier (Romans 3:26).

When Jesus took up the cross and invited us to do the same, He called each of us to let go of ego and selfish ambition. The one who seeks personal gain and fame will lose their soul. To follow Jesus is to lose our life in order to gain it. When Paul exhorts us to "be imitators of God," he goes right on to explain, "Walk in love, as Christ loved us and gave himself up for us, a fragrant offering and sacrifice to God" (Ephesians 5:1–2). Like Father, like Son. There's no right way we can claim God's promises as His children and not do the same.

Lesson 5: Trust the Holy Spirit.

At the moment of salvation through faith in Christ, the Spirit regenerates us. We are born of God, and we are indwelled and sealed. Whereas the baptism of the Spirit unites us spiritually to Christ and to His corporate body, the church, elsewhere Paul admonishes us to "be filled with the Spirit" (Ephesians 5:18). And in Romans 8:14–16 he says, "All who are led by the Spirit of God are sons of God. For you did not receive the spirit of slavery to fall back into fear, but you have received the Spirit of adoption as sons, by whom we cry, 'Abba! Father!' The Spirit himself bears witness with our spirit that we are children of God."

Whether implicitly or explicitly, churches often establish lists of external conduct by which believers must conform to demonstrate they're "in the faith." This isn't all bad. The New Testament itself has numerous commands against specific sinful behaviors. But external conduct is not the essence of Spirit-empowered Christian living.

Not only does the New Testament raise the bar for true spirituality, but it entirely shifts the model. Keeping rules by our own willpower is little different from living a worldly life; it's just self-effort to a given self-serving end. Instead, we're given a new law: the law of the Spirit (Galatians 5:16, 18; Romans 8:1), the law of Christ (Galatians 6:2), the law of love (Romans 13:8–10; 1 John

3:21–24). *This* law should control our lives by the power of God himself alive in us.

The Holy Spirit knows what's unholy in our lives, and so He begins His work of freeing us from those things that would destroy us. He sanctifies, making us truly *spiritual*, *Christlike*, *godly*. He guides us to rid us of sin and to lead us when we should share the gospel, sacrifice to do good, or pray. So trust the Spirit. In so doing you will experience God beautifying, filling, and empowering your life. The fruit of the Spirit will spring forth in your life because it forms from the life of God in you.

Lesson 6: Be kind but firm with deceivers and the deceived.

Perhaps you know some people who claim Christian faith but don't uphold the doctrine of the Trinity. Though we might admire the zealous door-to-door proselytization of Jehovah's Witnesses, their rejection of Jesus Christ as the eternal Son of God stands contrary to biblical truth. Many Mormons lead upright lives and may align with Christianity on many moral and practical issues, but they essentially believe in a different god. And Jesus-Only Oneness Pentecostals are certainly closer to the truth than Mormons and Jehovah's Witnesses, but their modalistic theology doesn't square with Scripture's insistence on *distinct* persons of the Trinity.

Theology matters. In such big issues as the Trinity, the difference is between heaven and hell—eternal life and eternal condemnation. With so much at stake, allowing people to embrace a false religion is the opposite of loving our neighbors. Rather, we must speak the truth in love (Ephesians 4:15).

When you confront crucial errors, though—and confront them we must—"do it with gentleness and respect" (1 Peter 3:15). When opposing such false doctrines, we're to prioritize Paul's advice to Timothy:

> The Lord's servant must not be quarrelsome but kind to everyone, able to teach, patiently enduring evil, correcting his opponents with

gentleness. God may perhaps grant them repentance leading to a knowledge of the truth, and they may come to their senses and escape from the snare of the devil, after being captured by him to do his will. (2 Timothy 2:24–26)

Lesson 7: Worship and glorify the triune God.

Good theology leads us to know, love, and obey God with all we are. Faced with the grandeur of God's revelation, Paul could hardly stop for breath, piling on one reason for rejoicing after another:

> I do not cease to give thanks for you, remembering you in my prayers, that the God of our Lord Jesus Christ, the Father of glory, may give you the Spirit of wisdom and of revelation in the knowledge of him, having the eyes of your hearts enlightened, that you may know what is the hope to which he has called you, what are the riches of his glorious inheritance in the saints, and what is the immeasurable greatness of his power toward us who believe, according to the working of his great might that he worked in Christ when he raised him from the dead and seated him at his right hand in the heavenly places, far above all rule and authority and power and dominion, and above every name that is named, not only in this age but also in the one to come. And he put all things under his feet and gave him as head over all things to the church, which is his body, the fullness of him who fills all in all. (Ephesians 1:16–23)

The truth about God is what forms the foundation and framework of our relationship with the Father, Son, and Holy Spirit. Yet for all that could be said, there comes a point when the magnificence of God Almighty is beyond expression. Again, Paul writes:

> Oh, the depth of the riches and wisdom and knowledge of God! How unsearchable are his judgments and how inscrutable his ways! "For who has known the mind of the Lord, or who has

been his counselor?" . . . For from him and through him and to him are all things. To him be glory forever. Amen. (Romans 11:33–36)

The nurturing of sound doctrine generates worship and love. The desk, the books, the computer, and the immense networks of information that point the way should bring us to our knees in adoration of the living God. Worship of the triune God is our eternal and privileged reason for being. Never forsake either private or corporate worship. Pray to the Father, through the Son, by the power of the Spirit. Worship the Father, Son, and Spirit with a faithful body of believers. Serve God by imitating Christ by the enabling power of the Holy Spirit. Make everything you say and do be to the glory of the triune God.

In the God-breathed words of the apostle Paul, "the grace of the Lord Jesus Christ and the love of God and the fellowship of the Holy Spirit be with you all" (2 Corinthians 13:14).

Snapshot of History

Four periods of church history—Patristic (100–500), Medieval (500–1500), Protestant (1500–1700), and Modern (1700–Present)— witnessed the doctrine of God developing in various ways. The following chart summarizes the major developments related to God, the Trinity, and Jesus Christ during four periods.[10]

Patristic Period (100–500)	Medieval Period (500–1500)	Protestant Period (1500–1700)	Modern Period (1700–Present)
• The Trinitarian "Rule of Faith" and baptismal form used as a standard for orthodox instruction.	• Councils of Constantinople II (553) and Constantinople III (680–681) apply the doctrinal definitions of the first four councils to new challenges.	• Major Protestant reformers reaffirm the doctrines of the Trinity, deity/humanity of Christ, and the personhood of the Holy Spirit.	• Modern liberal theologians reject the authority of councils, creeds, and Scripture, thus rejecting the classic orthodox doctrines of the Trinity, the deity and humanity of Christ, the virgin birth, and other core teachings.
• Death and resurrection of the God-Man central to the church's theology.	• Council of Nicaea II (767) declares "orthodox" the making of images of Christ and the saints.	• Many Protestant confessions affirm the doctrinal authority of the first four ecumenical councils.	• Alternatives to classic orthodox Trinitarian theism arrive, including Deism, Unitarianism, Panentheism, Pantheism, and eventually Agnosticism and Atheism (1700–1900).
• Tertullian first uses technical formulae "one nature/three persons" for the Trinity and "two natures/one person" for Christ (c. 200).	• Roman Catholic and Eastern Orthodox Churches split over the pope's addition of *"filioque"* to the Nicene-Constantinopolitan Creed (1054).	• Some "radical reformers" challenge the classic doctrine of the Trinity and deity of Christ.	• False teachers establish sects and cults founded on the rejection of Trinitarian and Christological orthodoxy (1800–1900).
• Church leaders defend orthodox teachings on the Trinity and Christ against Docetism (c. 90–200), Gnosticism (100–500), Adoptionism (100–300), Modalism (200–300), Arianism (300–400), Apollinarianism (350–400), Nestorianism (400–450), and Eutychianism (430–500).	• Anselm of Canterbury articulates his ontological argument for the existence of God and his attempts to prove the necessity of the incarnation based on reason alone in *Cur Deus Homo* (c. 1100).	• Michael Servetus burned at the stake in Geneva for stubbornly and vociferously rejecting the Trinity.	• Fundamentalism responds to liberalism by emphasizing the "fundamentals" of the faith, including Trinitarianism (1900–1950).
• Councils of Nicaea (325), Constantinople (381), Ephesus (431), and Chalcedon (451) provide Trinitarian clarification.	• Aquinas argues for the existence of God based on observable nature (c. 1270).	• Deism and Unitarianism rise in continental Europe and England.	

THREE

Fashioned and Fallen—
Humanity and Sin

Nothing was made evil by God, but all things good, yea, very good—but the sin in which man was concerned brought evil upon them. For when man transgressed, they also transgressed with him. For as, if the master of the house himself acts rightly, the domestics also of necessity conduct themselves well; but if the master sins, the servants also sin with him; so in like manner it came to pass, that in the case of man's sin, he being master, all that was subject to him sinned with him.[1]

—Theophilus of Antioch (c. 170)

We believe that man was created in holiness, under the law of his Maker; but by voluntary transgression fell from that holy and happy state; in consequence of which all mankind are now sinners, not by constraint, but choice; being by nature utterly void of that holiness required by the law of God, positively inclined to evil; and therefore under just condemnation to eternal ruin, without defense or excuse.[2]

—New Hampshire Baptist Confession (1833)

In Short . . .

Every Sunday school kid knows that Genesis 1 and 2 describe God's creation of everything from day and night to birds and fish, from sun and moon to Adam and Eve. If they stick to it long enough, those Sunday schoolers will learn about the temptation of the serpent, the eating of the forbidden fruit, and the expulsion from the garden of Eden (Genesis 3). In fact, many church kids have a fridge door full of coloring sheets to prove it!

But the biblical epic of creation and fall isn't confined to the first few chapters of Genesis. These central themes are carried throughout the Bible until the final consummation in the new heaven and new earth of Revelation 21:1. There the paradise of God is restored, the curse of sin and death is banished, and redeemed humanity is finally able to be all it was meant to be from the beginning.

God Created of Everything, Out of Nothing, for Someone and Something

When people ask "Why is there something instead of nothing?" we can respond as the Bible does: "In the beginning, God created the heavens and the earth" (Genesis 1:1). Creation is the art of the Artist, designed to reveal His reality. And because the Artist is the ultimate Good, His creation was originally "very good" (1:31).

As we saw in the last chapter, all things exist by the will of God the Father, through the mediating word of God the Son, by the agency of God the Holy Spirit (Genesis 1:1–2; John 1:1–3). This universe didn't just pop into existence as the result of random processes; nor is it careening in a purposeless path toward nothingness. Rather, "from him and through him and to him are all things" (Romans 11:36).

This understanding of creation should inspire us to worship the Creator, who is enthroned above His work. He is the sovereign Director of the course of history toward the fulfillment of His will. Between Genesis and Revelation, God's creation points to His power and prompts awe at His majesty (Psalm 8:1–9; Romans

1:20). It also provokes a posture of faith (Hebrews 11:3) and promotes worship even among the greatest of heavenly creatures
(Revelation 4:11). The Bible's teaching concerning creation does
more than answer the question *Where'd all this stuff come from?*
It explains the orderliness of existence from microscopic cells to
planetary orbits.

Humanity as the Crowning Work of God's Creation

Ancient polytheists (those who believe in many gods) held that
humans were slaves in a chaotic universe, subject to the whims of
squabbling deities. On the other hand, modern atheists often think
of "the human animal" as a fortunate accident of an evolving
universe. In either case humans are too small or the universe is too
big for humans to have any real meaning, purpose, or significance.

But the Christian teaching concerning humanity is a worldview
apart from such pessimistic perspectives. According to the Bible,
men and women were created in the image of God and according
to His likeness (Genesis 1:26–28). This teaching establishes the
uniqueness of human beings among all God's creatures, from angels to earthworms. As God's image-bearing co-regents on earth,
humans were to cultivate Eden and extend the rule of God over
the uncultivated earth (2:7–25).

In opposition to the classic Christian doctrine of the special
creation of humanity in the image of God (*imago dei*), the modern
theory of naturalistic evolution seeks to understand and explain
human origins apart from God. It assumes that humanity evolved
from a common ancestor by a process called "natural selection,"
more informally referred to as "survival of the fittest." Today the
theory of naturalistic (and often atheistic) evolution dominates
academic and scientific institutions.[3] Yet it reduces humanity
to the status of "more complicated animal," different from the
earthworm or even a single-celled amoeba only by degree, not
ultimately by nature.

But according to Scripture, humanity is the climax of God's purposeful, ordered account of creation. Humans have inherent dignity, created for loving relationships with God and others. More than merely physical matter, humans have an immaterial part that distinguishes them from other earthbound creatures. These two competing versions of human origins—the natural and the supernatural—profoundly impact how we approach moral issues such as abortion, genetic engineering, and euthanasia. Simply put, if humans are only natural products of random processes, then we're peasant subjects in the kingdom of chaos. But if humans are the crowning work of God's purposeful creation, then we're princes and princesses of the King of the cosmos.

We've Fallen, and We Can't Get Up!

Back in 1989, a company ran a television ad promoting a device worn around the neck to call a dispatch service for help if a person couldn't reach a telephone in an emergency. To illustrate how to use the device, the dramatized commercial shows an elderly woman who's fallen in the bathroom. She presses the device and exclaims, "I've fallen, and I can't get up!" Sadly, the actress portraying the woman was perceived to be so bad at her craft that her line became a joke in pop culture. But anyone who's experienced a debilitating fall firsthand—or helped nurse someone who's been injured in a fall—knows this isn't a laughing matter. Falls can be deadly!

The fact is humanity has fallen, and without divine help, they can't get up. Yet modern, "enlightened" minds scoff at the notion that humans have a fallen nature that renders them sinful. They would much prefer to regard themselves as basically good, just with a few bad habits or sinful behaviors. They would be offended to learn Scripture teaches that their fallen, sinful condition applies to both gross crimes and seemingly trivial imperfections.

> "After Adam's fall, all men begotten after the common course of nature are born with sin; that is, without the fear of God, without trust in him, and with fleshly appetite; and that this disease, or original fault, is truly sin, condemning and bringing eternal death."[4]
>
> Augsburg Confession (1530)

Because God originally created humanity good (Genesis 1:26–31), clearly something happened that resulted in the wickedness, war, corruption, oppression, suffering, and death so prevalent on earth. This is what we call "the fall," taught from Genesis to Revelation as the universal problem affecting not only humanity but all creation. And the Savior, Jesus Christ, is its only solution (1 Timothy 2:5).

Evil, Evil Everywhere

The question has nagged inquiring minds for centuries: If God is good, and He created everything good—including humans (Genesis 1:31)—where did evil come from? (We'll come back to this question later in the chapter.)

Most Christians throughout history have understood Satan as the leader of a large force of evil demons who wage war against the forces of God in heaven and on earth (Ephesians 6:12). Likely sometime before the creation of the first humans and their fall into sin, some angelic beings themselves fell from their original good and holy condition. According to classic interpreters, Satan and a host of angelic beings rebelled against God in heaven, becoming the evil adversaries of humanity (Ezekiel 28:12–16). Satan deceived and tempted the mother and father of humankind and instigated a history of evil that has invaded God's creation (1 Corinthians 15:21–22; 2 Corinthians 11:3).

In Adam and Eve's decision to abdicate their position as rulers over God's creatures, all the aspects of sin are present: unbelief, disobedience, and pride. The consequences of the fall match the seriousness of the prohibition. The Creator had formed humans from the dust of the earth, so to dust they would return (Genesis 3:19). This involved separation from the source of life, fellowship with their Creator. The separation also led to Adam and Eve's guilt before God and shame before each other (Genesis 3:10).

The sin of the first couple was representative. They led all humanity as their descendants and heirs of their nature into bondage to rebellion and the ways of death (Romans 5:12). Our sins are self-destructive, but they affect the lives of family, friends, peers, and society. Instead of Eden, the fall bequeathed a wasteland of thorns and thistles with unrest, sorrow, and death. Strife in families became conflict between families and developed into wars between tribes and nations. As a result, our good world has been infested by sin, suffering, death, and the devil.

In the Darkness, a Light

It must be admitted that the doctrines of humanity and sin leave us in a hopeless situation—at least when seen from a purely human perspective. But this is precisely the context into which the hope of Christianity steps. We would do well to remember the simple

> "For through the first man, Adam, nature is fallen and weakened by sin, and the punishment of that stain has fallen upon all mankind. Thus nature itself, which You created good and right, is considered a symbol of vice and the weakness of corrupted nature, because when left to itself it tends toward evil and to baser things."[5]
>
> Thomas à Kempis (c. 1400)

statement we made just a couple of short pages ago: *God created everything, out of nothing, for someone and something.* The rebellion of humanity didn't change God's plans; rather, the rebellion of humanity became the occasion for the greatest display of divine love and grace that could ever be imagined. As the promise in Isaiah hints, "the people who walk in darkness will see a great light; those who live in a dark land, the light will shine on them" (Isaiah 9:2 NASB).

Passages to Ponder

Philosophy versus theology . . . experience versus doctrine . . . science versus faith . . . common sense versus the sense of Scripture . . . These age-old tensions in doing theology reach a fevered pitch when it comes to the doctrines of creation, humanity, and the fall. Prevailing scientific theories seem to fly in the face of the biblical account of creation. Competing views of human nature among philosophers, biologists, psychologists, and sociologists challenge the Christian understanding of humans created according to the image of God. And individual feelings about good and evil, right and wrong, and wisdom and folly counter the teachings of Scripture regarding human fallenness, sinfulness, and death.

As we begin exploring matters of creation, humanity, and sin, it's necessary to establish a firm biblical footing. Of course, Christians don't always agree on every detail of what the Bible says about these things. But we do agree on the big picture: that God created all things out of nothing, humans were fashioned in the image of God, humanity fell through disobedience, and therefore, all people stand in desperate need of God's saving grace.

Once we've understood the following passages, we'll be ready to dig deeper into the theological and practical implications of creation, humanity, and sin.

(1) Genesis 1–2—The Doctrine of Creation as the Foundation of Christian Teaching

The appeal of atheism shouldn't surprise us. In a world without a Creator, people are free to do their own thing, be their own person, establish their own standards (or reject all standards)—as long as they tolerate everyone else's views on truth. This thinking is bound up in individualistic entitlements and an urgent agenda to be rid of "fundamentalisms" found in Christian, Jewish, and Islamic settings.

But the opening chapters of the Bible present the foundations of a completely different view of the world. They demonstrate that God's creation was orderly and suitable for life (Genesis 1–2) and declared "very good." It pronounces God's will for humanity in terms of rule and procreation. Further, the creation account in Genesis 1–2 teaches that men and women are meant to live in community with one another and in harmony with creation.

Beyond Genesis, the Bible continues to assume and build on the creation account (Exodus 20:11; Psalm 139:13–14). Not only did God create human existence as a whole, but He created us as individually distinctive human beings. Moreover, creation also reveals God's power and glory to all people (Psalm 19:1–2). Those

---

PASSAGES TO MASTER AND MEMORIZE

Genesis 1:26–28	Romans 3:23
Genesis 1:31	Romans 5:12
Genesis 2:7	Galatians 5:19–21
Genesis 3:17–19	Colossians 1:16
Romans 3:10–12	James 3:8–9

Note: Not all these passages are discussed in the text, but they'll all help you master the doctrines of creation, humanity, and sin.

who deny creation by God implicitly assume that all legitimate knowledge is only natural (no revelation) and is arrived at only by experience or experiment.

But creation is so intricate that our finite experiments can't even ask the right questions, much less provide satisfying answers. The more answers science produces, the longer the list of questions.

The biblical affirmation of creation is also seen in the New Testament. In Matthew 19:4–5, Jesus answered some Pharisees by saying, "Have you not read that he who created them from the beginning made them male and female, and said, 'Therefore a man shall leave his father and his mother and hold fast to his wife, and the two shall become one flesh'?" The apostle John keynoted his Gospel with a stunning restatement of creation, this time clarifying that the divine agent of creation was indeed the eternal Son of God, the preincarnate Word of God (John 1:1–3). And everything created good in the beginning, though having fallen into corruption in between, is part of a plan of redemption that will restore the entire creation to its intended glory (Romans 8:19–23; Revelation 21:1–5).

Yes, for eyes to see, creation displays order, purpose, and meaning. But these things can be appreciated only when one affirms that God is the Creator and Sustainer of the universe.

(2) Genesis 1:26–28 and James 3:9—Humanity Created in the Image of God

Perhaps as never before in history, we humans struggle to understand who we are and why we exist. In secular universities, the "soul" is increasingly perceived as an illusion, "a ghost in the machine." The human being is reduced to little more than DNA and behavioral conditioning. Nothing transcends the physical world. Personhood is defined in ways that exclude the unborn, and personal "identity" is whatever we want it to be.

So what are we? We are unique creatures of God, with bodies and souls forged together as an integrated whole—a reality we call "human nature." Neither merely spiritual like angels nor merely physical like animals, we are unique creations in God's grand display of living beings. We are, to use the Bible's own language, uniquely created according to the image of God (Genesis 1:26–27).

Jewish and Christian teachers have interpreted "image of God" (*imago dei*) through various lenses.[6]

The human being is often said to reflect divine personhood. Just as God has mind, will, and emotion, humans have mind, will, and emotion. As God is morally pure, humans have a moral sense called the "conscience" (Romans 2:15). As God is eternal, so people have, as it were, a sense of eternity in their hearts (Ecclesiastes 3:11). With all this said, such a perspective of the image of God is sometimes described as a "structural view," that is, our individual personhood in some sense derives from the God who is personal.

Another lens on the *imago dei* is the "relational view." Genesis 1:26–27 declares that God created humanity in the divine image as "male and female." Each complements the other; they're designed for each other. After creating the first man, God declared, "It is not good that the man should be alone" (2:18). When God presents the bride to Adam, he rejoices. Genesis 3:8 recounts that God "walked" in the cool of the day in the garden of Eden, indicating a personal relationship between God and the first humans. The

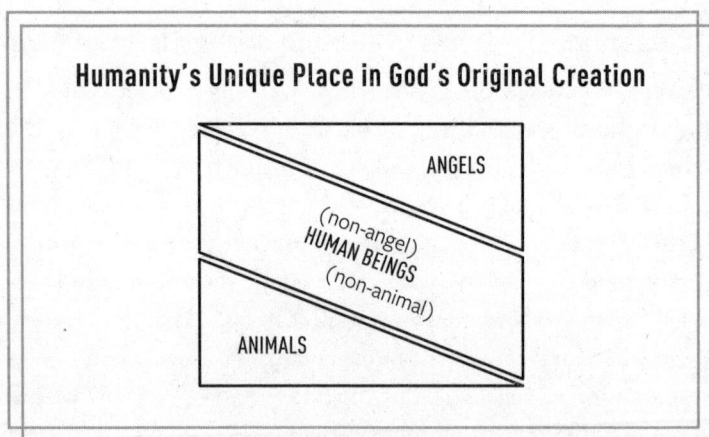

Humanity's Unique Place in God's Original Creation

ANGELS

(non-angel)
HUMAN BEINGS
(non-animal)

ANIMALS

relational view of the image of God is that humanity is made for companionship with others, analogous to how the Father, Son, and Holy Spirit relate to one another.

Yet another view of the image of God is the "functional view." Many modern scholars argue that a proper definition of the *imago dei* is best derived from the activities exhorted of the first couple: "Let them have dominion over . . . all the earth" (Genesis 1:26) and "Be fruitful and multiply and fill the earth and subdue it and have dominion over . . . every living thing that moves on the earth" (1:28; compare Psalm 8:6). In this view, humans were created as visible, physical representations ("images") of the invisible God in His creation, with a mission and mandate to care for and to rule over the world. To accomplish this, humans must multiply their number across the face of the earth.

Likely these views—the structural, the relational, and the functional—all contribute to the mystery of the *imago dei*, which like God himself contains more than can be expressed. One thing is clear, though: We are created to reflect the Maker and to enjoy relationship with Him. Genesis 1:26–27 tells us who we are as persons created in the image of God, and it tells why we exist: to be God's representatives, reflections, and even friends. As creatures created in the image of God, we are invited to know God and be like Him.

This doctrine of the *imago dei* is crucial for understanding the inherent worth of each individual. Because every person has been created according to the divine image, every person has been invested with dignity and value (Genesis 9:6; James 3:9). Someone's inability to manifest a particular aspect of the image of God does not prevent them from manifesting other aspects (such as personality or personal holiness). This fact is critical to current discussions about issues like abortion and euthanasia.

The bottom line is this: All humans maintain the dignity and responsibility implied by the image of God. All people have been made valuable and dignified, not just believers. And all people manifest the extraordinary abilities God gave humanity to rule under Him. The image of God is not determined merely by *function*; it's also indicated by *essence*. Any human being is human. Every fetus, child, adolescent, and adult deformed or in a persistent vegetative state is nonetheless human and thus has dignity.

(3) Genesis 2:7—Body and Soul: Material and Immaterial Aspects of Humanity

The human person is "animated dust," completely dependent on God for life (Genesis 2:7; Psalm 104:29–30), part of this physical world but more than this physical world. Throughout their history Christians have tried to describe the human person to account for our distinctive material and immaterial aspects.

Perhaps the most widespread view has been *dualism*, which holds that body and soul are distinct entities (sometimes called "substances" or "natures"). Some ancient Greek philosophies held that the body was irrational and inferior to the immortal soul (the immaterial person) and that the spiritual part would be freed from its bondage at death. Most Christian scholars throughout history believe such radical dualism loses the unity of the person, fails to explain its biblical complexity, and relegates the body to an inherently evil role.

Interestingly, Genesis 2:7 says though Adam's material aspects are formed from the earthly elements and his immaterial aspects are breathed in by a special act of God, all together the human creation—material and immaterial—is called a "living soul" (KJV). The term *soul* is the Hebrew word *nephesh*, roughly equivalent to the Greek word *psyche* and Latin *anima*. Sometimes it can be used of the immaterial part, but other times it can simply refer to living, animate beings—material and immaterial—as in Genesis 2:7.

In short, though we acknowledge that humans have both material and immaterial aspects, we should never think of a person as a "spirit trapped in a body" or as a "body that contains a spirit." Rather, we should understand the human person as a complex creature uniquely designed to live life on earth and commune with God in heaven.

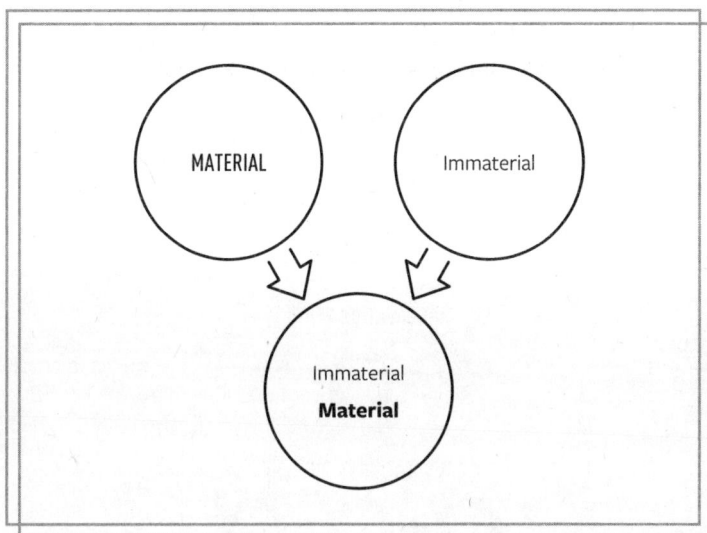

As for human reproduction, most everyone understands the formation of the body in the womb, but what about the person's immaterial aspect? Where does the "soul" come from?

A few early Christians adopted a Greek concept known as the *preexistence of the soul*. In this view, a person's immaterial part existed in a previous state prior to its union with the body. This view has not been popularly held in church history.

Another view more popular among orthodox believers, including many Roman Catholics and some protestant theologians today, is the *special creation of the soul* theory. The concept is that God directly creates each person's soul and joins it to the body in the womb. In this perspective, while our physical bodies come from our parents, our souls come by God's immediate, direct creation.

Finally, the view known as *traducianism* (or generationism, or procreationism) holds that the human species was immediately and directly created in Adam and that both material and immaterial aspects since have been procreated through human parents. This position had strong support in the early church and has gained many supporters since the Reformation.

Three Views on the Origin of the Soul

(black = body, white = soul)

PREEXISTENCE OF THE SOUL

SPECIAL CREATION OF THE SOUL

PROCREATION OF THE SOUL

O + O = O

---

(4) Colossians 1:16—Creation of the Invisibles

Without question, angels, demons, and Satan himself are finite beings created by God through the Son. Colossians 1:16 says, "For by him [Christ] all things were created, in heaven and on earth, visible and invisible, whether thrones or dominions or rulers or authorities—all things were created through him and for him." The reference to things "in heaven," "invisible," and even "thrones or dominions or rulers or authorities" explicitly includes angelic beings. And not only good angels of God, but wicked demons as well. Ephesians 6:12 defines "the rulers . . . authorities . . . and powers" as those who reign over "this present darkness" . . . "the spiritual forces of evil in the heavenly places."

Because the creation of angelic beings isn't specifically mentioned in Genesis 1 and 2, some point to Job 38:7, where the "sons of God"—presumed to be angels—are said to have shouted for joy at the creation of the world. If this is the case, then angels had to have been created prior to the physical world. Others have seen the creation of angels to have occurred on the first day of creation, and that the "light" spoken into existence by God included the bright angelic host (Genesis 1:3).

The first real indication of the existence of angelic beings seems to come in Genesis 3, where the serpent (a sub-human creature) enters the picture. This passage doesn't demonstrate that Satan is in view, but that point becomes clearer through a comparison of other passages (Romans 16:20 [with Genesis 3:15]; 2 Corinthians 11:3; Revelation 12:9; 20:2). So, then, by the time of the tempta-tion in the garden of Eden, angels had been created and Satan had fallen. Neither the creation nor the fall of Satan could have come later than Genesis 3.

These invisible, spiritual creatures known as angels "serve for the sake of those who are to inherit salvation" (Hebrews 1:14; compare Acts 21:1–19). These good angels who serve God's will have their wicked counterparts as well. Jesus said the punishment of eternal fire was actually created "for the devil and his angels" (Matthew 25:41). And the book of Revelation pictures the arch-angel Michael with his army of righteous angels engaged in heav-enly warfare against the dragon and his angels (12:1–2).

Until his ultimate defeat, how does Satan, as a creature, pro-mote chaos around the world? Many interpreters throughout his-tory have understood Satan and his demonic hordes functioning behind the scenes of godless nations and God-opposing religions. Some point to Ezekiel 28, where a different term is used for the ruler of Tyre (*prince*, 28:2) and the shadowy figure behind him (*king*, 28:12). This "king of Tyre" is described as having been "an anointed guardian cherub" (28:14), who was "in Eden, the garden of God" (28:13). He was "blameless" in his ways from the day he was created until unrighteousness was found in him (28:15).

Though not all interpreters agree, most Christians throughout history have seen the "king of Tyre" as a reference to Satan and his ancient fall, probably due to his jealousy at the creation of Adam and Eve. If Satan is in view here, then he's pictured as operating in the world by influencing political and military leaders, as he does in Revelation 13 and perhaps even in Isaiah 14.

Whatever the case may be regarding these specific passages, one thing is clear: God originally created all things "good," including angels. The fall of some angels into sin and rebellion came from an abuse of their creaturely freedom. While wicked spirits presently attempt to undermine God's kingdom and the salvation of His people, one day He will vanquish them forever, and they will never inflict evil on God's creation again (Revelation 20:10).

(5) Genesis 3—The Fall of Humanity

The first man and his wife were created in God's image with authority over the rest of creation (Genesis 1:26–30; 2:19–20). They were to exercise authority on God's behalf over the world. But through the deception of the serpent—the lowest of the creatures—this arrangement was turned on its head. As a creature meant to be under humanity's control, the serpent (no doubt controlled by Satan) tempted humanity to rebel against their Creator.

Perhaps this account would be more understandable if the first sin had been a capital crime—if Eve had struck Adam down in a rage or Adam had slaughtered all the animals just for fun. But eating a piece of fruit? On the other hand, God could have easily said, "I didn't ask for much. I gave you everything and demanded restraint in one little thing."

The fact is the simplicity of this command shows the importance of devotion and obedience to our Creator in everything, not just the things we believe are important. In other words, the eating of the fruit was a simple act that points to the far greater issue of rejecting God's authority and thus offending His honor.

The consequences of the fall for humanity anticipate a continuing struggle between good and evil as a primary problem in the world around us. And in Genesis 3 they point us to the origin of a host of common plights that have marred humanity throughout history:

- fear and insecurity (3:10)
- a sense of perpetual guilt (3:11)
- the need to blame others (3:12–13)
- alienation between God, humanity, and creation (3:8; 14–19)
- painful existence (3:16–18)
- death (3:19)

Genesis 3 shows us that Satan was allowed to put innocent humans to the test. The fundamental sin was prideful rebellion against God and His word of command. The original sin of Adam and Eve—along with their fallen, mortal condition and sinfulness—has been perpetuated by procreation. All, therefore, are born into the world not with the pure, innocent nature of Adam prior to the fall but with the corrupt, fallen nature Adam had after the fall.

FIVE "DEATHS" RESULTING FROM THE FALL

Spiritual Death—Separation from the life of God and resulting in depravity (Genesis 3:8–11; Ephesians 2:1; Colossians 2:13)

Physical Death—Unnatural separation of material and immaterial parts of humanity (Genesis 3:19)

Covenantal Death—Loss of blessing, now under cursed conditions (Genesis 3:14–19)

Relational Death—Interpersonal and social alienation from fellow humans (Genesis 3:16)

Cosmic Death—Breakdown and corruption of all creation (Genesis 3:17–19; Romans 8:20–23)

---

(6) Romans 3:9–23—Depravity of Fallen Humanity

More and more, the biblical concept of "sin" is rejected by the world. Why? Because it interferes with an optimistic appraisal of our self-worth. It gets in the way of the fun and happiness we pursue. It doesn't allow us to follow our hormones as "mutually consenting adults." In short, the concept of "sin" irritates people because it "holds them back." But when the Bible digs down a level deeper behind personal sins and introduces the concept of "depravity," that's when people are really offended!

Most will agree that the world contains depraved people like serial killers, genocidal maniacs, and terrorists, but we often view them as exceptions rather than the rule and let the rest of us "good" people off the hook. Not so fast. The Bible declares *everyone* guilty (Psalm 14:2–3; Ecclesiastes 7:20; 9:3; Isaiah 53:6), convicting *everyone* of sin (Romans 3:23; Ephesians 2:1–3). The fact is Scripture paints a gloomy picture of human depravity and its lingering, long-lasting results (Genesis 6:5; Jeremiah 17:9; Romans 8:7–8).

"Depravity" doesn't mean individuals or societies are always as bad as they *could* be. It means that apart from God's grace, they're *capable* of being that corrupt. It's the difference between saying "My bad!" versus admitting "I'm bad!" Depravity means we fall short of God's perfect standard of holiness (privation) and that we ourselves are twisted, corrupt, and tend toward sinful attitudes, actions, and addictions (perversion).

With one voice, orthodox Christians reject the idea that humans are born pure, innocent, and able to believe, think, and live rightly without the aid of God's grace. Around the year AD 400, the monk Pelagius taught the opposite: that humans are born innocent and can choose to be sinless. To Pelagius, a person's depravity is personal and determined by voluntary actions that can be reformed through human effort.

All orthodox Christians reject the optimism of Pelagianism, but not all Christians have agreed on the extent of depravity on fallen humanity. Around the same time as Pelagius, the monk John Cassian taught that humanity is mortal, prone to sin, and stands in need of God's saving grace. Yet Cassianism holds that people have freedom to respond to God's offer of salvation. This view is most common in the Eastern Orthodox churches and some Protestant traditions that emphasize human free will after the fall.

Another "partial" view, advanced at the Synod of Orange II in 529, is similar to the post-reformation view known as "Arminianism" (named after Jacob Arminius, who died in 1609). Though this view adheres to total depravity, Arminians believe humans have, by grace, been given a choice to accept or resist the offer of saving grace. This view of total depravity partially alleviated by the grace of God survives today in a large portion of orthodox Protestant churches, including the Wesleyan, Pentecostal, and many Baptist and free churches.

A final part of the Christian tradition has held to "total depravity." The fall of humanity and their ruin before God is *total*. Everyone stands in absolute need of God's grace even to understand the gospel and choose to accept it. This view of total depravity is classically expressed in the fifth-century theology of Augustine of Hippo and is shared by Reformed traditions that identify with Calvinist theology.

FOUR CLASSIC VIEWS ON HUMANITY AND SIN

Pelagianism	Cassianism	Orange II	Augustinianism
• Adam's sin harmed only himself.	• Adam's sin harmed all humanity.	• Adam's sin destroyed all humanity.	• Adam's sin destroyed all humanity.
• All people are born spiritually alive and innocent.	• All people are born spiritually sick and in need of healing.	• All people are born spiritually dead and guilty.	• All people are born spiritually dead and guilty.
• Humans are able to do good in their own power.	• Humans are able to cooperate with God's grace.	• Humans are enabled by grace to cooperate with God.	• Humans are unable to do good in their own power.

In short, though all orthodox, Protestant, Bible-believing Christians reject Pelagianism as unbiblical, they aren't completely in agreement on the effects of depravity on the individual. Their positions range from a view of "partial depravity" to what is called "total depravity."

(7) Romans 5—The Doctrine of Original Sin

The first man's disobedience initiated a history-long bondage to sin and the just judgment of death (Romans 5:12, 15, 17). According to Romans 5, sin is a deadly condition we humans are born with, a condition that can be reconciled only by the gracious gift of life through Jesus Christ (5:15, 17, 21). All actual sins flow from the fallen condition of humanity that first entered our race when Adam sinned (Mark 7:21–23). This doctrine of "original sin" is part of our inheritance as orthodox Protestant Christians. It's a doctrine taught by Scripture and affirmed throughout church history. The doctrine of original sin can be expressed most simply by saying that when Adam sinned, all humanity fell into sin.

Theologian Charles C. Ryrie defines "original sin" as the "sinful state into which all people are born . . . because Adam's original sin produced that moral corruption of nature that was transmitted by inheritance to each succeeding generation."[7] That is, original sin is that corruption of human nature that started with Adam's sin and infected all humans since. Simply put, we're fallen, depraved sinners because our mommies and daddies were fallen, depraved sinners. And they (and all humans) were fallen, depraved sinners because the first humans—Adam and Eve—were fallen, depraved sinners.

Now, this same idea of a corrupt human nature arises from several passages of Scripture, not just Romans 5 (our current passage to ponder). We've included a small box full of them so you can see for yourself.

ADDITIONAL PASSAGES RELATED TO ORIGINAL SIN

Genesis 5:3	Romans 3:10–12
Genesis 8:21	Romans 5:12
Psalm 51:5	Romans 8:20–22
Psalm 58:3	Galatians 3:22
Proverbs 22:15	1 John 5:19
Ephesians 2:3	

Admittedly, none of those passages in the box use the actual words *original sin*. But they show up in the works of Christian leaders and thinkers throughout the centuries, cited as evidence for the concept of original sin. Major figures in the history of the church have agreed that the Scriptures, even though they may not be as explicit as we would like, teach the doctrine of original sin. Though any given tradition may describe the concept differently or emphasize different aspects of the doctrine, the church throughout its history has understood that Adam's original sin plunged all humanity into sin, death, and condemnation. Only the person and work of Jesus Christ can rescue us from the effects of Adam's original sin.

It's worth noting that some theologians in the Protestant tradition, in framing their understanding of original sin, include not only the corruption of human nature but also the guilt arising directly from Adam's sin—reckoned directly to each and every human. Most theologians call this latter element "imputed sin," which raises an important point: Some regard original sin as *including* imputed sin, and some (like Ryrie) do not.

While we can't resolve this difference of perspectives here, we can clarify it. For purposes of our discussion, think of it this way: *I'm a fallen, depraved sinner because my parents were fallen, depraved sinners. They, like all humans who preceded them, are*

129

Imputed and Inherited Sin Compared

IMPUTED SIN Romans 5:12-21	INHERITED SIN PSALM 51:5; EPHESIANS 2:3
Adam Each Person Me	Adam ↓ All People ↓ Me

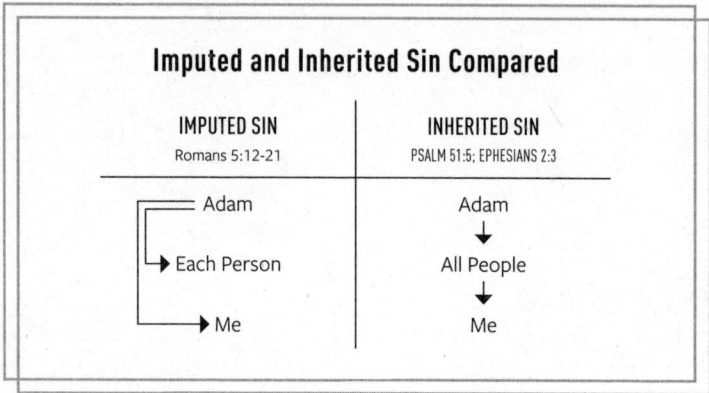

fallen, depraved sinners because the first humans—Adam and Eve—were fallen, depraved sinners. This is the basic definition of original sin. Some theologians, in wrestling with Romans 5:12 coupled with 2 Corinthians 5:21, take one additional theological step and affirm that the sin of Adam is directly reckoned, or imputed, to each human.

Realities to Remember

Probably, few millennials or those younger have ever watched a single episode of the original 1950s drama *Dragnet* . . . or its 1960s revival . . . or its 1989 remake . . . or even its failed 2003 reboot. But older generations will never forget some of *Dragnet*'s classic trademarks: its "names have been changed to protect the innocent" voiceover, its "dummm-duh-*dum*-dum!" title theme,[8] and especially its most (mis)quoted catchphrase, "Just the facts."[9]

Picture the mythic scene. Two LA detectives dressed in suits and ties interview an eyewitness to a crime. The elderly woman, obviously shaken up, begins gushing with personal opinions and irrelevant insights that distract the unflappable Sgt. Joe Friday and his terminally dour partner from their investigation. With a raised hand, Sgt. Friday stops the woman and sets her back on track: "All we want are the facts, ma'am."

When it comes to the essentials of Christian theology, all we want are the facts—the basic foundations that hold all the details together. Yes, we can spend a lifetime investigating all the intricate issues, debated questions, and logical implications of creation, humanity, and sin, but first we need to sort out the central truths around which everything else revolves.

Reality 1: The triune Creator is the foundation for a Christian worldview.

"Why is there *something* instead of *nothing*?"

To this fundamental question about existence are really only three main answers. Atheism says there is no God, so something has always existed. Pantheism asserts that God is everything, and everything is God. Theism believes in a personal Creator who made everything that exists out of nothing.

These different answers from atheists, pantheists, and theists aren't merely the irrelevant musings of philosophers or theologians with too much time on their hands. They're extremely vital to everyday life because they affect a person's "worldview." James Sire explains, "A worldview is a commitment, a fundamental orientation of the heart, that can be expressed as a story or in a set of presuppositions . . . which we hold . . . about the basic constitution of reality, and that provides the foundation on which we live and move and have our being."[10]

Scripture acknowledges that "competing" views of creation are out there. Many "gods" and "lords" or other theories and philosophies lead to all sorts of different answers to the question *Why is there something instead of nothing?* In response to these countless claims, the apostle Paul wrote:

> Although there may be so-called gods in heaven or on earth—as indeed there are many "gods" and many "lords"—yet for us there is one God, the Father, from whom are all things and for whom we

exist, and one Lord, Jesus Christ, through whom are all things and through whom we exist. However, not all possess this knowledge. (1 Corinthians 8:5–7)

The author of Hebrews notes that this foundation of a Christian worldview ultimately rests not on scientific proofs, philosophical speculations, personal experiences, or logical arguments, but on faith: "By faith we understand that the universe was created by the word of God, so that what is seen was not made out of things that are visible" (Hebrews 11:3).

Christians believe that all things came into existence by the triune God—the good, all-powerful, all-knowing Father who has revealed himself through His Son by the power of the Holy Spirit. This changes everything. Contrary to atheism and pantheism, the world has purpose, meaning, order, and beauty because it's the handiwork of the Creator. And humans have a framework, grid, and belief system through which they can understand the world, make decisions, and establish values.

We must remember that the triune Creator is the foundation for a Christian worldview.

Reality 2: All humans are created in the image of God and have inherent dignity.

Alternative accounts of human origins corrupt or destroy human dignity. If humans have somehow evolved by a process of blind natural selection, unaided and unguided by the hands of a creative God, then our complexity might give us an edge for survival among other beasts. But it doesn't make us distinct from them.

That humans—and no other earthly creatures—are uniquely created according to the image of God is the foundation of every person's dignity. Though as earth creatures we share similarities with other creatures whose "ingredients" come from the earth (Genesis 1:24; 2:7), humans have been endowed with physical, intellectual, and spiritual capacities that make us uniquely fitted for a special calling in God's ordered creation.

Today more than ever, the question of what is human and what is a person generates intense controversy. People's lives are on the line here. The Bible declares that we're created in God's image. From the unborn to the dying, from the unrepentant sinner to the self-sacrificial saint, from a man living in the White House to a man living under a bridge—all people have inherent dignity and worth as image-bearing creatures of God. No matter what gender, no matter what age, no matter what race, no matter what economic level, every human being is singularly significant. No other worldview can genuinely affirm human equality.

The creation of humans—all people and each person—in the image of God is therefore a reality we must remember.

Reality 3: All are sinners, all have sinned, and all need a Savior.

We're not sinners because we sin; we sin because we're sinners. And because we're sinners who sin, we need a Savior who didn't, doesn't, and can't.

Though humans were originally created good, the fall from that original goodness and innocence plunged all of humanity into sin and guilt. The apostle Paul wrote, "Sin came into the world through one man, and death through sin, and so death spread to all men because all sinned" (Romans 5:12) and added, "One trespass led to condemnation for all men" (5:18). In short, "All have sinned and fall short of the glory of God" (Romans 3:23).

Fish swim. Birds fly. Snakes slither. Sinners sin. It's in our fallen nature. Nobody can escape it. If you're human—a natural descendant from Adam and Eve—then you're born into a family of fallen sinners. We've inherited their humanity as well as their fallenness—their mortality, weakness, imperfections, guilt, and condemnation.

But there's a way of escape. Jesus Christ, born of a woman but not of a man, was free from the guilt, stain, and condemnation of sin. In fact, Christ was tempted in every respect as other humans, but "without sin" (Hebrews 4:15). As such, He alone is able to serve as a perfect, acceptable sacrifice and "stand-in" for sinners: "For our sake he made him to be sin who knew no sin, so that in him we might become the righteousness of God" (2 Corinthians 5:21).

So though we must never forget that all people are sinners and all have sinned, we must also remember that we have a sinless Savior.

Reality 4: Angels and demons are finite creatures of an infinite Creator.

Many baseless, unbiblical, and even silly beliefs about angels, Satan, and demons are floating around out there.

A lot of folk theology teaches that angels are actually the spirits of good humans who died. So poor old Uncle Bob, bless his heart, went to heaven because God needed another angel to sing in the choir, play the harp, or serve as guardian angel for little children. Perhaps, then, the ghosts of bad people are demons who might haunt the living. All the more reason for good Angel Bob to do his thing!

Others think angels are everywhere: cushioning children from bumps and bruises, catching babies when they fall, and reserving parking places when impatient people pray. In modern popular mysticism, angels often play the role of magical protector, spiritual comforter, or invisible companion—similar to imaginary friends or security blankets for small children.

And who knows how many religious people live in fear of the devil and his rogue band of cronies hell-bent on terrorizing unsuspecting victims. They've seen one too many movies where innocent victims are attacked by demons or Satan himself, and the only thing they can do is call a professional exorcist in to save the day!

With all this confusion, it's important to keep one fact straight: Angels, Satan, and demons are finite, limited creatures who operate under the sovereignty of their Creator. Angelic beings, both good and evil, can do only what God allows them to do.

Yes, God does, for His own reasons, grant Satan and demons a long leash of latitude to test, tempt, deceive, and even attack humans. But the Bible clearly teaches that demons can't do any of this without God granting them leave to do so (Job 1:9–11; Luke 22:31–32; 2 Corinthians 12:7–9). And when we remember that God's good angels are "ministering spirits sent out" by God "to serve" His will (Hebrews 1:14), we should realize that praying to angels for help is pointless when we have direct access to their Boss (Ephesians 2:18; Hebrews 4:16). And while talking to the only One who's absolutely sovereign over all created things, we might as well ask Him to protect us from the forces of evil and the devil himself (John 17:15; Ephesians 6:16; 2 Thessalonians 3:3).

We must remember that angels and demons are finite creatures subject to the sovereignty of an infinite Creator.

Reality 5: God is not the author of evil.

We've already seen, over and over again, that in the beginning God created all things good (Genesis 1:31). And the New Testament says "every good gift and every perfect gift is from above, coming down from the Father of lights" (James 1:17) and that "God is light, and in him is no darkness at all" (1 John 1:5).

But if all this is true, that God is light and God is good, why is so much darkness and evil in the world? Didn't He create everything? How could this be?

Most Christians throughout history—and even today—have followed Augustine's *theodicy*, a term that means "an explanation of evil in light of an omnipotent, morally perfect Creator." This argument is often called the "free will defense." That is, the all-powerful God of goodness created finite beings good and gave them freedom of choice. Though He knew some would choose against Him (thus, the *possibility* of evil), God himself is not culpable for their free choices against Him. Therefore, evil in the universe is a consequence of those personal choices; natural evil includes the consequent physical judgments these have brought about (Genesis 3).

Theologian Thomas Oden writes:

> Christian teachers have worked cautiously to preserve the teaching of the holiness of God from the charge that God directly causes evil. The *freewill defense* has become a time-tested response to the charge that God is the author of sin. Accordingly, it is not God that causes sin, but rather it is human freedom, which is a good but distortable creation of God, that elicits sin. We do the sinning ourselves; God does not do it. It is not sin with which God cooperates, but human freedom. God cooperates by empowering free will to act and by providing the secondary arena of natural causality in which our freedom is able to stand, though liable to fall. . . . Hence the memorable formula: *God concurs with the effect but not with the defect of our actions.*[11]

Personal experiences of pain and suffering, affliction and injustice, tragedy and death will sometimes tempt us to shake our fists heavenward and blame God for the sin, evil, and suffering of this present world. But God is no more responsible for sin than the sun is responsible for casting a dark shadow behind things that block its light. Sin itself is not a thing. Evil is not an inky substance that flows from place to place, causing untold destruction. Death is not a shadowy figure claiming victims at random. Sin, evil, and death are *negations* of righteousness, goodness, and life. As such, God didn't *create* them but temporarily tolerates them until that great day when "death shall be no more, neither shall there be mourning, nor crying, nor pain anymore" (Revelation 21:4).

Even in the midst of the deepest darkness of this fallen world, we must remember that God is not the author of evil.

Errors to Avoid

Though children think cautions only spoil their fun and squelch their freedom, as we grow older we realize warnings are meant to protect us from harm. Often the warnings come after others have learned the hard way, experiencing accidents with injuries or even fatalities. Heeding the warnings can save us from similar pain and heartache.

The study of Christian theology has its own dangers too. Throughout history certain doctrinal and practical errors have repeatedly infected the body of Christ. In response, Christians have developed a battery of immunizations in the form of stern warnings against fringe beliefs, unhealthy practices, and disastrous heresies. But each new generation needs to be vaccinated against these dangers, or they run the risk of succumbing to avoidable pain and suffering. If they don't, they'll pass these doctrinal diseases and practical plagues on to the next generation.

The following "errors to avoid" represent some of the most serious and urgent threats to right thinking and healthy living with regard to the doctrines of creation, humanity, and sin. In order to remain spiritually healthy in our own generation and to better prepare the next, we need to inoculate ourselves against the threat of infection by heeding these warnings.

Error 1: Skepticism's Scientific Seduction

As techno-savvy as you think you are, chances are you've never heard of the Bowmar Brain—a pocket calculator with four—count 'em, *four*—functions: add, subtract, multiply, and divide! And the red LED display made the 1970s users of the device feel like they were living in a science-fiction movie. Go ahead and search for "Bowmar Brain" on your smartphone. As you do, consider that what you hold in your hand not only has more computing power than the Bowmar Brain but more than the 1969 Apollo 11 astronauts had in their command module and lunar lander.

Let's admit it. Not only is technology cool, but the advances in science that underlie all our helpful, time-saving devices have benefited humanity in many ways. There's simply no denying that scientific discoveries have provided innumerable solutions to everyday problems. From technology to medicine and from industry to agriculture, science has revolutionized the world over the last couple of centuries. None of us could—nor should—deny this.

But there's a seductive side to some science that leads to a warning. It's almost as if some in the scientific world would want us to become little "Bowmar Brainlesses." Some skeptics (and the scientific community seems to have a disproportionate number of them) suggest that we can believe only what science can confirm. "Follow the evidence!" they say. And that quest leads such skeptics to doubt or even deny the existence of a Creator. They ditch their faith (if they ever had any), and they trash the faith of others. They ridicule all religions, including Christianity.

But what these skeptics are unwilling to admit is this: They've exchanged one faith for another faith. Their perspective, which they claim is grounded in evidence, has no evidence to explain the origin of life or the origin of the universe.[12]

So the error here is this: Listening to the sweet song of science can stultify our thinking, and we can mistakenly follow science further than it's qualified to lead us. When it comes to improving on the "Bowmar Brain," we can give science a long and loud round of applause. But don't listen to the voice of science when it pretends to offer something that would dislodge your faith. That part of science's song is a lie.

Error 2: The Fallacious Fall

Several times in this chapter, we've mentioned the Christian doctrine of original sin. As you remember, this is the teaching that Adam's sin plunged all of humanity into spiritual ruin. This teaching, as we saw in Passages to Ponder (Romans 5), has been consistently taught and believed by the church ever since the New Testament era. This is because the New Testament leaves us no other valid option. Adam's sin brought spiritual ruin upon all humanity.

This is where the danger arises. Modern scientific theories of evolution have little room for a historical Adam and a historical Eve. Many scientists say they never existed—at least not the way Scripture speaks of them. If Adam and Eve existed at all, science claims, they weren't like the picture painted by Scripture. They were hominids just like every other hominid of their generation, and they just happened to be the source of all the genetic material we currently see in humanity. They were our ancestors, but they were nothing special—at least they weren't physically unique. This is demanded by the modern scientific theory of common descent.

But what just happened here? As it turns out, science has effectively denied a part of the Christian faith that's been affirmed for centuries on the basis of both Scripture and tradition. The doctrine of original sin is well grounded theologically. But if science says there was no real historical Adam, then it's obvious that Adam's fall did nothing to humanity. It's just as if a character in your favorite movie died, a death that does nothing to you but stir a few emotions if you happened to develop an attachment. Besides that, the death is irrelevant.

So where does that leave us? Is this a competition between scientific "fact" and Christian "faith"? Not quite. You see, modern science doesn't like to admit this, but scientific theories of biological descent are themselves based ultimately on a kind of faith, not fact. (Shock! Gasp!) So it's ultimately a question of faith (science) versus faith (Christian teaching). The case of Richard Dawkins is instructive here. As Antony Flew (a former atheist) writes:

> Dawkins himself has elsewhere confessed that his atheistic view of the universe is based on faith. When asked by the Edge Foundation, "What do you believe is true even though you cannot prove it?" Dawkins replied: "I believe that all life, all intelligence, all

creativity and all 'design' anywhere in the universe, is the direct or indirect product of Darwinian natural selection. It follows that design comes late in the universe, after a period of Darwinian evolution. Design cannot precede evolution and therefore cannot underlie the universe." At bottom, then, Dawkins's rejection of an ultimate Intelligence is a matter of belief without proof.[13]

The simple truth is *we don't have the scientific facts regarding origins*. Instead, modern science begins with a philosophical pre-supposition (their own version of faith) and interprets the data gathered by science in accordance with that faith.

So that's the error. Many scientists and historians tell us Adam didn't really exist. Stories of his fall are just myths and legends, they claim. But when Christians jettison their faith because of the dogmatic pronouncements of science, they're *not* choosing facts over fiction, and they're *not* making the only reasonable choice. Instead, they're choosing a Johnny-come-lately kind of faith that can't even withstand the scrutiny of the atheists of yesteryear over a faith that's much more coherent and intellectually honest.

Don't do that. Be a person of *faith seeking understanding*.

Error 3: I'm OK, You're OK

In the late 1960s, psychiatrist Thomas Harris first published a book titled *I'm OK—You're OK*.[14] The book applied a new psychiatric theory called "transactional analysis" to the average person, hoping to change the world by encouraging a generation to adopt a new view of life (thus the summary "I'm OK—You're OK"). That book played a major role in establishing the entire self-help genre of books. So the next time you're in a bookstore and see four aisles of books like *How to Increase Your Hamster's IQ*, you can thank Thomas Harris and *I'm OK—You're OK*. At least partly.

To be clear, there's much good in adopting a life view that's accepting of other people. No argument here. In fact, because all humans are made in God's image, every last one of them deserves to be treated with dignity. This is a biblical concept. But somewhere along the way, at least in some cultures, a similar idea arose with respect to God's acceptance of us all.

The idea runs like this: "All humans are basically good. And yet we all make mistakes. Surely God will recognize the good in us and understand the mistakes we make. Surely God will accept all of us." This idea could be called the *spiritual* version of "I'm OK—You're OK." But this idea, according to Scripture, is a lie. This idea suggests that we humans don't really have a spiritual problem. Some versions admit that we have a spiritual problem but say we have the ability in ourselves to fix it. Both versions deny the truth of Scripture.

The first lie this view teaches is that our sin problem is either not a problem or a manageable problem—something we can fix on our own. But Romans 6:23 says, "The wages of sin is death, but the free gift of God is eternal life in Christ Jesus our Lord." Houston, we have a problem. And we can't fix it. And it's going to kill us. Forever. *This* is the truth of Scripture: "All have sinned and fall short of the glory of God, and are justified by [God's] grace as a gift, through the redemption that is in Christ Jesus" (Romans 3:23–24). Only God can fix our sin problem.

The bottom line is this: I'm *not* OK, and you're *not* OK. Apart from the free gift of God in Christ, we're doomed. To teach otherwise is to provide a false hope, based on a perverted lie.

Error 4: Good Ghost in a Bad Host

If pressed, just about everyone could look in a mirror and find flaws with what they see. For some, those flaws rarely cross their minds. For others, physical flaws dictate, in sometimes profound and painful ways, how they are in the world—the places they'll go, the activities they'll engage in, and the people with whom they'll spend time. This latter group is especially prone to the negative effects of the danger that says our true, immaterial selves are waiting to be set free from the sin-tainted and broken-down bodies that hold us captive.

This view has been around the church since the heretical Gnostics, influenced by Platonic philosophy, taught that the created world—and everything physical in it—was wicked, a punishment upon we humans, who were essentially spiritual beings. Today, while some teachers will occasionally indict the physical flesh as the source of all our problems, this particular danger most often crops up in the yearning to escape the pain of this world for an overly spiritual heavenly existence. In this imagined heaven, human beings would float through an ethereal world without the encumbrances of our broken bodies.

But this kind of "hope" couldn't be further from the biblical teaching. The Bible proclaims we're not just spiritual beings "trapped" inside a wicked and broken physical body. The real "me" is not my spirit or soul. Our bodies are not simply attachments onto our true, immaterial, spiritual selves. Rather, they're fundamental to who we are as created human beings. The healing ministry of Jesus makes this clear, as the Lord often healed both the physical and the spiritual maladies of those He encountered (Matthew 9:1–8; Mark 10:46–52; Luke 17:11–19).

The "good ghost, bad host" perspective leads, then, to profound problems. Some who hold this view tend to see the body as little more than disposable trash. Consider the devastating consequences for those people who agonize most over their physical flaws, having yet one more reason to see themselves as worthless, broken, and beyond help.

Others will take the "good ghost, bad host" view and see the body as the source of all that's wrong in the world. For these, the body hinders their true spiritual selves from the good life with God. But this view ignores the reality that God wants to work in and through us as embodied creatures.

But how, then, should we see the body? Psalm 139:13–14 affirms the particular care God has for us as His created beings, revealing a kind gentleness in God's creative act. Genesis 2:7 presents God as crafting the first human in a most intimate fashion, making something beautiful and extraordinary (a body) from material that most of us would consider filthy and common (dirt). When God breathed life into that body, human beings were from then on a *psychosomatic* unity (*psychosomatic* is a Greek term meaning "soul/body"). We are *meant* to be body and soul in one person.

Ultimately, our hope is in Christ, because of whom we have the promise of the resurrection of *this* body—that God will make new that which He has created (Ezekiel 37:1–9; 1 Corinthians 15:53–54; Revelation 21:5). In that day, the union of body and soul broken by death will once again be reunited to the glorious unity that God has always intended for human beings.

Error 5: The Devil Made Me Do It!

Not all of God's multitude of creations has the power of choice. While people make heady decisions all the time, and even animals can "decide" to stand and get a drink of water, a plant lives or dies based on whether it receives the proper nourishment from ground and sky. Too much sun or too little water can spell doom for these delicate creations.

People often seem to paint themselves in the guise of the earth's plant life when it comes to temptation, able only to receive whatever the world around them dishes out. Therefore, if sin and temptation crouch at our doorstep, the thinking goes, we'll have to give in. For someone like this, sin isn't about their own failings but about the presence of Satan, his demons, or other wicked people wreaking havoc in their life.

This approach to life has been labeled lots of different ways. Some call it rationalization. Others talk of making excuses or pointing the finger. Whatever we call it, the practice is nearly as old as humanity itself. Way back in Genesis 3, in the moments after the first act of disobedience, both Adam and Eve pointed their fingers away from themselves to place the responsibility on someone else (Genesis 3:11–13). The reality for the first couple was simple: They had failed in their obligation to God. No one else could stand between them and the responsibility they bore for their choices. They had to own up to what they'd done.

Many people today still engage in this kind of blame game. As with any effective strategy of self-preservation, there's some truth in it. The world is full of fallen people, and Satan and his demons are certainly part of the problem we face with sin and temptation. But this is only one part of the problem. We simply cannot say the devil is the direct cause of all sin, sickness, and suffering in the world. To do so would be to completely absolve ourselves of personal responsibility for our own sinful deeds. And it's not biblical.

The problem of sin in the world is more complicated than simply claiming "The devil made me do it!" We're also part of the problem. And on top of that is our deteriorated world, which groans under the weight of sin (Romans 8:20–22). Each of these things contributes to the wickedness in the world. And though a demon, another person, a destructive hurricane, or even our own sinful desire might tempt us directly or indirectly, only *we* make our own sinful choices.

Therefore, when we sin, we need to own up to it. And while the many representatives of wickedness in the world victimize people repeatedly, we need to keep watch lest we fall prey to the danger of blaming others for those sinful deeds that are our own.

Lessons to Live

Not to stereotype, but have you ever noticed how most boys in the age range of about seven to eleven are, well, a *mess*? If their hair isn't disheveled, it's in upheaval. If their face isn't dirty, it's because they wiped it with their T-shirt. And if they managed

144

to put on clothes that actually fit and match, some item is likely inside out or upside down.

Thankfully, as they go from "tween" to "teen" to "young adult," most boys start doing the one thing that turns them from little piglets to little princes: They actually look at themselves in the mirror. And not just to make funny faces. They really look intently at themselves and notice "I'm a slob!" Only then, after actually seeing themselves in the mirror, can they take steps to pull themselves together.

James has the same idea in mind when he urges his readers to not be just *hearers* of the word but *doers* of the word (James 1:23–25). If we stop our study of creation, humanity, and sin at pondering passages, remembering realities, and avoiding errors, we'd be no better than those unkempt, grubby tweens who couldn't care less about what they look like in the mirror. Instead, we need to gaze intently at God's Word and look closely at ourselves, taking opportunities to tidy our thoughts, wash our attitudes, and clean up our actions.

The following four lessons should give us something to not only ponder but to live out.

Lesson 1: Worship and glorify God as Creator.

In Revelation 4, we encounter an arresting scene. The apostle John leads us into a vision he was given, and in the vision we see the throne room of heaven. The One sitting on the throne was dazzling. And around His throne, twenty-four elders sat on thrones of their own. We also see four living creatures. We're not told exactly what they are, but we are told exactly what they do: "Day and night they never cease to say, 'Holy, holy, holy, is the Lord God Almighty, who was and is and is to come!'" (4:8).

And whenever the living creatures do this (and it sounds like they do it fairly often), the elders fall down, cast their crowns before the throne of God, and proclaim God's worthiness. They say,

"Worthy are you, our Lord and God, to receive glory and honor and power, for you created all things, and by your will they existed and were created" (4:11).

This sounds a little bit out of place, doesn't it? Perhaps you were expecting them to say something about God's character or the impressiveness of His being. Or at least something about Jesus and His second coming in the clouds. But no! They praise God for His role as the Creator.

On further reflection, this may be even more awesome than we ever imagined. In one compact statement, the elders praise God by acknowledging not only what He is (the only One with power to create all things) but also what He's done (He has, in fact, created all things).

By wrestling with this passage, we learn the proper response to the cosmos. It's *not* to presume that the universe is some physical accident, some *quantum fluctuation in nothingness*. And the universe isn't a self-centered glory-hog, beckoning us to obsess over *it*, live our lives for *it*, or even worship *it*. On the contrary, the created order is a signpost. It points us toward God. And this is the first responsibility of all creatures: to recognize the Creator and praise Him as the Creator. If this is important enough to be the centerpiece of one of the few heavenly vignettes we find in Scripture, it must be important enough for us to put into practice.

Lesson 2: Enjoy God's creation as a gift from His hand.

Ever since God cursed the ground in the aftermath of Adam's fall, human beings have been in conflict with the created realm. Backbreaking work, blasphemous art, and broken relationships provide ample reason for humans to shrink from the created world.

But simply avoiding the wickedness of the world doesn't offer a viable solution to the Christian who understands the world as a creation of Almighty God. One of the best ways to embrace the truth of God as Creator is to enjoy that creation as a gift. The apostle Paul made it clear to Timothy that "everything created by God is good, and nothing is to be rejected if it is received with thanksgiving" (1 Timothy 4:4).

For many Christians, this exhortation extends to the world of nature. The biblically minded among us will recall the advice of the proverb that says to consider the ways of an ant and recognize that there is much to learn in our observation and appreciation of the created world (Proverbs 6:6). To benefit from what God has made is a blessing, one we should respond to with gratitude.

But our appreciation of the created world should extend beyond the beauty of nature and into those realms given to us through the agency of God's creative image-bearers: art, music, medicine, architecture, film, and technology, among many others. When we make things, we image our Creator. As Dorothy Sayers argued, "The characteristic common to God and man is apparently . . . the desire and ability to make things."[15] Such commonalities should be appreciated rather than avoided.

Any appreciation of the created world also implies the responsible use of the resources made available to us. That humanity has found so many ways to use so many of the resources in the earth's air, water, and ground suggests something about the many ways God's gift of creation can be employed. Yet our use of the creation should always stay true to the original creation mandate of exercising dominion—a practice that carries with it the notion of care.

As created beings we should receive God's creation with joy and thanksgiving. The many facets of the created world bring beauty and life to us. And while we should avoid over-indulgence and gluttony, we should also avoid an ascetic approach to the created world that would keep us from God's majestic, revelatory creation (Romans 1:20).

Lesson 3: Treat all people with dignity as bearers of the image of God.

One of the most ironic teachings in Scripture arises from the recognition that all humanity is lost. We're all corrupted as fallen humans, and our guilt is compounded by our own willing acts of defiance and rebellion. We're sinners who sin, and we sin because we're sinners.

But ironically, even though we're *warped*, we're not *worthless*. Even though we're *vitiated*, we're yet *valuable*.

This is the teaching of Scripture. We've discussed the nature of man's sinfulness and depravity at great length. And the Bible abundantly affirms this principle: We're so broken by sin that it's not possible to repair ourselves. Divine action is required to repair that breakage.

But Scripture portrays us as valuable even in our broken condition. Humanity was created in the image of God, and that image—though defaced—is not erased. And because we're all made in the image of God, we have value. Dignity. Worth.

Apparently, this is *not* the result of God's saving work. According to James 3, all of humanity must be considered made in the image of God. It doesn't matter if someone is unborn or dying. It doesn't matter if someone is a prisoner or homeless. Diseased, disabled, rich, poor, believing, unbelieving, gay, straight, religious, nonreligious, male, female—every last one of us is made in the image of God and deserves to be treated with dignity. James 3, as we have already seen, informs us that it's unfitting even to curse those made in God's image if we're going to use the same mouth to bless God.

This is where many Christians have a problem. We focus so much on Scripture's honest commands regarding holiness, every one of which contains valid, binding principles. (See Jude 23—"hating even the garment stained by the flesh"; 1 Thessalonians 5:22—"abstain from every form of evil"; and 2 John 11—"whoever greets him takes part in his wicked works.") But in so doing we sometimes end up treating most other humans as cursed. In our desire to pursue holiness, we violate the very principle of James 3. My brothers and sisters, these things ought not be this way!

The lesson to live is this: Treat all humans as made in God's image—as having a built-in dignity.

Lesson 4: Admit that you're a helpless, hopeless, hapless sinner in desperate need of a Savior.

We have some bad news: You're not a sinner because you sin. Nobody gets off that easy. You sin because you're a sinner to the core. And there's nothing—absolutely *nothing*—you can do to fix that. Go ahead and try. You're helpless. And because you're helpless, you're hopeless. And because you're hopeless, you're hapless—both a victim of the sins of others and a perpetrator of sins against God, yourself, and other sinners like you.

Oh, and *you're not alone*. We're in the same condition. And so is everyone else in the whole world. We're *all* born not merely with an inclination to sin but guilty of sin. Since the wages of sin is death (Romans 6:23), we're by nature subject to punishment by God. Once we've all conceded that we're sinners—accepting the tragic news—what can we do? Yes, admitting that fact is the first step, but if we end with that step, it'll be a misstep.

The good news of the incarnation, death, and resurrection of Jesus Christ is our only hope. Remember how we just said "everyone else in the whole world" is a sinner? Well, there was and is only one exception—Jesus Christ, the Son of God. Through that one Savior, God provided *for* us what we can never accomplish for ourselves. He gave His Son as a source of new life while we were still spiritually dead in our trespasses and sins.

Before we can accept the solution—the good news of Jesus Christ—we must acknowledge the problem: our sinfulness. Ironically, we put this principle in practice not by doing something, but by receiving something. How then do you receive the free gift of life that comes only through Jesus Christ? You "believe in the Lord Jesus." Then and only then "you will be saved" (Acts 16:31).

Snapshot of History

Throughout the eras of church history known as the Patristic (100–500), Medieval (500–1500), Protestant (1500–1700), and Modern (1700–Present), the doctrine of humanity and sin has undergone development. The following chart summarizes the twists and turns related to these doctrines throughout history.[16]

Patristic Period (100–500)	Medieval Period (500–1500)	Protestant Period (1500–1700)	Modern Period (1700–Present)
• All Christians believe God made humans in His image, body and soul, but they fell from innocence to sin and death (100–500) • *Imago dei* in humans is increasingly viewed as the rational capacity (100–500) • Against fatalism, early church fathers insist on human free will (400) • Pelagius: humans are born spiritually alive with ability to earn eternal life (c. 410) • Augustine: humans are born spiritually dead, unable to do good without grace (c. 410) • Cassian: humans are spiritually sick, can cooperate with God's grace but are unable to save themselves without His help (c. 420) • Council of Ephesus (431) condemns Pelagianism	• Eastern Orthodoxy holds a more optimistic view of the human condition, upholding free will to respond to God's grace (500–1500) • Orange II (529) in the West affirms an Augustinian view of total depravity and need for grace, rejects Eastern view of partial depravity • Doctrines of Orange II forgotten as Roman Catholic theology drifts toward Pelagianism (1000–1500) • God's image in humanity, linked to reason and free will, seen as partially intact in fallen humans, enabling them to respond freely to His grace (1000–1500) • Some late medieval scholastics teach doctrines of sin similar to Pelagius	• Against what they saw as Pelagian-like Roman Catholic teachings, reformers such as Luther and Zwingli reassert Augustine's teachings on original sin and total depravity (1500–1550) • Luther says God's image in humans was lost in the fall, only restored through Christ (1520); other major reformers believed it was damaged but not destroyed • Anabaptists and Arminians react to Augustinian and Calvinist doctrines of original sin and total depravity, taking a softer view similar to Cassianism (1500–1700)	• Enlightenment thinkers reject classic doctrines of original sin and total depravity (1700–1800) • European Christendom succumbs to Enlightenment views of humanity, leading to the birth of liberal theology and a high view of human reason and ability (1700–1900) • North American Christianity experiences a slower, more gradual loss of classic views on humanity and sin (1750–1850) • Second Great Awakening (1790–1840) sees a major departure from classic views on depravity and original sin • Darwin's theory challenges the creation of humans in God's image and all classic doctrines of humanity and sin (1860–Present)

151

FOUR

Saved by Grace Through Faith— God's Rescue of Sinners

And we, too, being called by His will in Christ Jesus, are not justified by ourselves, nor by our own wisdom, or understanding, or godliness, or works which we have wrought in holiness of heart; but by that faith through which, from the beginning, Almighty God has justified all men; to whom be glory for ever and ever.[1]

—Clement of Rome (c. 95/96)

The righteousness of God is the cause of salvation. Here, too, *"the righteousness of God"* must not be understood as that righteousness by which he is righteous in himself, but as that righteousness by which we are made righteous (justified) by Him, and this happens through faith in the gospel.[2]

—Martin Luther (1530)

In Short . . .

In the beginning, the triune God created all things and placed His image-bearing humans in a privileged place as His agents of

153

dominion in the world (Genesis 1–2). But instead of carrying out that mission in obedience to God, they disobeyed and fell into sin. Not just a little moral boo-boo but a total plunge into the depths of depravity (Romans 3:23). The result? A severe lostness of all people who, left to themselves, have nothing to look forward to but death and judgment.

Sounds bleak? It is. But that's just the bad news—the first part of the Christian story.

Now for some good news—the gospel of Jesus Christ.

What Is the Gospel?

The word *gospel* means "good news." What's the Bible's good news?

In 1 Corinthians 15:3–8, Paul summarizes the gospel as the death and resurrection of Christ. In Romans 1 he rests the gospel firmly on the person of Christ as the son of David and Son of God (Romans 1:1–5). In Galatians 1, the same apostle writes, "Grace and peace to you from God our Father and the Lord Jesus Christ, who gave himself for our sins to rescue us from the present evil age, according to the will of our God and Father, to whom be glory for ever and ever" (Galatians 1:3–5 NIV).

Paul also wrote to Timothy, encouraging him to do this:

Join with me in suffering for the gospel, by the power of God. He has saved us and called us to a holy life—not because of anything we have done but because of his own purpose and grace. This grace was given us in Christ Jesus before the beginning of time, but it has now been revealed through the appearing of our Savior, Christ Jesus, who has destroyed death and has brought life and immortality to light through the gospel. (2 Timothy 1:8–10 NIV)

Finally, Peter provides an extended explanation of the gospel:

Praise be to the God and Father of our Lord Jesus Christ! In his great mercy he has given us new birth into a living hope through

the resurrection of Jesus Christ from the dead, and into an inheritance than can never perish, spoil or fade. This inheritance is kept
in heaven for you, who through faith are shielded by God's power
until the coming of the salvation that is ready to be revealed in the
last time. In this you greatly rejoice. (1 Peter 1:3–6 NIV)

We can conclude there are a variety of ways to summarize the
gospel yet several essential components. Whether the point is made
explicitly, the message of salvation in the gospel is rooted in the
work of the triune God. It's God's eternal plan, ordained before
the creation of the world but accomplished in time and space in
the life, death, and resurrection of Christ. The gospel provides
hope—Christ's resurrection is the basis of our resurrection—and
the gospel promises that He will complete the work He started,
that the second coming is the fulfillment of the hope of the gospel
(Philippians 1:6).

How does a person receive this free gift of salvation through
Jesus Christ? That's the great news of the good news: We're saved
from our sin by grace alone, through faith alone, in Christ alone.

By Grace Alone, Through Faith Alone, In Christ Alone

Grace—undeserved blessing—is always free, never earned, and
can never be repaid. Grace is the center of the Christian faith, the
storyline of the Bible. Grace is what distinguishes Christianity
from the world's religions, which are rooted in the law of sowing
and reaping, in gods (or impersonal forces) that give people what
they earn or deserve. They're founded in the law of karma, the
view that "in this world nothing happens to a person that he does
not for some reason or other deserve."[3] Christianity, on the other
hand, is all about grace.

The Christian doctrine of salvation can be summarized in that
single word, *grace*. In the gospel, because of the person and work
of Christ, sinners can be saved, become righteous, be reconciled
to God, and have the hope of a life that never ends. And these

blessings are *never* earned. Rather, our own works deserve nothing but death (Romans 3:23). Salvation—deliverance from the consequences of sin—isn't something anyone can earn or merit. Rather, the blessings of God are received by grace through faith in Christ.

Salvation is by grace alone, through faith alone, in Christ alone. This is the testimony of the Scriptures and the confession of Bible-believing Christians everywhere.

What's Broken Will Be Fixed

God didn't create the world as it now is. His creation was good. In Genesis 1, the repeated refrain that God saw what He'd made as good emphasizes this fact, culminating in the declaration that everything was "very good" (Genesis 1:31). But everything broke in Genesis 3. When Adam and Eve listened to the serpent instead of God, when they rebelled against their Creator, they introduced evil, corruption, decay, and death into the world. Fallenness and brokenness are the result of sin and the major plotline of every earthly story.

But God loves the world He created. And since His knowledge is comprehensive, human rebellion against Him in the garden didn't catch Him by surprise. It didn't destroy His plans for His creation. It didn't even require Him to switch to "plan B."

"He took on Himself death on our behalf, and He makes Himself an offering to the Father for our sakes. For we had sinned against Him, and it was meet that He should receive the ransom for us, and that we should thus be delivered from the condemnation. . . . For just as darkness disappears on the introduction of light, so is death repulsed before the assault of life, and brings life to all, but death to the destroyer."[4]

John of Damascus (c. 740)

Human sin brought condemnation and judgment; the whole creation was cursed because of their rebellion. But God had taken their rebellion into consideration as a component of His eternal purposes. Beginning in Genesis 3, He's been at work to redeem His creation. And His plans won't be thwarted by the creatures' rebellion against Him.

The Bible is the story of God's gracious and loving response to the rebellion of His creatures. He didn't destroy the rebels or the world He created. Instead, He responded in accordance with His character (Exodus 34:6–7). God's gracious and faithful love triumphs over evil and rebellion.

Grace fixes what's broken.

Jesus Christ, the Only Savior

The central person in God's plan of redemption is Jesus Christ. All Old Testament Scriptures point forward to the work of redemption in the Messiah (compare John 5:39). In His incarnation, the Word added full humanity to His full deity and came into the world He'd created (John 1:14). Jesus' teaching and healing ministry and His proclamation of the coming kingdom brought opposition from the religious leaders of the day. They conspired to have Him put to death at the hands of the Roman governor Pontius Pilate.

Jesus' death appeared to be the end of the story. In fact, two of His disciples expressed their loss of hope: "We had hoped that he was the one who was going to redeem Israel" (Luke 24:21 NIV). But Jesus was dead, and with Him their hope of redemption was buried.

But the Son of God didn't stay in the tomb. On the third day after His death, He was resurrected. Then over a period of forty days, Jesus appeared to many before ascending to God the Father. His ascension, however, was accompanied by the angels' promise that He would come back in the same way He left (Acts 1:11). His work wasn't finished in His first advent. There's much more work for Him to do until all His enemies are defeated.

But the first advent did accomplish the work of atonement—the work necessary to secure salvation for lost humanity. Jesus' death on the cross was the fulfillment of the promises of sacrifice for sins. He died as a substitute, as the Lamb of God who takes away the sin of the world (John 1:29). "It is finished," He declared, and then He died. No further sacrifice for sins is needed (Hebrews 10:10–14).

Having taken on himself the sin of the world, Jesus experienced the consequences of sin. He became sin for us, Paul declares (2 Corinthians 5:21). But it's not possible for sin and death to defeat the giver of life, the One who is Life itself. Three days later He walked out of the tomb. His resurrection not only proves His sacrifice was accepted and that everything He taught was true but provides hope. *His resurrection is the heartbeat of the gospel*—the good news that death doesn't have the final word, that one day everything will be made right (1 Corinthians 15).

Wise unto Salvation

We live in the space between Christ's first and second coming, between the cross and the crown, between His coming to suffer and die and His return to establish an eternal kingdom of life and peace. And during this time, we've been given stewardship of the gospel of grace, "the power of God for salvation to everyone who believes" (Romans 1:16). We have the privilege of being ambassadors of God, imploring people to be reconciled to Him (2 Corinthians 5:20). We are witnesses who make disciples of all nations (Acts 1:8; Matthew 28:18–20).

Our message isn't "Work harder," or "Do this and don't do that," or "Say these words," or "Make this pilgrimage," or "Give this much money," or even "Lay down your life for others." Our message is that the Creator became a creature—becoming the God-Man—to provide for us what we can never provide for ourselves. God sent His Son for us while we were still sinners, in

The Gospel of the Person and Work of Christ

THE GOSPEL

PERSON OF CHRIST

2 Timothy 2:8

2 Corinthians 4:4

Romans 1:1–4

RESPONSE: FAITH

WORK OF CHRIST

Romans 2:15–16

2 Timothy 2:8

1 Corinthians 15:1–5

Romans 1:16–17
Galatians 1:6–9; 2:14–16; 3:1–3

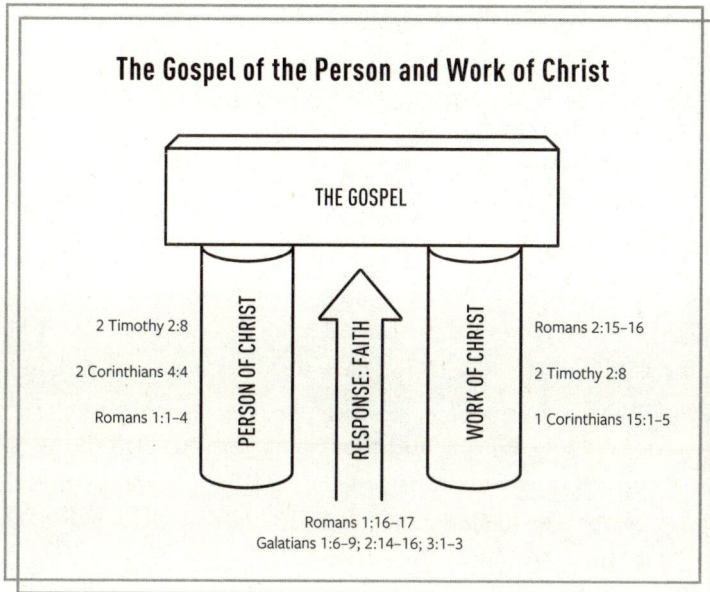

rebellion against Him (Romans 5:8). Salvation is His gift, by grace alone, through faith alone, in Christ alone.

Passages to Ponder

The Bible is the story of God's work of redemption of His creation.[5] Everything He does is rooted in the plan to make all things new through the work of His Son. He carries out His work in a variety of ways through a variety of people in a variety of contexts. But there's one unified redemptive plan.

The following passages from the Old and New Testament Scriptures have been selected to introduce key issues and significant developments in salvation history. Clearly, they're not comprehensive but representative. Many more could be considered. But these will provide an overview of major elements of God's work of grace. Thoughtfully considering these major passages will help the student of Scripture interpret and understand the rest of the Bible.

(1) Genesis 15:6—Abraham's Justifying Faith

In Genesis 12, God chose one man from Ur, Abram (later called Abraham), to be the mediator of blessing to all peoples on earth (Genesis 12:1–3). Then God made a covenant with the patriarch Abram in Genesis 15, ratifying in the form of an ancient "grant treaty" the promises He made in Genesis 12. This covenant is the foundational biblical covenant of redemption. When the Lord appeared to Abram, He promised him a great reward (Genesis 15:1). The patriarch reminded the Lord that he was childless, and if he died childless, how would God mediate his blessing to succeeding generations?

The Lord took him outside, showed him the stars in the heavens, and said, "So shall your offspring be" (15:5). In response to this promise, Abram "believed the LORD, and he counted it to him as righteousness" (15:6).

The significance of this verse is apparent from its multiple uses in the rest of the Scriptures. In Habakkuk 2:4, God may allude to Genesis 15:6 to emphasize the contrast between the wicked and the righteous: "Behold, his soul is puffed up; it is not upright within him, but the righteous shall live by his faith."

In the New Testament, both Paul and James quote Genesis 15:6. In Romans 4, the phrase appears three times. Paul begins with the assertion that Abraham was not justified by works. Instead, he declares that the Scriptures say "Abraham believed God, and it was counted to him as righteousness" (Romans 4:3). Paul contrasts wages, which are earned, with faith, which is a gift (4:4–5). A gift can never be earned. After using David as an example, Paul returns to the assertion that "faith was counted to Abraham as righteousness" (4:9).

Then Paul argues that since Abraham's faith was credited to him prior to his circumcision, Abraham is "the father of all who believe," both the circumcised and uncircumcised (4:11–12). Later, Paul returns to Genesis 15 when he writes, "In hope he believed against hope, that he should become the father of many nations, as he had been told, 'So shall your offspring be'" (4:18; compare Genesis 15:5).

Even when Abraham was a hundred years old, "no unbelief made him waver concerning the promise of God, but he grew strong in his faith as he gave glory to God, fully convinced that God was able to do what he had promised. That is why his faith was 'counted to him as righteousness'" (4:20–22). Note that this is the third time Paul quotes Genesis 15:6.

Then he draws this application: "The words 'it was counted to him' were not written for his sake alone, but for ours also. It will be counted to us who believe in him who raised from the dead Jesus our Lord" (4:23–24). Abraham is the perennial example of how an unrighteous person can be declared righteous.

In Galatians 3:6, Paul uses Genesis 15:6 to rebuke the opponents of the gospel. As in Romans 4, he draws a contrast between salvation by works and by grace: "Does he who supplies the Spirit to you and works miracles among you do so by works of the law, or by hearing with faith?" (Galatians 3:5). The answer is clear: "Just as Abraham 'believed God, and it was counted to him as righteousness' . . . it is those of faith who are the sons of Abraham" (3:6–7).

Paul then makes the bold claim that the gospel was announced in advance to Abraham when God promised him, "In you shall all the nations be blessed" (3:8; compare Genesis 12:3). He then reaffirms salvation by grace through faith and not works.

Finally, James quotes Genesis 15:6 in his argument that a living faith is vitally connected to works: "Faith by itself, if it does not have works, is dead" (James 2:17). A living faith, according to James, is characterized by works. James then castigates the person who would deny the proper connection between faith and works. He calls his imaginary opponent a "foolish person" (2:20) and uses Abraham as an example. According to James, when Abraham offered his son Isaac (Genesis 22), "faith was active along with his works, and faith was completed by his works" (2:22). This incident fulfills the Scripture that said, "Abraham believed God, and it was counted to him as righteousness," and thus Abraham was "called a friend of God" (2:23).

Abraham believed God and was justified by his faith. Justification is never earned. It's a gracious gift of God. Only by grace can an unrighteous person be declared righteous. For Paul and James, Abraham's justification is the model for all those who are justified.

(2) Isaiah 53—The Prophecy of the Suffering Servant

The prophet Isaiah describes a figure he refers to as the servant of the Lord in four passages: Isaiah 42:1–9; 49:1–13; 50:4–11; 52:13–53:12. In the first three, the servant brings justice to the nations (Isaiah 42:1), is a light for the Gentiles (42:6), restores Israel to God (49:5), brings salvation to the ends of the earth (49:6), and endures suffering but is ultimately vindicated (50:4–9). In all three, the servant mediates justice and reigns in righteousness. But the description in the fourth song is different.

PASSAGES TO MASTER AND MEMORIZE

Genesis 15:6	1 Corinthians 15:51–52
Isaiah 53:5–6	2 Corinthians 5:17–21
Matthew 20:28	Galatians 2:16
Matthew 28:18–20	Ephesians 2:8–10
Romans 1:16–17	Hebrews 10:19–22
Romans 8:1	James 2:26
Romans 9:14–16	1 Peter 1:3–5

Note: Not all these passages are discussed in the text, but they'll all help you master the doctrine of salvation.

Although the servant will act wisely, he will be disfigured and marred (Isaiah 52:14). Isaiah describes his appearance and his suffering:

> For he grew up before him like a young plant, and like a root out of dry ground; he had no form or majesty that we should look at him, and no beauty that we should desire him. He was despised and rejected by men; a man of sorrows, and acquainted with grief; and as one from whom men hide their faces he was despised, and we esteemed him not. (Isaiah 53:2–3)

But this servant's suffering was not for himself; it was substitutionary: "Surely he has borne our griefs and carried our sorrows. . . . But he was pierced for our transgressions; he was crushed for our iniquities; upon him was the chastisement that brought us peace, and with his wounds we are healed" (53:4–5).

Although Isaiah uses past-tense verbs, he was describing a servant who was from his vantage point still future: the Messiah, the Lord Jesus. The cause of this suffering is declared to be God: "We esteemed him stricken, smitten by God, and afflicted" (53:4). Isaiah concludes, "All we like sheep have gone astray; we have turned—every one—to his own way; and the LORD has laid on him the iniquity of us all" (53:6).

The description of the suffering servant continues:

> He was oppressed, and he was afflicted, yet he opened not his mouth; like a lamb that is led to the slaughter, and like a sheep that before its shearers is silent, so he opened not his mouth. By oppression and judgment he was taken away; and as for his generation, who considered that he was cut off out of the land of the living, stricken for the transgression of my people? And they made his grave with the wicked and with a rich man in his death, although he had done no violence, and there was no deceit in his mouth. (Isaiah 53:7–9)

163

Isaiah then returns to language that attributes the suffering and death to the Lord: "Yet it was the will of the LORD to crush him; he has put him to grief; when his soul makes an offering for guilt, he shall see his offspring; he shall prolong his days; the will of the LORD shall prosper in his hand" (53:10). Surely there is a tension here that can't be easily resolved. It's possible to over-emphasize Isaiah's language to create a caricature of the atonement, where an enraged Father is satisfied only by the death of His Son.

On the other hand, it's equally possible to recoil in horror from the portrayal of the Suffering Servant and thus deny the language of this text. What Isaiah predicts is that the Servant, Jesus, took on himself the punishment that sinners deserved; His work of suffering and death was a substitute for ours. The innocent died so that the guilty could be forgiven and become righteous (2 Corinthians 5:21). In so doing, the justice of God was satisfied.

But thanks be to God, the story doesn't end at the cross, at the suffering and death of Jesus. Isaiah predicts the vindication of the servant:

> Out of the anguish of his soul he shall see and be satisfied; by his knowledge shall the righteous one, my servant, make many to be accounted righteous, and he shall bear their iniquities. Therefore I will divide him a portion with the many, and he shall divide the spoil with the strong, because he poured out his soul to death and was numbered with the transgressors. (Isaiah 53:11–12)

He will be rewarded because "he bore the sin of many, and makes intercession for the transgressors" (53:12). Because He's the righteous one, He doesn't die for His own sin. Because He died on behalf of the unrighteous and sacrificed himself for them, He has merited reward. He's able to share that reward with those who come to Him in faith. In Romans 3:26, Paul says the atoning work of Christ demonstrates God's justice and allows Him to "be just and the justifier of the one who has faith in Jesus."

In this sense, the New Testament affirms that "the Son of Man came not to be served but to serve, and to give his life as a ransom for many" (Matthew 20:28). Jesus, as the fulfillment of the suffering servant of Isaiah 53, declared that His purpose in coming was to be a ransom, to pay the redemption price for those who are slaves of sin. He came to redeem sinners. Later, the apostle Paul put it this way: "You are not your own, for you were bought with a price" (1 Corinthians 6:19–20).

The price required to set the slave free has been paid in full. According to Jesus, this was the reason He came—to give His life as a ransom. Beyond that, His model of self-sacrifice was to be followed by those who claim His name (Philippians 2:3–8).

(3) Romans 1:16–17—Righteous by Faith

After a personal greeting to the church in Rome, Paul boldly declares, "I am not ashamed of the gospel, for it is the power of God for salvation to everyone who believes, to the Jew first and also to the Greek. For in it the righteousness of God is revealed from faith for faith, as it is written, 'The righteous shall live by faith'" (Romans 1:16–17).

The content of that gospel is stated earlier in this first chapter of Romans. Paul identifies himself as a "servant of Christ Jesus" who was "set apart for the gospel of God" (1:1). This gospel, he says, was "promised beforehand through [God's] prophets in the holy Scriptures, concerning his Son, who was descended from David according to the flesh and was declared to be the Son of God in power according to the Spirit of holiness by his resurrection from the dead, Jesus Christ our Lord" (1:2–4).

The gospel is the good news that Jesus Christ, who is both fully human and fully divine, died and was raised from the dead. In His resurrection, through the power of the Holy Spirit, He conquered the enemy of every living thing.

This gospel brings Paul confidence because it alone is the means of salvation for everyone, both Jews and Gentiles. Jesus is the

Jewish Messiah. His first disciples were Jews. But very quickly, the good news spread to the Gentiles too. In Christ, Jews and Gentiles are reconciled to God and to one another. And in Christ, the unrighteous become righteous. This can happen only through the righteousness of Christ, by grace alone, through faith alone, in Christ alone.

What follows in the next two and a half chapters of Romans is an extended defense of the claim, summarized in "all have sinned and fall short of the glory of God" (3:23). The only hope of righteousness for those who are unrighteous is Christ's righteousness given to them by grace: they are "justified by his grace as a gift, through the redemption that is in Christ Jesus" (3:24).

(4) Romans 8—There Is No Condemnation

Paul's argument in the book of Romans reaches its crescendo in the eighth chapter. Having demonstrated that all are sinners and thus in need of redemption, and that this salvation comes by grace through faith, Paul unpacks several implications.

Those justified by grace through faith are no longer under the threat of divine condemnation (Romans 8:1). The grace of God accomplished what the law never could: It set sinners free (8:2–3). Paul explains that God accomplished our redemption through His incarnate Son (8:3–4). Having been set free from the law of sin and death, Christians live by the Spirit (8:9). Having the Spirit grants believers the hope of resurrection: "If the Spirit of him who raised Jesus from the dead dwells in you, he who raised Christ Jesus from the dead will also give life to your mortal bodies through his Spirit who dwells in you" (8:11).

Believers face the struggles of life in a fallen world with confidence in the hope of the resurrection. Salvation doesn't mean believers no longer suffer (compare 2 Timothy 3:12). Rather, it means suffering and death won't win in the end. Believers share with creation itself the hope of redemption: "For the creation

166

was subjected to futility, not willingly, but because of him who subjected it, in hope that the creation itself will be set free from its bondage to corruption and obtain the freedom of the glory of the children of God" (Romans 8:20–21).

Paul explains that creation has been groaning since the fall, and that "we ourselves, who have the firstfruits of the Spirit, groan inwardly as we wait eagerly for adoption as sons, the redemption of our bodies" (8:23). The Spirit doesn't remove suffering from our lives; He comforts us and gives us hope in the midst of suffering. And we know that the promise of resurrection is sure because the One who promised is trustworthy.

We can have confidence that God is working for good, that the sovereign Creator of the universe has a plan, and that He will accomplish it. The summary statement, "We know that for those who love God all things work together for good" (8:28), is followed

Variety of Views on a Believer's Security

Perseverance of the Saints
The saved will persevere in faith and good works by the power of the Spirit. (*Classical Calvinism*)

Eternal Security
The saved will be kept forever by the power of the Spirit. (*Moderate Calvinism*)

Voluntary Security
The saved will remain saved unless they reject salvation by their own free choice. (*Moderate Arminianism*)

Conditional Security
The saved will endure providing they don't fall into unrepentant sin or apostasy. (*Classical Arminianism*)

Potential Security
The saved have the ability to remain saved as long as they pursue righteousness. (*Classical Finneyism*)

Insecurity
Christians can never be sure whether they are actually saved. (*Radical Finneyism*)

by an order of the steps in God's work of salvation (8:29–30). The link between these terms provides hope and assurance for those who are already justified but not yet glorified. God will carry out His purpose from beginning to end.

What follows is one of the most well-known passages in the Bible. Paul declares his confidence that "neither death nor life, nor angels nor rulers, nor things present nor things to come, nor powers, nor height nor depth, nor anything else in all creation, will be able to separate us from the love of God in Christ Jesus our Lord" (8:38–39). What an amazing, confidence-boosting declaration! Our salvation is secure in Christ.

(5) Romans 9—God's Sovereign Choice

The blessings promised to the descendants of Israel, like the blessings promised to the descendants of Abraham, are for those who share the faith of Abraham, Isaac, and Jacob, not merely for those who share their DNA. The blessings of God are always mediated by grace through faith, not simply through a particular bloodline.

Paul illustrates this through God's selection of Isaac, not Ishmael (Romans 9:7–9), and Jacob, not Esau (9:10–14), to be the line through which the Messiah will come. He explains that God's choice of Jacob and rejection of Esau wasn't due to genetics (they were "children by one man" [9:10]), nor to anything either one had done (9:11), but only because of God's sovereign choice (9:11–12). Neither genetics nor works were the basis for God's choice of Jacob. And in Paul's argument, this example establishes the principle that nobody "earns" or "deserves" divine election.

God's selection of Jacob ("Jacob I loved") and rejection of Esau ("Esau I hated") raises the question of justice. If God's choice isn't rooted in what those two have done, isn't God unjust (9:14)? Paul's answer is to quote from God's response to Moses, "I will have mercy on whom I have mercy, and I will have compassion on whom I have compassion" (9:15; compare Exodus 33:19). The choice isn't dependent on "human will or exertion, but on God, who has mercy" (9:16). Paul uses Pharaoh, of whom God had said, "For this very purpose I have raised you up, that I might show my power in you, and that my name might be proclaimed in all the earth" (9:17; compare Exodus 9:16), to further illustrate the freedom of divine choice.

In short, Paul insists that God has the right and prerogative to do whatever He chooses, as the potter has the right to make whatever He chooses out of His clay (9:20–21).

Despite two thousand years of Christians debating the nature of predestination, free will, and election, we have not all settled on a final answer to all the questions. But Paul's overall point is still clear: God's choice is not based on merit, a favored bloodline, the faith of our parents, our good works, or even good intentions. Salvation is based on His own sovereign grace and mercy.

(6) 2 Corinthians 5—The Ministry of Reconciliation

Paul often encourages Christians to walk by faith and not by sight (2 Corinthians 5:7), to live in light of the hope of resurrection, and to acknowledge that to be at home with the Lord is preferable to being in this mortal tent (5:1–6). In every situation, our primary goal is to please Christ (5:9).

Further, because of the promise of future resurrection, Christians should be motivated to persuade nonbelievers to believe in Christ today: "For the love of Christ controls us, because we have concluded this: that one has died for all, therefore all have died; and he died for all, that those who live might no longer live for themselves but for him who for their sake died and was raised" (5:14–15).

Paul then issues another well-known saying: "If anyone is in Christ, he is a new creation. The old has passed away; behold, the new has come" (5:17). A few have taken this as a declaration that Christians are completely new creations, no longer capable of sin.

This seems contradicted by human behavior and the reality of universal death. Others take it as a statement about the positional salvation that occurs in justification. In this view, sanctification—or growth in holiness—is the practical application of this positional reality. An alternative view is that Paul is describing the future hope of the resurrection. When we're resurrected, we'll be a new creation, and we'll live in a new creation.

Having been reconciled to God, we've been given a ministry of reconciliation. That ministry is certainly our responsibility in the here and now—between Christ's first and second coming. We are "ambassadors for Christ, God making his appeal through us" (5:20). Then Paul says to his readers, "We implore you on behalf of Christ, be reconciled to God" (5:20). Having confidence in the saving person and work of Christ and hope in the resurrection, we are empowered in the ministry of encouraging people to be reconciled to God through faith in His Son.

Second Corinthians 5 concludes with a summary statement that draws together the work of Christ and our hope: "For our sake he made him to be sin who knew no sin, so that in him we might become the righteousness of God" (5:21). He who had never sinned still suffered and died as if He had. He who had no sin of His own became sin for us. His work of redemption was for us and for our salvation. This isn't merely a clear statement of substitutionary atonement—the death of the innocent for the guilty—but a clear statement of the hope of our receiving the righteousness of God. We who are not righteous can be declared righteous by the gift of God's grace.

(7) Galatians 2–3—The Just Shall Live by Faith

The issue that led to Paul writing to the Galatian churches is apparent from the early section of his epistle. He expresses his astonishment that although they had trusted in the grace of Christ for salvation, a message they'd heard from Paul, they had then turned to a "different gospel," which is really a false gospel (Galatians 1:6–7). Paul's condemnation of this perverted gospel is clear and strong: "Even if we or an angel from heaven should preach to you a gospel contrary to the one we preached to you, let him be accursed!" (1:8; he repeats this in 1:9).

Apparently, the Galatians had been "bewitched" (3:1) by an appeal to human effort: "Are you so foolish? Having begun by the Spirit, are you now being perfected by the flesh?" (3:3). This "different gospel" adds the requirement of works, of human effort, to salvation. This false teaching must be rejected and condemned.

To demonstrate the truthfulness of the gospel he'd preached to them, Paul reminds the Galatians of what the Old Testament taught. Abraham was justified by faith (Galatians 3:6; compare Genesis 15:6). The means by which Abraham was justified is the only means by which a sinner can be justified, and this is true for both Jews and Gentiles. Those who rely on following the law are cursed (3:10). Salvation can never be earned by keeping the law (3:21–22).

Thus, Paul condemns the misunderstanding that the Law of Moses was a means of salvation. As Isaiah puts it, "All our righteous deeds are like a polluted garment" (Isaiah 64:6). Failing to keep the law perfectly means that one is a transgressor of the law, and thus unrighteous. Salvation could never be accomplished by works. Paul shows how the story of Abraham teaches this: Abraham was justified before the Law was given (Galatians 3:17), and the Law cannot set aside the promise God made to Abraham. Abraham's inheritance could not depend on the Law, for then it would no longer be dependent on the promise God gave to Abraham (3:18). The Law was given, Paul explains, "until Christ came, in order that we might be justified by faith" (3:24).

The "gospel" announced to Abraham was the good news that all nations would be blessed through him (Galatians 3:8; Genesis 12:3). This doesn't mean all without exception will be saved, but it does mean all *peoples* can be saved. When the work of redemption is complete, people of every tribe and tongue will be represented in the body of the redeemed (Revelation 7:9–10). The means by which the blessings would be mediated to all peoples is through the "seed" (or "offspring") of Abraham, and the "seed" is Christ (Galatians 3:16).

Salvation for people of all nations is through faith in Christ. Of the redeemed, Paul writes, "In Christ Jesus you are all sons of God, through faith. For as many of you as were baptized into Christ have put on Christ. There is neither Jew nor Greek, there is neither slave nor free, there is no male and female, for you are all one in Christ Jesus" (3:26–28).

(8) Ephesians 2—Justification by Grace Through Faith

The "good news" of the gospel is rightly contrasted with the "bad news" about us. And Paul makes this contrast clear in Ephesians 2. All this good news is contrasted with bad news, which makes the good news all the better. The bad news is that apart from Christ, we were dead in our "trespasses and sins" (Ephesians 2:1), we were "following the course of this world, following the prince of the power of the air, the spirit that is now at work in the sons of disobedience" (2:2), and we lived in rebellion against God and were "by nature children of wrath" (2:3). Apart from the grace of God, in our rebellion against Him, we were hopeless and helpless to do anything about it. This is the doctrine of depravity; we were "essentially and unchangeably bad apart from divine grace."[6]

Things are different for us now, though, "because of the great love with which he loved us" (2:4). God's motivation in providing salvation is His love for us, because He's "rich in mercy" (2:4). He's a God of mercy and compassion, abounding in love and faithfulness (Exodus 34:6). Our salvation is found in Jesus Christ, who has been raised from the dead and seated at the right hand of the Father (Ephesians 1:20). And all those who are "in

Christ" have been raised with Him and are seated with Him (2:6; compare Romans 6:1–10). From that position of union with Him, we wait for our resurrection from the dead and the redemption of all things.

It's also important to note that, according to Paul, God "made us alive together with Christ" even when we were "dead in our trespasses" (Ephesians 2:5). Salvation is God's work on our behalf. He acted for us when we were unable to do anything. When we were dead, He made us alive. *Salvation is an act of grace* from a gracious God: "By grace you have been saved" (2:5). Salvation is God's gift.

In his summary statement, the apostle affirms this: "By grace you have been saved through faith. And this is not your own doing; it is the gift of God, not a result of works, so that no one may boast. For we are his workmanship, created in Christ Jesus for good works, which God prepared beforehand, that we should walk in them" (2:8–10).

Salvation is by grace, not by works. Elsewhere Paul explains that works earn wages, while grace is a gift (Romans 4:1–5). What we have earned from God is death and condemnation, but God offers us salvation as a free gift (6:23). Salvation can never be earned. Since we all fall short of God's standard of righteousness, all we can contribute to salvation is our need.

Salvation is by grace *through faith*. Faith is the means by which the blessings of salvation are received. Faith is not a work. It's not something we can do. While some Christians don't hesitate to call faith a gift to those God has predestined for salvation, others argue that faith itself is not the gift but our response to God's gracious initiative. Either way, we should agree that faith is not a work but a response to God's work. Otherwise, salvation would be by works, and Paul has clearly ruled that we are saved "not by works" (Ephesians 2:9).

Salvation is by grace through faith *in Christ*. Throughout Ephesians 1–2, Paul stresses that salvation is through the work of Christ. In Ephesians 2:10, he affirms that we were "created in Christ Jesus." In the next section, he describes the work of Christ in bringing Jews and Gentiles together in His work of salvation by means of His blood. He accomplished His purpose of making "one new man in place of the two, so making peace, and might reconcile us both to God in one body through the cross" (2:15–16). God's plan of salvation is part of His "eternal purpose that he has realized in Christ Jesus our Lord" (3:11) in His work in His first coming, a purpose that will culminate in the age when God will "unite all things in him, things in heaven and things on earth" (Ephesians 1:10).

Although Paul doesn't say it precisely this way, he's affirming that salvation is by grace alone, through faith alone, in Christ alone. He explicitly rejects that salvation is by works (2:8–9). If it's by grace and not works, then it's by grace alone. If it's through faith and there is no salvation apart from faith, then it's through faith alone. And if salvation is rooted in Christ and His work, then it must be in Christ alone.

Salvation is by grace alone, through faith alone, in Christ alone, but the faith that saves is never alone. Salvation culminates in good works. We are not saved *by* good works; we're saved *for* good works (2:10). God has ordained these for us, and we can have confidence that His plans always come to fruition.

> "Satisfaction is something Christ gives to God, but forgiveness is something God gives to us. Forgiveness amounts to grace, not vis-à-vis Christ, but vis-à-vis us. For God, Christ's satisfaction opens the way—without violating his rights—to forgive sins out of grace and so to justify the ungodly. . . . For a perfect satisfaction (atonement) is the guarantee of absolute, irrevocable, and eternal forgiveness."[7]
>
> Herman Bavinck (1896)

Realities to Remember

Every teacher has experienced delivering a powerfully engaging lecture or facilitating a life-changing lesson in the classroom only to hear a student ask, "Will this be on the test?" At its worst, the question is rooted in pragmatism; the only time this student cares to pay attention is if the class will be responsible for the material on a test. After all, since we all have limited ability to recall information, their focus should be only on the material over which they'll be tested, right? But a more charitable response would be to recognize that some facts, some details, are more important than others.

Here are several realities about salvation particularly important for us to remember. These concepts not only help us remember to keep the main thing the main thing but help us understand *why* the main thing is the main thing.

Reality 1: Only when we understand our need do we better grasp God's grace.

Deep in the heart of Carlsbad Caverns National Park in New Mexico is an area called the King's Palace. On park ranger–guided tours there, rangers turn off the electric lights and extinguish their lanterns so everyone is plunged into such black darkness that they can't see their hands in front of their faces. Then the rangers relight their lanterns, and that tiny, welcome flame expels the darkness, giving visitors a new appreciation for light.

In a similar way that lantern light expels the darkness, the good news of the cross, resurrection, and return of Christ is directly proportionate to our understanding of our desperate need.

Because of human rebellion in the garden, every descendant of Adam is born "in him." We're born not merely with an inclination to sin but guilty of his sin. Since the wages of sin is death (Romans 6:23), universal death proves universal sin. It's only a matter of time until every living thing dies. Although medical advances might

175

extend life, no one gets out alive. We're both hopeless and helpless to do anything about it.

Into this darkness and depravity shines the light of the gospel. Unlike the small flame from a lantern in that cavern, the gospel is the brightest of lights. The gospel is our only hope. God provides for us what we could never accomplish ourselves. He loved us while we were sinners. He gave His Son to make us His friends while we were His enemies. He gave us the gift of life while we were dead in trespasses and sins. We love Him because He first loved us.

In short, we've already contributed everything we ever can to our salvation: our desperate need. We're born guilty of original sin. We regularly and consistently affirm our sinfulness by what we do. We're broken people who continue to break things. We need someone to do for us what we could never do for ourselves. And that's what Christ has done and what He continues to do.

Reality 2: Salvation is by grace alone, through faith alone, in Christ alone.

Salvation is the work of the Father, Son, and Holy Spirit on our behalf. The Father knew those who would be saved even before the foundation of the world. He sent the Son to become one of us, to give His life to pay the penalty of our sins, and to be raised from the dead to give us the hope of eternal life. We received the Holy Spirit as a deposit, a down payment, a seal, and as the firstfruits of our inheritance (Romans 8:23). The Spirit is not our inheritance; He's the beginning of an indescribable inheritance yet to come (Ephesians 1:14).

We were—every one of us—born in Adam. Because of the work of the triune God, we're now in Christ, united to Him by the will of the Father by the power of the Holy Spirit. What's true of Christ is true of us, not because we're divine but because of His incomparable grace. What's promised to Christ is promised to us, not because we deserve His inheritance (an inheritance can never be earned) but because of His incomparable grace. We died with

Him, were buried with Him, and we have the assurance that we will be raised with Him.

We have this hope because of His incomparable grace. Our identity, our destiny, our hope, our life itself is found in Him: "Christ in you, the hope of glory" (Colossians 1:27).

We're saved not through ourselves, by our own works, or because of something good in us. We must never forget that we're saved by grace alone, through faith alone, in Christ alone, by the work of the triune God alone.

Reality 3: Salvation has the end in view.

Many Christians have a too-narrow, truncated view of salvation. They often believe "salvation" refers only to what happened when they believed in Jesus—being "born again" or "regenerated" by grace through faith in Christ. To the question "When did you get saved?" they point to a moment when they said a prayer, trusted Christ, or responded to an altar call. But this emphasis on the "moment of salvation" doesn't exactly square with the Bible's teaching that salvation is much, much bigger than "getting saved."

Without in any way minimizing the importance of coming to trust Christ for salvation, the focus of salvation in the New Testament is ultimately forward-looking. Salvation isn't merely what's

---

THE WORK OF THE HOLY SPIRIT AND SALVATION

1. Baptizes into the body of Christ—1 Corinthians 12:13
2. Imparts life—2 Corinthians 3:6
3. Seals for redemption—Ephesians 1:13–14
4. Indwells for relationship—John 14:16–17; 1 Corinthians 6:19
5. Fills for transformation—Ephesians 5:18–21
6. Works in believers to produce fruit—Galatians 5:22–23; Philippians 2:12–13

---

happened to us at some point in the past, when we were converted, or justified, or regenerated. Rather, salvation has a future focus, a future hope. Having been granted the firstfruits of our inheritance, we look forward to the fulfillment of God's promise of a new heaven and a new earth (Romans 8:22–25). The trajectory of God's plan of redemption draws us forward, provides us the courage to stand, and gives us the perseverance to endure because the One who has promised is faithful.

We are people of hope, but not because if we work hard enough we can create a better world. Rather, we're people of hope because God promised us a new creation, and His promises are sure and secure. His promises are true not only for individuals but for all creation, because the whole creation comes from the One who made everything out of nothing and redeems that which is broken. We trust in the God of our father Abraham, the God "who gives life to the dead and calls into existence the things that do not exist" (Romans 4:17).

Reality 4: Salvation has the church in view.

We were saved as individuals, chosen by God and set apart in the hope of our calling. We will be saved as individuals at the regeneration of all things (Matthew 19:28). But salvation doesn't end with the individual.

We've been redeemed and joined to Christ along with multitudes of other members of His body. We're joined to a family that transcends time and space, made up of all believers in Jesus throughout history and throughout a diversity of cultures. Joined to Him, we're joined to one another so that by our love for God and love for one another people will see that love and come to know and understand that the Father sent the Son into the world so that all might be saved through Him (John 13:34–35; 17:23). We are His ambassadors, calling others to believe in Jesus Christ and be saved, and to become part of this holy nation, royal priesthood, the incarnation of the Son of God on earth (1 Corinthians 12:12–27).

Yes, Christ died for *you*—in your place. He saved *you*—by the regenerating work of the Spirit. But just as important is the corporate aspect of Christ's saving work—past, present, and future. The apostle Paul reminds us of this oft-neglected reality when he notes that Christ "loved the church and gave Himself up for her, so that He might sanctify her, having cleansed her by the washing of water with the word, that He might present to Himself the church in all her glory, having no spot or wrinkle or any such thing; but that she would be holy and blameless" (Ephesians 5:25–27 NASB).

The church—the communion of saints called together and united by the Holy Spirit—is just as much an object of Christ's saving work as is the individual.

Reality 5: The world displays God's grace—if we have eyes to see.

A change in perspective changes everything. One person looks at the world and sees evidence of decay, desolation, and destruction. She is dominated by fear and despair. Another person looks at the same world, and although aware of what's wrong with the world, he sees the beauty in the world God has made. Even in this fallen world, one hears echoes of Eden in creation and in the works of artists.[8] To a great extent, we see what we expect to see.

When God delivered His people out of slavery in Egypt, He demonstrated His power, protection, and preservation of them as He poured out plagues on the land of Egypt. At the Red Sea, He again delivered His people from the peril of Pharaoh's army. He gave them water to drink and manna to eat. He led the people in a pillar of fire by night and a cloud during the day. He was present with His people. The Egyptians and the surrounding nations saw His power as a threat. The Israelites saw it as protection and provision.

As Jesus taught His disciples, He encouraged them with these words: "He who has ears, let him hear" (Matthew 13:9; compare

Matthew 11:15, Revelation 2:21). He even pronounced a blessing on them: "Blessed are your eyes, for they see, and your ears, for they hear" (Matthew 13:16). Seeing is both an act and result of blessing. Paul describes unbelievers as blinded by the "god of this world" and thus kept from "seeing the light of the gospel of the glory of Christ" (2 Corinthians 4:4).

Through regeneration, the indwelling Spirit has "shone in our hearts to give the light of the knowledge of the glory of God in the face of Jesus Christ" (2 Corinthians 4:6). And "his invisible attributes, namely, his eternal power and divine nature, have been clearly perceived, ever since the creation of the world, in the things that have been made" (Romans 1:20; compare Psalm 19). Philip Yancey puts it succinctly: "If God exists, and if our planet represents God's work of art, we will never grasp why we are here without taking that reality into account."[9]

God isn't merely visible through His creation; He's also revealed in His Son and the body of His Son, the church. Paul says the church "now" reveals "the manifold wisdom of God" (Ephesians 3:10), and "in the coming ages" God will "show the immeasurable riches of his grace" in the church (Ephesians 2:7). Perhaps most clearly, Paul explains that, in the midst of a "crooked and twisted generation," the church is to "shine as lights in the world, holding fast to the word of life" (Philippians 2:15–16). Grace is visible where it's present, and it's everywhere present.

May God open our eyes to see and ears to hear what He wants us to see and hear.

Errors to Avoid

A standard set of traffic signs warns drivers of possible danger ahead. They're usually diamond-shaped with a yellow background and black letters or symbols. They alert drivers there's about to be a sharp curve, bump, or dip in the road; that animals might be crossing in front of them; or that a surface might be slippery. A safe driver pays attention to these warnings. A foolish or reckless driver ignores them at his own peril and puts himself, passengers, and other drivers—not to mention those animals—at risk.

We've looked at five realities to remember. Now we'll consider several errors to avoid. Some of them are denials of what the Bible teaches about salvation. Others arise from a misplaced focus or emphasis. In every case, ignoring the danger signs can put ourselves and others in error.

Error 1: Resting on Works

Salvation is either by grace alone, through faith alone, in Christ alone—or it's not. There's no middle ground. Salvation by grace plus works wouldn't be salvation by grace alone. Thus, making any aspect of salvation dependent upon works would be a heretical position.

If humans are born sinners, if we're guilty of Adam's sin, if we've rebelled against God, then we're in need of salvation. We're in need of help from someone else. We've contributed everything we can to salvation—our own desperate need. In short, we've done enough. Anything we add can't detract from, distract from, or destroy what we've already done. There's no way to undo the damage we've done by our sin and rebellion against God.

What the gospel promises us is that God loved us in our sin and rebellion. He took the initiative to do for us not only what we couldn't do for ourselves but what we had no desire to do for ourselves. While we were sinners Christ died for us (Romans 5:8).

But salvation isn't limited to the past. It's rooted in Christ's work on the cross, His resurrection, and His ascension. Having been justified by grace, we're also sanctified by grace through faith, not works. The hope of resurrection and the re-creation of all things is God's work, not ours.

If any aspect of salvation is by works, then salvation is not by grace alone, through faith alone, in Christ alone. Salvation is a gracious gift of God to sinners and rebels. It's not our work.

Error 2: Resting from Works

If works righteousness is one danger to avoid, the opposite error is every bit as dangerous. This is the antinomian heresy. If there's nothing we can do to save ourselves, if salvation is all God's work, does that make us passive? Does that mean we don't do anything?

The Bible is full of commands to be followed. When Jesus was asked which commandment was the greatest, He responded, "'Love the Lord your God with all your heart and with all your soul and with all your mind.' This is the first and greatest commandment. And the second is like it: 'Love your neighbor as yourself.' All the Law and the Prophets hang on these two commandments" (Matthew 22:37–40 NIV).

And the apostle Paul asserts that all the commandments of God are summarized "in this one command: 'Love your neighbor as yourself.'" He follows by saying, "Love does no harm to a neighbor. Therefore love is the fulfillment of the law" (Romans 13:9–10 NIV). Surely love is active. Surely these commands are to be obeyed. Surely the Christian life is not passive.

This is likely a tension that cannot be resolved easily, if at all. Salvation from beginning to end is God's work for us. The faith that saves is active and visible. The Christian life is an active life. Rather than resolve the tension, in Philippians 2:12–13 Paul states it clearly: "Continue to work out your salvation with fear and trembling, for it is God who works in you to will and to act according to his good purpose" (NIV).

In that most famous of hymns, "Amazing Grace," John Newton expressed the tension this way: "'Twas grace that taught my heart to fear, and grace my fears relieved."[10] Grace teaches us to fear the awesome God of the universe, but grace also attracts us to Him and relieves our fears. We are set free to serve freely and enthusiastically through the grace of the gospel.

Error 3: "Just-as-if-ication"

Translating complex theological concepts into simple phrases and word pictures is a challenging but worthwhile goal. But sometimes the desire to simplify leads to error. Many of us have heard the Trinity compared to an egg, which is an inaccurate analogy of the one God who exists eternally in three persons, each of which shares the same essence.

Maybe some of us were taught that justification means "just as if I never sinned." This description, although clever and easy to remember, has the decided disadvantage of being completely and uselessly wrong. More than that, it cheapens and minimizes the glorious provision of divine grace in the gospel.

When God created Adam and Eve, they were innocent, perfect, and without sin. When they rebelled against God by eating from the forbidden fruit, they became guilty of sin. That sin destroyed their relationship with God and brought condemnation, and ultimately, they received the wages of sin: death.

The promise of the gospel is that sins will be forgiven. Jesus promised forgiveness through the new covenant (Matthew 26:28). Forgiveness comes finally and ultimately through the atoning work of Christ (Ephesians 1:7). Forgiveness removes the guilt of sin, restoring the guilty person to a state of innocence. The slate has been wiped clean.

But the provision of the gospel doesn't end with a clean slate. The gospel isn't merely about the negative, the removal of sins. Justification is positive, promising that the believer will be henceforth regarded as righteous. So to be justified is to be "declared righteous." Not merely innocent, but completely righteous, as righteous as the Righteous One is righteous. In justification, the righteousness of Christ is imputed to the believer (Romans 3:21–26; 4:24).

According to protestant theology, justification is a legal term, whereby the Judge declares the unrighteous to be righteous by imputing or crediting it to the believer. In Romans 4:1–6, Paul argues for this using the example of Abraham, whose faith was credited to him as righteousness.

In summary, it seems that justification is the declaration that the believer is just, or righteous. Since no one but God alone is righteous, this declaration must be rooted in the imputation of the righteousness of another to the account of the one who is unrighteous. Romans 3:21–22 says, "But now apart from the law the righteousness of God has been made known, to which the Law and the Prophets testify. This righteousness is given through faith in Jesus Christ to all who believe" (NIV).

The only way an unrighteous person can become righteous is through the substitutionary atoning work of the Righteous One. Paul declares, "God made him who had no sin to be sin for us, so that in him we might become the righteousness of God" (2 Corinthians 5:21 NIV).

Error 4: Holding Salvation Back (in the Past)

Salvation has past, present, and future aspects. Charles Ryrie explains, "From God's perspective salvation includes the total work of God in bringing people from condemnation to justification, from death to eternal life, from alienation to filiation. From the human perspective it incorporates all of the blessings that being in Christ brings both in this life and the life to come."[11]

Ryrie further describes the three tenses of salvation: "(1) The moment one believed he was saved from the condemnation of sin (Ephesians 2:8; Titus 3:5); (2) That believer is also being saved from the dominion of sin and is being sanctified and preserved (Hebrews 7:25); (3) And he will be saved from the very presence of sin in heaven forever (Romans 5:9–10)."[12]

The term *salvation* is often used as a synonym for conversion. In this usage, "salvation," the point of conversion, is distinguished from "sanctification," the process of growth in godliness, or discipleship. As indicated above, people sometimes describe the time they "got saved," or when they "were saved." By that language, they don't really mean to imply that salvation is entirely in the past. They mean that at some point in the past they came to the point of believing the gospel message and trusting Christ alone for salvation.

It might be more helpful to think of salvation as a point, a process, and then another process. Salvation is rooted in the past but has ongoing effects into the present and the future. In salvation, we come to faith in Christ and at that point in time move from being an enemy of God to being His friend. Then there's a long process of growth in godliness (often called sanctification), which culminates in another process—the resurrection of the dead and the restoration of all things, also known as glorification.

Error 5: Jesus Loves ~~Even~~ Only Me

God saves individual sinners by means of the atoning sacrifice of His Son. But He places those individuals into a corporate body. The believer is saved by grace alone, through faith alone, in Christ alone—but God never intends for the believer to be saved alone.

In 1 Corinthians 12, Paul uses the metaphor of the body to describe the church. The comparison is between the unity of the human body, made up of many individuals who fulfill unique roles in the larger body of Christ. Saved as individuals, "we were all baptized by one Spirit to form one body—whether Jews or Gentiles, slave or free—and we were all given the one Spirit to drink" (1 Corinthians 12:13 NIV).

Elsewhere Paul describes our relationship to one another in the body of Christ this way: "Speaking the truth in love, we will grow to become in every respect the mature body of him who is the head, that is, Christ. From him the whole body, joined and held together by every supporting ligament, grows and builds itself up in love, as each part does its work" (Ephesians 4:15–16 NIV).

Salvation is individual and corporate, but it's also cosmic. The work of redemption won't be complete until all of creation is redeemed. Creation groans in hope of being set free from bondage to corruption. Creation's redemption is tied to our redemption, the resurrection of our bodies (compare Romans 8:18–25).

In the conclusion of the redemption story, God ushers in a new heaven and a new earth and makes His dwelling on the earth with us forever (Revelation 21:1–4). Ryrie's summary is true:

> Soteriology, the doctrine of salvation, must be the grandest theme in the Scriptures. It embraces all of time as well as eternity past and future. It relates in one way or another to all of mankind, without exception. It even has ramifications in the sphere of angels. It is the theme of both the Old and New Testaments. It is personal, national, and cosmic. And it centers on the greatest Person, our Lord Jesus Christ.[13]

Error 6: Halving the Gospel

Beyond controversy, the atonement requires the sacrifice of Christ on the cross. From the beginning of the biblical story, the cross has cast a shadow over all of God's work in the world.[14] The atonement through Jesus' death on the cross was ordained before the creation of the world (Revelation 13:8).

But is the cross the *focus* of the gospel? The apostle Paul seems to say so: "For the word of the cross is folly to those who are perishing, but to us who are being saved it is the power of God" (1 Corinthians 1:18). Then Paul asserts that "we preach Christ crucified, a stumbling block to Jews and folly to Gentiles" (1:23). Later, he's even more explicit: "For I decided to know nothing among you except Jesus Christ and him crucified" (2:2). At first glance, Paul seems to be making "Christ crucified" the summary of the gospel he preached.

Reading more of Paul's first epistle to the Corinthians reveals that he's using "Christ crucified" and "the message of the cross" as a synecdoche, a figure of speech that uses the part for the whole. He makes this clear a little later in the same letter to the Corinthians, where he describes the gospel: "Christ died for our sins in accordance with the Scriptures, that he was buried, that he was raised on the third day in accordance with the Scriptures" (15:3–4).

According to Paul, *the gospel message includes the death, burial, and resurrection of Jesus, not just His death.* Of course, the cross is an essential prerequisite for resurrection. Only the dead can be raised, and only through the shedding of blood is forgiveness possible (Hebrews 9:22).

Although Paul uses "the cross" as a summary of the gospel, in 1 Corinthians 15 he declares that without the resurrection, there is no gospel. If Christ is not raised, "then our preaching is in vain and your faith is in vain" (15:14), "we are even found to be misrepresenting God" (15:15), "your faith is futile and you are still in your sins" (15:17), and "we are of all people most to be pitied" (15:19). But because Christ has been raised, we too shall be raised: "For as in Adam all die, so also in Christ shall all be made alive" (15:22). And "just as we have borne the image of the man of dust, we shall also bear the image of the man of heaven" (15:49). Then death will be "swallowed up in victory" (15:54).

Lessons to Live

Salvation is the grand story of the Bible. It's the focus of God's activity in this world. It was "for us and for our salvation" that the Son of God became incarnate and undertook the work of redemption.[15] Remembering these realities and avoiding significant errors are important. But so what? How do these ideas impact and influence the way we should live?

What follows are several suggestions of lessons to live. This isn't a comprehensive list, but it's presented in the hope of stimulating further reflection on the significant aspects of the great salvation God has provided for us and promised to us.

Lesson 1: Trust that God's promises are sure and that He'll complete what He started.

Every one of us is fallible. We make promises to people, and then for any number of reasons we fail to follow through. Sometimes our failure is due to a change of mind. Sometimes we forget the promise. Other times we simply over-promise despite our good intentions. God, on the other hand, is not fallible. His memory isn't flawed. And His power and ability are never inadequate. God never promises what He cannot or will not complete.

When God makes promises, His character and attributes create confidence in His faithfulness. God is omniscient; when He makes promises He's aware of all the possibilities and actualities, as well as having comprehensive knowledge of everything that will happen in the future. His promises take all that into consideration. Nothing catches Him by surprise. God's knowledge is comprehensive.

God is omnipotent; He has sufficient power to accomplish what He sets out to do. His will never be thwarted since no one has power to undo what He's done or to prohibit what He plans to do. God's power is sufficient.

God has planned our redemption in advance. His plan was dependent upon the work of Christ in time and space. Jesus came to earth at the perfect time, according to God's plan, and accomplished what God had planned (Galatians 4:4–5; Ephesians 2:10). If the first coming of Christ was at the right time and accomplished God's will perfectly, we can trust that His second coming will also be according to God's will.

Trusting God to complete His work of salvation provides a confident outlook on life. In the midst of uncertainty and tension, the foundation of God's faithfulness provides stability. Paul concludes his defense of the doctrine of resurrection in 1 Corinthians with this admonition: "Therefore, my beloved brothers, be steadfast, immovable, always abounding in the work of the Lord, knowing that in the Lord your labor is not in vain" (15:58). We can give ourselves to the service of God and others with total abandon because God is trustworthy.

Nothing can thwart God's plans. Nothing can stop Him. Nothing can derail His goals. And nothing can separate us from Him. Paul exclaims, "For I am sure that neither death nor life, nor angels nor rulers, nor things present nor things to come, nor powers, nor height nor depth, nor anything else in all creation, will be able to separate us from the love of God in Christ Jesus our Lord" (Romans 8:38–39).

Lesson 2: Seek opportunities to practice grace.

Grace isn't merely the beginning of the Christian life; it's the whole of salvation. And grace is a powerful, transformative, redemptive force. It changes everyone and everything it touches.

Unlike karma, grace is not a zero-sum game. Grace is extravagant; the more it's given, the more there is. When grace is hoarded, it fails to work its power as intended, but when grace is freely given, it changes both the giver and the recipient. Grace wasn't given to us to be preserved and protected; we're recipients of grace so we'll bless others.

When Jesus sent out His twelve disciples, He asked them to go with this lesson: "You received without paying; give without pay" (Matthew 10:8). Everything we have has come from God. What we have is given to us so we'll use it wisely. God blesses us so we might be a blessing. The old hymn puts it this way: "Is your life a channel of blessing? Is the love of God flowing through you? . . . Make me a channel of blessing today."[16]

What does that kind of grace look like? Paul tells us, "Be kind to one another, tenderhearted, forgiving one another, as God in Christ forgave you" (Ephesians 4:32). That's easier said than done.

We need a reconditioning to accept the implications of the Bible's teaching on grace. Grace provides the basis for our hope that one day all things will be made right. Grace is also the power to transform our lives here and now. Grace forever transforms our relationship with God, with one another, and with all creation. We should live as people of grace. If grace will one day change the world, it's also the means of transforming the world here and now.

Lesson 3: Admit your faith struggles and help others through their own.

Whether faith is understood as a gift of God or the human response to divine grace, it can't be dependent upon anything in us. Faith is a good thing, but it can't be produced unaided by a creature who's "essentially and unchangeably bad."[17] Becoming a person of faith is not the end, though. It's the beginning of a lifelong learning to walk by faith.

John Calvin defined faith as "a firm and certain knowledge of God's benevolence toward us, founded upon the truth of the freely given promise in Christ, both revealed to our minds and sealed upon our hearts through the Holy Spirit."[18] But, Calvin acknowledges, faith is always mixed with unbelief:

> While we teach that faith ought to be certain and assured, we cannot imagine any certainty that is not tinged with doubt, or any assurance that is not assailed by some anxiety. On the other hand, we say that believers are in perpetual conflict with their own unbelief. In the course of the present life it never goes so well with us that we are wholly cured of the disease of unbelief and entirely filled and possessed by faith. Hence arise those conflicts; when unbelief, which reposes in the remains of the flesh, rises up to attack the faith that has been inwardly conceived.[19]

In Calvin's view, as long as we're in the flesh, until the resurrection, we'll never be free of doubt, uncertainty, and unbelief.

How then should the believer deal with the struggle of the faith? Calvin's advice is helpful:

> But if in the believing mind certainty is mixed with doubt, do we always come back to this, that faith does not rest in a certain and clear knowledge, but only in an obscure and confused knowledge of the divine will toward us? Not at all! For even if we are distracted by various thoughts, we are not on that account completely divorced from faith. Nor if we are troubled on all sides by the agitation of unbelief, are we for that reason immersed in its abyss. If we are struck, we are not for that reason cast down from our position. For the end of the conflict is always this; that faith ultimately triumphs over those difficulties which besiege and seem to imperil it.[20]

In short, that faith is mixed with doubt is a constant reminder of (1) the grace of God that is ours through faith, and (2) God's promise that one day there will be no more need for faith—when faith becomes sight (1 Corinthians 13:11–13; 2 Corinthians 5:7).

Lesson 4: Never outgrow your need for the Savior.

"We have (still) a great need for a Savior and a great Savior for our need."[21] That need doesn't decrease as we grow in grace. But growth in grace perhaps intensifies our realization of our need.

The degree to which we understand the doctrine of original sin is the degree to which we appreciate the grace of God. The degree to which we understand the depth and breadth of depravity is the degree to which we appreciate the grace of God. The degree to which we understand the effects of the fall on us and the world in which we live is the degree to which we appreciate the grace of God.

There seems to be an intimate and necessary connection between hamartiology (the doctrine of sin and depravity) and soteriology (the doctrine of salvation). By this we don't merely mean that the good news of the gospel demands a robust understanding of original sin and depravity. That is important, though. For if we think humans are sick and need healing, are weak and need strength, are lazy and need motivation, are malnourished and need to be fed, or are ignorant and need more information, our view of the gospel is that it is helpful.

But if we understand the depth of our own depravity and the effects of original sin on all creation, the gospel becomes our only hope. And yet if we remain sinners in need of redemption after conversion, remain capable of sinning, and regularly demonstrate that capacity by our sinful choices, then we're increasingly dependent on and desperate for the love of our Savior.

The old hymn "Come, Thou Fount of Every Blessing" becomes our prayerful testimony: "O to grace how great a debtor daily I'm constrained to be! Let Thy goodness, like a fetter, bind my wandering heart to Thee. Prone to wander, Lord, I feel it, prone to leave the God I love; Here's my heart, O take and seal it, seal it for Thy courts above."[22]

Lesson 5: If you love God, love others.

Love God and love others—these are the two great commandments (Matthew 22:36–40). According to Jesus, "On these two commandments depend all the Law and the Prophets" (22:40).

What is the relationship between these two commandments? It could be that the first, "You shall love the Lord your God with all your heart and with all your soul and with all your mind" (Matthew 22:37) is the most important and should be the first priority. In that case, the second, "You shall love your neighbor as yourself" (22:39) would be secondary. According to this view, love for others would pale in comparison to love for God, for love for God is love of an infinite being while love for others would be love for inferior creatures.

Another option would be that love for others is the evidence or manifestation of the reality of love for God. This might be one way to read 1 John 3:14–20. Love for others would validate love for God: "Little children, let us not love in word or talk but in deed and in truth. By this we shall know that we are of the truth and reassure our heart before him" (3:18–19).

A preferable approach avoids separating the two commands; they need to be distinguished but can never be separated. Those related to God as children of their Father love Him. In fact, John says, "God is love . . . We love because he first loved us" (1 John 4:16, 19). He continues, "If anyone says, 'I love God,' and hates his brother, he is a liar; for he who does not love his brother whom he has seen cannot love God whom he has not seen. And this commandment we have from him: whoever loves God must also love his brother" (4:20–21). Love for God and love for others are inextricably linked. We can't do one without the other, but the two are not the same.

Thus, Jesus can say, "On these two commandments depend all the Law and the Prophets" (Matthew 22:40). Elsewhere He can say love for others is the focus without mentioning love for God: "So whatever you wish that others would do to you, do also to them, for this is the Law and the Prophets" (Matthew 7:12).

Similarly, the apostle Paul affirms, "Owe no one anything, except to love each other, for the one who loves another has fulfilled the law" (Romans 13:8); "Love is the fulfilling of the law" (13:10); and "The whole law is fulfilled in one word: 'You shall love your neighbor as yourself'" (Galatians 5:14). People loved by God love God, and they love what God loves. Those loved by God love others, for God is love (1 John 4:8).

Lesson 6. Rest your assurance on Christ, not in memory or emotions.

In some communities of faith, conversion testimonies are treated as the basis of assurance of salvation. One might regularly hear stories of people who can recall the time and place they placed their faith in Christ. This certainty of the timing of the miracle of new birth is then used to assure the community that salvation has occurred. Some believers even write their "spiritual birthday" in the front of their Bible, right under their physical birthdate.

For those who don't have such a conversion story, the result might be feelings of inferiority and a lack of assurance. The impression that God's grace is most clearly seen in spectacular conversion stories can be unintentionally communicated. And the flip side of that message can be devastating: Does God do nothing for those who grew up in the church and came to faith early in life?

It should *always* be encouraging to hear stories of God's grace in conversion. Each one is different. No two stories of salvation are the same since each person is unique. The value of telling those stories is that one story connects with one person and not another. So someone who met Jesus one night in a jail cell connects with some people in a way that another person's story of growing up in Sunday school never will, and vice versa. But conversion stories are not the basis of our assurance of salvation; they're simply one part of the story.

Salvation is God's gift to us. It's not dependent upon our work. Even more importantly, assurance can't be based upon our memory of something we did. Surely the assurance of someone with Alzheimer's can't be dependent upon the memory of a conversion. We rest, quite simply, in the loving arms of our Savior. *His* work brings assurance, for He who began a good work in us will complete it. Thanks be to God for His amazing grace.

Snapshot of History

Throughout the eras of church history known as the Patristic (100–500), Medieval (500–1500), Protestant (1500–1700), and Modern (1700–Present), the doctrine of salvation has undergone some amazing development. The following chart summarizes the twists and turns related to this doctrine throughout history.[23]

Patristic Period (100–500)	Medieval Period (500–1500)	Protestant Period (1500–1700)	Modern Period (1700–Present)
• Christ's person/ work are central to salvation (100–500)	• Eastern Orthodoxy thinks of salvation in terms of deification by union with Christ through the church (500–1500)	• In protest of Rome, Luther, Zwingli, and many other reformers reassert Augustine's teachings on depravity, election, grace (1500–1550)	• Enlightenment attacks classic protestant doctrines on salvation, birthing modern liberal theology (1700–1800)
• Free will for cooperating with grace mostly prevails (100–400)	• Synod of Orange II (529) in the West affirms Augustine's view of total depravity and need for grace, without fully adopting his teachings on predestination, perseverance	• Protestants teach salvation by grace alone, through faith alone, in Christ alone (1500–1700)	• First Great Awakening yields unity among Calvinists such as Edwards and Whitefield and Arminians such as Wesley
• Pelagius says humans can merit salvation apart from grace (c. 410)		• Reformed doctrinal system (*Institutes*) sends Calvinist salvation views worldwide (1550–1700)	• Second Great Awakening emphasizes Arminian theology, free will, and emotionalism to persuade repentance
• Augustine teaches total depravity, unconditional election, perseverance of the saints (c. 400–430)	• Most affirm a measure of free will and human cooperation with God's grace (600–900)		
• Council of Ephesus (431) condemns Pelagianism, doesn't support all of Augustine's views	• Increasingly semi-Pelagian Roman Church opposes strong Augustinians (1000–1500)	• Anabaptists, Arminians react to strong Calvinism and assert a view of free will and cooperation like ancient Cassianism (1550–1700)	• Personal conversion experiences and point-in-time salvation emphasized (1800–Present)
• Cassian, Eastern Orthodox Church affirm middle way between Augustine and Pelagius (430)	• Protests from Augustinian reformers such as Wycliffe and Hus result in persecution and execution (1300–1400)	• Roman Catholic Council of Trent (1545–1563) condemns protestant views of salvation	• Conservative evangelicals face liberal redefinitions of salvation as mere social and ethical reform
• Most believe baptism and the Eucharist are the means of saving grace (100–500)			

FIVE

The Communion of Saints—
The Church as the
Growing Family of God

As in the sea there are islands, some of them habitable, and well-watered, and fruitful, with havens and harbors in which the storm-tossed may find refuge, so God has given to the world which is driven and tempest-tossed by sins, assemblies—we mean holy churches—in which survive the doctrines of the truth, as in the island-harbors of good anchorage; and into these run those who desire to be saved, being lovers of the truth, and wishing to escape the wrath and judgment of God.[1]

—Theophilus of Antioch (c. 180)

Wherever we see the Word of God purely preached and heard, and the sacraments administered according to Christ's institution, there, it is not to be doubted, a church of God exists.[2]

—John Calvin (1559)

In Short . . .

For Christians who attend church on a regular basis and seek to grow in Christlikeness, the doctrines of the church (ecclesiology) and spiritual growth (sanctification) are immensely and immediately practical. Almost anything we think or say about these subjects applies directly to the lives of believers—right away. If you want practical theology, this is it!

But this also poses a challenge, because these areas—the church and spiritual growth—are two of the most hotly debated topics in Christian theology. Whole denominations have been named after their views on how churches should be led (Presbyterian, Congregational, Episcopalian) or their perspectives on water baptism (Baptists), or even their approach to sanctification (Methodists) or the work of the Spirit in the lives of believers (Pentecostals).

In short, the areas of theology addressed in this chapter are riddled with metaphorical land mines. Even professional theologians often shy away from venturing into these areas too hastily.

But if we focus on the big picture—things on which all (or at least most) Protestant Christians agree, we can avoid the proverbial land mines and learn some foundational truths along the way—truths that are, again, immensely and immediately practical.

The Starting Point: Jesus Christ

Both the starting point and center point of our spiritual life (sanctification) and life in the community of the Spirit (ecclesiology) is Jesus Christ. All aspects of our spiritual skill set—and every spiritual relationship we have—point always, only, inexorably, to one person: Jesus Christ. To be "in Christ" is to have a real, saving relationship with God by grace alone, through faith alone, in Christ alone, by a union affected by the Holy Spirit. Thus, there is no authentic, growing relationship with the Holy Spirit or with the people of God apart from a saving relationship with Jesus Christ.

But as we all know, the nature of that saving relationship is that it's invisible. You can't "see" someone's genuine faith. No bright yellow halo hovers above the heads of authentic saints. There's no tiny blue LED planted in a believer's ear to indicate they participate in a saving relationship with Jesus Christ. And it doesn't matter what congregation or denomination a person belongs to either—for genuine Christians participate in some seemingly "dead" churches, and non-Christians hang out in some apparently "alive" churches. In protestant Christian theology, every church "is a mixed body."[3]

But this invisible relationship with Jesus Christ through the work of the Holy Spirit should not be an excuse to neglect the sanctifying relationship with fellow believers in the church through the work of that same Holy Spirit. As the saying goes, you can't claim to love Jesus but hate His bride.

You may have heard it said that Christianity isn't a religion; it's a relationship. Sometimes people use that cliché to dismiss the "visible church" from their lives and focus just on their personal, private, individual experience with the cool Guy named Jesus in what they call the "invisible church." But that misuse—or even abuse—shouldn't detract us from what is nevertheless true about the cliché. It isn't an excuse to dismiss the visible church as irrelevant. Rather, our invisible spiritual relationship with Jesus Christ is the one thing that makes the visible church eminently relevant. We love the body of Christ because we love Jesus.

The Church: A Community Son-Centered and Spirit-Formed

The study of the church starts with the saving relationship between the Redeemer and the redeemed. That is, the community of the redeemed is Son-centered. Jesus Christ is the center and source of the church, which is the community of the redeemed under His headship. But that's not the only thing that unites Bible-believing Christians with respect to the doctrine of the church. The community is also Spirit-formed. The Holy Spirit of God forms the church of Jesus Christ.

> "If you say that Christ's Church must have a head here on earth, so it is, for Christ is Head, who must be here with His Church until the day of doom, and everywhere by his Godhead."[4]
>
> John Wycliffe (c. 1380)

This is the message of Scripture and the consistent affirmation of Christians throughout history. As a result, the church finds its unique identity as the community of the redeemed because of a spiritual relationship with Jesus Christ through the work of the Holy Spirit. Only because of the Spirit's ministry do we have invisible union with our Savior and visible unity with His people.

Thus far we've been speaking of what's often called the "invisible" church conceived of in its broadest sense—the church "universal." But the visible expressions of that Son-centered and Spirit-formed community are primarily seen through local congregations with leadership, membership, ordinances like baptism and communion, ordered worship, and mission. While Christians pretty much see eye to eye on the invisible and universal notions of the church, their essential unity is displayed in a diversity of beliefs regarding local church practices.

Spiritual Growth: A Life Son-Centered, Spirit-Formed, and Community-Minded

Having been united to Christ and to the body of Christ, the church, by the power of the Holy Spirit, and having been joined to the visible community of fellow Christians, now what? This is where the doctrine of spiritual growth or "sanctification" picks up.

Despite the diversity of views on the best means for growing in our faith toward Christlikeness, all Christians agree that our sanctification rests on the invisible saving relationship between the Redeemer and the redeemed. Once again, this is the necessary starting point, precisely because no one can even dream of living the Christian life unless they're already united to Christ in salvation and therefore indwelled by the Spirit of God—the one who makes us "holy" as He himself is holy. Simply put, authentic sanctification flows out of genuine justification. Because we have been declared righteous (justified) and united to Christ by the Spirit, we're now being made more righteous (sanctified) by the same union with Christ by the Spirit.

Here the essential intersection between our doctrine of the church and our doctrine of the spiritual life becomes evident. Sanctification is not *me*-oriented; it's *we*-oriented. The focus of sanctification is Christ, by the power of the Spirit, but the means and goals are community-oriented. Sanctification as the growth in holiness of individuals who are savingly related to Christ has as its purpose the strengthening of Christ's body, the church. As justified individuals grow in their relationship with Christ and one another through the work of the Spirit in the context of their local church communities, the worldwide body of Christ also grows in holiness, magnifying Christ's name and bringing glory to God the Father.

"The church is one, finding its oneness in Christ. The church is holy, set apart from the world to mediate life to the world and bring forth the fruits of the Spirit amid the life of the world. The church is catholic in that it is whole, for all, and embracing all times and places. The church is apostolic in that it is grounded in the testimony of the first witnesses to Jesus' life and resurrection, and depends upon and continues their ministry."[5]

Thomas Oden (1992)

Passages to Ponder

The following passages form the foundation and structure for Christian ecclesiology and sanctification. Numerous additional passages could be included, but by carefully considering these, you'll be able to establish your own understanding of the Christian community and the Christian life with a firm footing. Along with a basic discussion of the points of agreement and disagreement among various Bible-believing Christians regarding the meaning of these passages, you'll also find verses to commit to memory.

(1) Acts 2—The Day of Pentecost and the Coming of the Holy Spirit

Ten days after Christ's ascension to heaven, something changed, marking a major turning point in the outworking of God's plan of redemption. During the Jewish festival of Pentecost, the Holy Spirit descended upon the small gathering of Jesus' disciples in Jerusalem.

The world would never be the same.

In Acts 1, the author, Luke, recounts how Jesus told the disciples to wait in Jerusalem for "the promise of the Father," which, Jesus said, "you heard of from Me" (Acts 1:4 NASB). What was that promise? He said, "You will be baptized with the Holy Spirit not many days from now" (1:5 NASB). This promise is consistent with Jesus' earlier teaching concerning the coming of the Spirit recorded in John 14:16–17: "I will ask the Father, and He will give you another Helper, that He may be with you forever; that is the Spirit of truth" (NASB). This Spirit, Jesus said, "abides with you and will be in you" (14:17 NASB). The baptism of the Holy Spirit at Pentecost fulfills that promise of the indwelling of the Spirit.

While different Christian traditions see the import of the Spirit's baptism in different ways, it's clear that Acts affirms the following three things.

First, the ministry of the Spirit that appears on the day of Pentecost must be called the baptism of the Holy Spirit. Why? Because this very event—predicted by Christ—was called the baptism of the Holy Spirit (compare Acts 1:5; 2:1–4). Later, the event that solidified the position of Gentile believers in this fledgling movement is also the baptism of the Holy Spirit (compare Acts 10:47; 11:15–16).

Second, the baptism of the Holy Spirit is something new; it's a turning point in the ministry of the Holy Spirit. When Jesus told the disciples to wait in Jerusalem for what the Father had promised (Acts 1:4), it's clear they were to wait for something that had not yet occurred. And Jesus acknowledged that while the disciples knew of the Holy Spirit and that the Spirit had been "with them," when they received the baptism of the Spirit, He would be "in them" (John 14:17). That's a new experience unheard of prior to Pentecost.

Third, the baptism of the Holy Spirit is foundational for the subsequent mission of the apostles and the existence of the New Testament church. Everything the apostles did in the remainder of Acts was predicated upon and driven by the baptism of the Holy Spirit. Beyond this, the baptism of the Holy Spirit drives the identity of the fledgling community of the redeemed—the church. No longer was the covenant community restricted to Jews. Now it's open to all who believe in Christ—Jew or Gentile. This equal reception of the Holy Spirit dramatically demonstrated the equality of all who believe in Christ.

Although there is great agreement on the signal importance of the Spirit's ministry in defining the church since Pentecost, significant disagreement persists among Bible-believing Christians over exactly how to understand the boundaries of the church. Should those who came to God in faith before the baptism of the Spirit still be considered part of the church? That is, were Old Testament believers like Enoch and Abraham part of the church? Or did the church begin at Pentecost, constituting an entirely new covenant community distinct from the Old Testament people of God?

This raises one of the most-discussed questions in protestant ecclesiology: When did the church begin? The following chart shows three of the responses to this question:

View	Representative	Reasoning
The church began with Adam	R. B. Kuiper[6]	All people ever saved are saved through one Savior and through one way of salvation—through faith in Christ. Old Testament saints, then, are saved through faith in Christ as prophesied in the OT. Thus, all OT saints are members of the one church, the body of Christ. The logical beginning of this saving faith is found in Adam and Eve, who thus constituted the first church.
The church began with Abraham	D. Douglas Bannerman[7]	Because of the significance of the role played by Abraham in Scripture, and the nature of the promises given to him that turn out to be corporate in nature, it may be said that "the Church of God, built upon the Gospel and the covenant of grace, was distinctly and visibly set up in connection with God's dealings with Abraham."
The church began on the Day of Pentecost	Millard Erickson[8]	The way the term ecclesia is used in the New Testament, and the way Jesus speaks of His church as yet future in Matthew 16, along with the significance of the gift of the Spirit in Acts 2, allows one to conclude that the church began at Pentecost.

(2) 1 Corinthians 12:12–31—The Body of Christ and Its Members

Even a half-conscious perusal of all social media platforms will provide ample evidence that body image is big business. Advertisements bombard us with images of the assumed (and usually younger) ideal human form. You'll see concoctions to combat balding, creams to erase wrinkles, and AI apps to instantly airbrush your mediocre mugshot into a billboard-worthy portrait. No doubt, we live in a hyped-up, over-charged, body-conscious world.

With all the attention we devote to our bodies, it's rather surprising that we've missed one of the most important messages of all: We as Christians *ought* to be body-conscious. But the body to which we ought to devote such attention is not our own, individual, physical body but rather the body of Christ. This teaching leaps from the text of 1 Corinthians 12.

Chapter 12 begins with a discussion of spiritual gifts. In the first part of the chapter, we learn that the body of Christ exhibits a number of different gifts, but this diversity all comes from the same sovereign source: the Holy Spirit. So, with respect to giftedness, the body of Christ displays God-intended unity amid diversity.

This same principle—unity and diversity—carries over into the main body of chapter 12. Beginning in verse 12, Paul repeatedly confronts the reader with the truth that every believer is unique, and yet every unique believer is part of the same body. What's more, this is precisely the result intended by the Spirit of God, whose work it is to baptize all believers into the one body of Christ (12:13). No physical body could ever work effectively if it were composed of only one part, reduplicated some insane number of times. This is the import of Paul's observation: "But as it is, God

---

PASSAGES TO MASTER AND MEMORIZE

Matthew 28:18–20	1 Corinthians 12:4–7
Acts 1:4–5	Galatians 5:22–23
Acts 2:38–42	Galatians 6:15–16
Romans 6:12–14	Ephesians 2:19–21
Romans 7:22–23	Ephesians 4:20–24
Romans 11:19–21	Philippians 3:20–21
1 Corinthians 11:23–26	1 Peter 2:5, 9

Note: Not all these passages are discussed in the text, but they'll all help you master the doctrines of the church and the Christian life.

---

arranged the members in the body, each one of them, as he chose. If all were a single member, where would the body be? As it is, there are many parts, yet one body" (12:18–19).

The teaching of this passage reemphasizes the point made in Acts 2—the Spirit's distinctive work since the day of Pentecost is to "baptize" believers into the body of Christ, the church. The invisible spiritual reality undergirds authentic membership in the community of the redeemed. In 1 Corinthians 12:13, this incorporation into the gift-sharing community in which spiritual growth occurs is clearly referred to as being "baptized" by the Spirit.

But the truth about the members and the body—the diversity and the unity—leads to another very practical end: "That there may be no division in the body, but that the members may have the same care for one another" (12:25). The upshot of this teaching is that each member in the body of Christ ought to view every other member with honor and compassion in authentic community life played out in the local church, where we are to be committed, participating members not for ourselves but for one another.

(3) 1 Peter 2:4–10—The Church as a Royal Priesthood

In this brief but powerful passage, we find the same pattern of agreement and disagreement that by now has become a familiar refrain: Some Christians see the church as the recipient of Old Testament promises given to Israel, whereas others see Old Testament citations as illustrative in helping the inspired New Testament author make his point about the nature of the church.

In this particular case, Peter uses a number of Old Testament passages to make the point that the church is a community of individual, living stones being built up "as a spiritual house" to be a holy priesthood and "to offer spiritual sacrifices acceptable to God through Jesus Christ" (1 Peter 2:5). On this point we see firm agreement among Bible-believing interpreters. The Old Testament language here paints a powerful picture, for the mental images of temple and sacrificial system illustrate clearly the author's plan to explain the nature of the church.

In cutting through the disagreements that swirl around the question of the relationship between Israel and the church, this passage emphasizes the saving and sanctifying relationship between Redeemer and redeemed. This relationship comes by grace, through faith, wrought by the miraculous work of the Holy Spirit.

But this passage also highlights the corporate nature of our worship and service. Throughout the passage, the second person "you" is plural—you all, believers in Jesus, are being built up to serve as priests (1 Peter 2:4–5). And because priests in the Old Testament were called to intercede with God on behalf of others, the New Testament concept of the priesthood of all believers means each one of us is called to exhort, encourage, and build up the other (Romans 14:19; 1 Thessalonians 5:11).

The point, again and again, is that the church *is* the community of the redeemed. It starts with a saving relationship that comes by grace through faith, and it proceeds along the lines of obedience created by that relationship for the purpose of contributing to the spiritual growth of our fellow believers. The redeemed are ushered into a real community of fellow saints for sanctification, and this communion begins with the work of the Holy Spirit in an eternal relationship with God through Christ.

(4) Ephesians 2:11–3:13—The Church and the Mystery of Gentile Inclusion

Think about a mystery you've read or watched, with its unexpected twists and turns or surprise ending. Whether wrought by masters such as authors Agatha Christie and Sir Arthur Conan Doyle or filmmaker Alfred Hitchcock—even this century's writer and director M. Night Shyamalan—a well-crafted, well-executed mystery always hits the audience with an "I-didn't-see-that-coming" moment. Looking back, we sometimes see little clues that point in the direction of the great reveal, but hindsight, as they say, is 20/20.

The same is true, we're told, with the great mystery of the church. According to Ephesians 2, Gentiles were not, prior to the appearance of the church, included in the covenant people of God. The text says Gentiles were "separated from Christ, alienated from the commonwealth of Israel and strangers to the covenants of promise, having no hope and without God in the world" (2:12). Before God revealed the mystery, the former situation prevailed: Gentiles were not a normative part of the people of God, nor were they partakers in the promises of God.

But the work of Christ and the coming of the Spirit changed all that. Paul articulates the revelation of this mystery: The work of Christ and the work of the Holy Spirit have made the two formerly opposing parties into one. Whereas before the time of Christ only Israel could claim to be the heir of the promises of God, now in Christ both Jews and Gentiles can be partakers in God's gracious blessing. "This mystery," Paul says, "is that the Gentiles are fellow heirs, members of the same body, and partakers of the promise in Christ Jesus through the gospel" (3:6).

What great news that was for those who were not direct descendants of Abraham, Isaac, and Jacob!

Now all peoples are able to partake of the promises of God in Christ. Because of what Christ did on the cross (Ephesians 2:16), and because of the ministry of the Holy Spirit in incorporating all who believe into the body of Christ (Ephesians 2:8), persons of any language, tribe, or ethnicity—Jew or Gentile—can be "fellow citizens with the saints and members of the household of God" (2:19).

(5) Matthew 28:18–20—Baptism

Here in the passage often called "the Great Commission," we find the basis for the church's practice of water baptism. And again, we find virtual unanimity among Bible-believing Christians who see this passage as the authority for the ordinance or sacrament of water baptism. Water baptism in the name of the triune God is an essential mark of confession of faith and incorporation into the visible church.

In this foundational passage, Jesus was speaking after His resurrection but prior to His ascension. In what becomes a rather powerful climax for the Gospel of Matthew, Jesus says:

> All authority in heaven and on earth has been given to me. Go therefore and make disciples of all nations, baptizing them in the name of the Father and of the Son and of the Holy Spirit, teaching them to observe all that I have commanded you. And behold, I am with you always, to the end of the age. (Matthew 28:18–20)

The clarity of this command from the lips of our Lord is compelling enough to create this widespread agreement in the Christian world throughout history: Our task is to make disciples by baptizing them and teaching them to keep the commandments of Jesus. Yes, diversity does exist and always has regarding the most

---

OTHER NEW TESTAMENT PASSAGES RELATED TO BAPTISM

Though churches and denominations differ on whether all of these following passages refer to water baptism or to Spirit baptism, they're generally regarded as key texts that inform a Christian understanding of baptism.

Matthew 28:18–20	Romans 6:3–4
Mark 16:16	Ephesians 4:4–6
Acts 1:4–5	Ephesians 5:25–26
Acts 2:37–41	Colossians 2:12
Acts 8:14–16	1 Peter 3:21–22
Acts 10:44–48	Hebrews 9:14
Acts 18:8	Hebrews 10:22
Acts 22:16	

---

appropriate candidates for receiving water baptism (only those who profess faith? or the children of believers too?).

Christians also disagree on the proper mode of baptism (dunking, sprinkling, or pouring?), and the specific words and actions associated with the rite (personal testimonies, confession of faith in Christ's person and work, a Trinitarian creed?). But Christians of every stripe believe that water baptism continues an accepted ordinance or sacrament in the church of Jesus Christ, that it seals a person as a disciple of Jesus and member of the body of Christ, the church.

(6) 1 Corinthians 11:17–34—Communion or the Lord's Supper

The Gospels of Matthew, Mark, and Luke all portray the acts of our Lord at the Last Supper in a way that could be considered merely descriptive. First Corinthians 11 indicates that the observance of the bread and wine was meant to be a continuous and frequent practice in the gathered community (11:20, 26, 33–34). The Last Supper wasn't simply to be a meal Jesus had with His disciples in the past, but a meal they were to have in memory of Him from that time forward.

This passage also has as its audience a gathering of primarily Gentile believers (no doubt with some Jewish believers present), and as a result the questions that could possibly be raised against the prescriptive nature of the Gospel accounts are resolved here. "I received from the Lord what I also delivered to you," Paul says (1 Corinthians 11:23). In this statement he connects the authority of the Lord with the continuing practice of the Lord's Supper in the church—a fact on which all Bible-believing Christians agree.

Now, different Christians may call the practice by different names (Communion, the Lord's Supper, the Lord's Table, or the Eucharist), and we may practice it with varying frequencies (weekly, monthly, or quarterly). We may observe it in different ways (leavened or unleavened bread, grape juice or wine, open to

NUMBER OF SACRAMENTS THROUGHOUT HISTORY

Early Churches: Many "signs" were "sacramental"—that is, mysterious in pointing to spiritual truths—but baptism and the Eucharist held central places as the rites of initiation and continued consecration; in some places penance began to be practiced for admitting wayward baptized Christians back into the fellowship of the church.

Medieval Church: Seven sacraments of saving and sanctifying grace began with baptism, included the Eucharist, and grew to include a system of penance, confirmation of those who'd been baptized as infants, marriage to expand the church physically, orders (or ordination) to expand the church spiritually, and unction (or anointing) in preparation for death.

Reformation Church: Baptism and the Lord's Supper (or Communion) were restored as the visible church's two sacraments, or ordinances; other activities were seen as means of grace for sanctification. Many practices such as confirmation, orders, and anointing are maintained in some traditions but not usually with sacramental status.

Modern Evangelical Churches: Baptism and the Lord's Supper are generally upheld as the sacraments or ordinances; other activities are practiced as means of testimony or spiritual growth.

all believers or closed to only church members), and we may even believe different things about the relationship between the elements and Christ's presence (real, spiritual, or memorial).

Unfortunately, these differences of doctrinal opinions and practices will almost certainly continue until Christ returns. But this shouldn't distract us from the fact that all Christians agree that the Lord's Supper is an essential mark of a properly constituted church community, a sign of our essential unity amid our diversity.

(7) Romans 6:6–14—Regeneration, Sin, and the Believer

If we're saved by grace through faith and not by works, as we've discussed earlier in this book, then doesn't this mean we can "live it up," "go hog wild," or "do anything we want"? If you haven't heard this line of argument from any young or immature believers, you will. But this kind of confused reasoning isn't new. In fact, it's as old as the good news of God's grace itself.

Romans 6 forms one of the central passages on the doctrine of sanctification precisely because it asks and answers a key question regarding the life of the believer: "Are we to continue in sin that grace may abound?" (6:1). And in this time-honored passage, we learn a vital truth about the relationship between regeneration (being "born again" or "saved" or "justified") and sanctification ("growing spiritually" or "becoming more Christlike").

The death of Christ has become our death because of our identification with Him: Those who have been "baptized into Christ Jesus were baptized into his death" (6:3). Similarly, the resurrection of Christ, according to this passage, is not only our hope of bodily resurrection (6:8) but the pattern of our present life after conversion. For "just as Christ was raised from the dead by the glory of the Father, we too might walk in newness of life" (6:4).

While this concept finds broad acceptance within the Christian world, exactly *how* regeneration forms the basis for sanctification is debated. Perhaps the best way to introduce this is to turn to that stellar example of all things theological, Dr. Seuss's wildly influential work, *The Cat in the Hat*.[9]

You probably know the story. If you don't, you should. Two kids are left at home on a rainy day. Mother is gone, and Father isn't even mentioned. With nothing to do because of the rain, the kids are bored out of their minds. Suddenly, a cat strides through the front door. But not just any mangy feral feline trying to escape the rain. This one's dressed like a gentleman: *the Cat in the Hat*! The Cat leads the two kids in all kinds of fun activities, making quite a mess along the way. All the while the family's fish, who plays the role of the moral compass, continually tells the kids they should make the Cat leave.

After a while, the Cat brings out a big red box, and from that box two little beings emerge: Thing One and Thing Two. These two "Things" begin to fly kites in the house and make an even bigger mess.

In the midst of all kinds of Thing-caused-chaos, we catch a glimpse of Mother walking up the sidewalk toward the house. Now, anyone can see that the mess is too large to be cleaned up in the amount of time it will take Mother to enter the front door. But the Cat in the Hat has one last trick up his sleeve: a massive, multi-armed, automated cleaner-upper-machine! Just in the nick of time, the house is clean and the Cat flees the scene. As the book ends, Mother steps into a clean house with two well-behaved children sitting right where they were when we first met them.

Let's rewind and highlight Thing One and Thing Two in this story. The story's climax of maximal fun (or maximal domestic damage, as the case may be) coincided with the arrival of Thing One and Thing Two, when they emerged from the box and started "helping" the children play. This is actually a helpful image to recall the range of perspectives on sanctification. We all see two "things" involved in the process (and progress) of sanctification.

Thing One might correspond roughly to the divine element in sanctification—the work of God in bringing about spiritual growth. Thing Two might correspond to the human element in sanctification—our own working in the pursuit of holiness. Both Thing One and Thing Two are involved. Very few Christians would dream of ascribing the entire work of sanctification to *only* Thing One or *only* Thing Two. They must somehow play together. Even theologians who are strong proponents of predestination typically affirm that the work of sanctification involves *some kind* of responsible participation of the human will with the will of God—even if the description of roles must be finely nuanced.[10]

The point here is this: Christians all agree that both divine action (Thing One) and human action (Thing Two) occur in the process of sanctification. But they disagree on just how the two fit together and which one, if either, predominates.

(8) Romans 7—The Battle with Sin

In this controversial passage, Paul—using singular personal pronouns "I" and "me"—paints a picture of a person at war within himself: "I do not do what I want, but I do the very thing I hate" (Romans 7:15). And beyond this, he says, "I have the desire to do what is right, but not the ability to carry it out. For I do not do the good I want, but the evil I do not want is what I keep on doing" (7:18–19).

Everyone reading this passage agrees that the situation depicted here is troubling. But in speaking about himself—a believer—is Paul also representing any believer? Or is he recalling his own past experience as an unbeliever, portraying the struggles any unbeliever faces?

Some commentators suggest that, using his own experience, he's representing not an unbeliever but a believer—someone who's already experienced regeneration and now faces the battle of living the Christian life. In this view, believers desperately want to fulfill the Christian life, but something within causes them to do what they don't want to do.[11] Instead of living a life of obedience, they find they actually engage in the evil they don't want to do.

On the other hand, some insist this is far too bleak a picture to be true of a regenerate person. Instead, this must be the portrait of an unregenerate (unsaved) person who just can't do what's right because they don't have the life-giving Spirit.[12] In that view, this passage must be Paul referencing his previous life as a nonbeliever.

Both of these perspectives run into difficult questions. For those who suggest that in Romans 7 Paul describes a believer, one might ask, "Doesn't this understanding give far too much credit to the

The following chart summarizes different views on the identity of the singular personal pronouns "I" and "me" in Romans 7:14–25.[13]

WHOM IS PAUL PORTRAYING?

Two views on Paul representing the believer	Two views on Paul representing the nonbeliever
• Paul describes his present experience as a Christian struggling with sin, thus applicable to even the most mature believers.	• Paul vividly recalls his past experience in struggling against sin prior to becoming a Christian, thus typical of all unbelievers who try to live moral lives.
• Paul rhetorically places himself in the shoes of Christians who must be delivered from their immaturity or "carnality" to live a victorious Christian life.	• Paul figuratively places himself in the position of non-Christian Jews who struggle with sin—those who know the Law but just can't seem to live by it.

power of sin? Doesn't this understanding make the power of God in Christ look just a little too weak?" For those who suggest that instead Paul is depicting an unbeliever, the question becomes, "How can it be said that an unbeliever delights in the law of God? This would seem to be impossible for an unregenerate person."

Wherever we land on the question regarding Romans 7 itself, other passages, such as Galatians 5—which we'll discuss next—*do* indicate that the authentic Christian life involves struggle against sin. Even for (or maybe *especially* for) the Spirit-led believer.

(9) Galatians 5:16–26—The Holy Spirit and the Battle with Sin

This classic passage gives vivid color and texture to the relationship between the Spirit's ministry in the life of the believer and the challenging process of progressive sanctification. "Walk by the Spirit," Paul says, "and you will not gratify the desires of the flesh" (Galatians 5:16). Here Paul portrays the battle involved in sanctification as a conflict between the desires of the Spirit and the desires of the flesh—the divine will and human unwillingness. But in this case, Paul gives numerous examples of the works of the flesh (5:19–21) and the fruit of the Spirit (5:22–23).

This passage makes one thing clear: *Sanctification is directly related to the ministry of the Holy Spirit in our lives.* Small wonder, then, that many use the phrase *the spiritual life* as roughly equivalent to "sanctification" or "the Christian life." The disagreement comes primarily in attempting to answer this question: How does one actually *do* this thing described in Scripture as walking *by the Spirit*?

For those who take a Reformed (or "Calvinistic") view of sanctification, the empowering grace of God in Christ looms over the process. Progress in sanctification, then, ultimately depends on God's work, even though this work of God shows up in the life of the believer as the believer's good works. On the other hand, some in the broader Wesleyan or Arminian traditions emphasize the human element in their understanding—God comes to the aid of willing hearts, which have been enabled by regeneration to cooperate with God's grace. Others speak in terms of a mysterious "cooperation" between the will of God and the will of regenerate hearts without daring to define the process.

So what gives?

To help us understand the toe-to-toe stand-off between two extremes (and the various perspectives in between), allow us to draw another analogy from a lesser-known story by Dr. Seuss: "The Zax." In that brief narrative, two odd-looking creatures—a "North-going Zax" and a "South-going Zax"—meet face-to-face in the prairie of Prax. Instead of easing even one inch to the right or left to let the other pass, these opposites on the spectrum of "Zaxdom" face off forever, unable to make way for the other.[14]

Not that theologians are frowning, furry who-knows-whats folding their arms and refusing to budge, but these two positions—God's sovereignty and human responsibility—will always stubbornly (and necessarily!) assert themselves in any thinking about the doctrine of sanctification. Why? Because both contribute essential elements of a mysterious truth held in tension. While some traditions might emphasize one or the other and other traditions seek to balance the two tendencies, the tension will always remain.

Who's Responsible for Sanctification?

$\longleftarrow$ $\longrightarrow$

A WORK OF GOD	A WORK OF GOD	A WORK OF MAN
Humans Passive	Humans Active	Humans Active
What God Does for Us	What God Does In and Through Us	What We Do for God
Essential for Salvation	Result of Salvation	Unrelated to Salvation

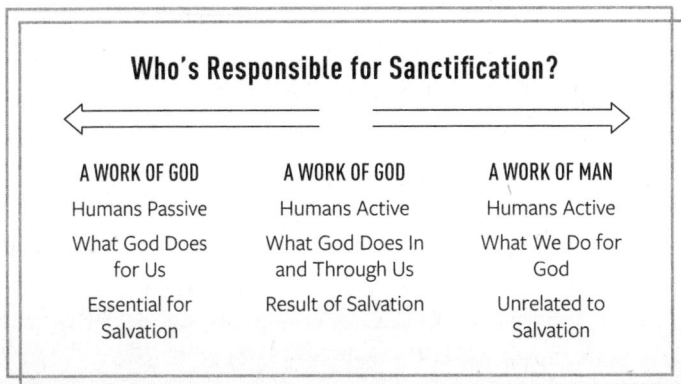

Realities to Remember

If you've ever coached Little League baseball, you've probably found yourself saying six words over and over and over again: "Keep your eye on the ball!" Those miniature sluggers ("Baby Ruths"?) are still developing the hand-eye coordination required to hit a baseball, and long experience has proven that the first item of business in learning to do that is indeed to *keep your eye on the ball.*

It's now time to examine some of the key concepts related to the foundational doctrines of the church and spiritual growth. These concepts help us understand how Bible-believing Christians see the doctrines of ecclesiology and sanctification. If we keep our eyes on these "realities to remember," we won't strike out when it comes to a proper understanding of these immensely practical areas of Christian theology.

Reality 1: The central principle of ecclesiology is our invisible relationship with Christ.

In the study of theology, one encounters phrases traditionally preserved in Latin. One such phrase is *sine qua non*. Literally translated "without which not," it typically refers to conditions or elements that are indispensable or necessary. To say it another way, *sine qua non* refers to that without which something could not exist. In orthodox protestant theology, the *sine qua non* of the true church is a saving relationship between the Redeemer and the redeemed.

If God had not reached down into our world and entered into a saving relationship with human beings, there would be no church. Oh yes, there could still be church buildings, church members, church activities, and church programs, but none of these would constitute the true church: the communion of *saints*, that is, truly born-again, Spirit-indwelled believers in Jesus Christ.

The church is composed of those who have been given spiritual life. The gift of salvation is what results in the church; the invisible relationship gives rise to a visible communion. One passage that demonstrates this is Ephesians 5:25–30. When we focus on the statements Paul makes in that passage regarding the relationship between Christ and the church, we see one stunning feature: Christ loved the church and gave himself up for her for the purpose of sanctifying her.

If the church exists precisely because of an invisible relationship that itself is a gift of God, then everything about that church ought to serve the development of the invisible relationship. To express this in reverse, if we emphasize the visible aspects of the church over the invisible, then we deny the priority of a relationship offered by God, and we insist that the visible church is the source of salvation.

Rather, the ministries and mission of the visible church—our local communities gathered to worship God and serve one another—must be centered on and empowered by the invisible saving relationship with Christ and the sanctifying work of the Holy Spirit.

Reality 2: Variety (or diversity) in the body of Christ is God's design.

The body of Christ is composed of many different individuals, each one gifted in unique ways by the same Holy Spirit that baptizes them into the body of Christ. Each person—each part of the body—is unique and valuable, according to 1 Corinthians 12.

Further, this is part of God's design for the body. This diversity, according to Scripture, is the very wisdom and blessing of God for the church. As a matter of fact, at one point (see Ephesians 4:11–16), the variety is actually portrayed as "gifts" given by Christ to the church for building her up.

But from a human perspective, this diversity is often seen as a pain in the church. Different people, different perspectives, different gifts, different concerns . . . this all adds up to difficulty. Friction. Conflict. In fact, some historic Christian traditions and denominations shake their fingers at diversity. For them, unity of the body—visible, institutional unity—can be achieved only through uniformity. They must all read from the same Bible translation, all pray the same prayers, all participate in the same liturgy, all submit to the same authorities, or all believe the same things about baptism, the Lord's Supper, spiritual gifts, and the end times.

The fact is, though, Christians within a single church and even between different churches already have spiritual unity based on their shared saving relationship with Jesus Christ. And this means they can experience visible unity based on the essential truths of the Christian faith despite their different beliefs and practices on less foundational matters.

Variety in the body of Christ is God's design. What's more, our response to this variety ought to be to honor one another in compassion while celebrating the unity of the body in Christ. Of course, we must never allow these differences to lead to division and disunity to the point that we deny a genuine brother or sister in Christ our love and fellowship. We can disagree on less-central doctrines without being disagreeable.

Reality 3: Sanctification is inseparably bound together with justification.

Chances are you've never heard the legend of "Greyfriars Bobby."

The story goes like this: Sometime in the mid-1800s, a man named John "Auld Jock" Gray worked for the city of Edinburgh in

Scotland. He happened to have a wee Skye Terrier named Bobby, and Auld Jock and Bobby were inseparable. So inseparable, in fact, that according to the legend, after Auld Jock died in 1858, Bobby stood guard over his master's grave until the dog himself died in 1872. That's fourteen years!

The townspeople of old Edinburgh were so moved by Bobby's loyalty that they erected a commissioned statue in his honor. It can still be seen just across from Greyfriars Kirkyard in front of Greyfriars Bobby's Bar.

Bobby's refusal to be separated from his master is a helpful illustration of another inseparable bond: the bond between justification and sanctification. Sanctification (or "spiritual growth") is inseparable from justification (or "spiritual birth"). If God begins the divine work of salvation in the form of justification, then He will most assuredly continue that work in sanctification—and complete it in glorification, when we're resurrected in glorious bodies at Christ's return.

This fact is important for two reasons. First, a "babe in Christ" should be nourished and nurtured toward maturity, and so we should both expect growth and promote growth. In fact, that's one of the functions of the church, the body of Christ—to gather together to encourage one another toward love and good works (Hebrews 10:24–25). Of course, just as in natural birth and growth people develop at different rates and in different ways, Christians mature differently as well. We should be patient toward others in their own spiritual journey, often characterized by sporadic fits and starts.

Second, we shouldn't expect those who haven't experienced the spiritual rebirth through faith in Christ to live as if they have. Christians are responsible for urging fellow believers to walk in a manner worthy of their calling, but they're not responsible for making sure outsiders who don't know the Lord are living according to the Christian code of conduct (1 Corinthians 5:9–13).

While we must rightly distinguish between justification and sanctification theologically, these two things should never be separated practically.

Reality 4: Sanctification is a work of the Holy Spirit, involving the responsible participation of the believer.

This might be the most important practical fact in the doctrine of sanctification. Christians agree doctrinally that both the divine work and human participation are involved in the process of sanctification. This very recognition leads some to emphasize the first—God's role—resulting in a view of sanctification that *can* sometimes become so lopsided that it ends up laying the responsibility for a believer's sin at God's feet, blaming Him for not making us perfect.

On the other hand, some emphasize the second—our responsibility—to such an extent that sanctification is no longer seen as the work of the Holy Spirit but our own voluntary response to God, accomplished through our own strength. As such, sanctification is seen as entirely optional.

Neither of these conclusions should sit well with Christians reckoning with the whole teaching of Scripture on the matter of spiritual growth toward Christlikeness. Instead, we would do well to admit that sanctification, while inseparably bound together with justification, is nonetheless distinct from it. That distinction can be seen in this way:

Justification is a once-for-all act of God in declaring us righteous when we personally exercise faith in Christ. Sanctification is an ongoing process, worked in us by the Holy Spirit (Philippians 2:12–13), which, to quote theologian Anthony Hoekema, "involves our responsible participation."[15] And because we can grow more and more in holiness and Christlike living, sanctification is never completed in this life. We await the future work of glorification—entirely the work of God—when we'll be resurrected and conformed perfectly to Christ (Philippians 3:20–21).

Reality 5: Sanctification is a team sport.

Sanctification isn't merely a personal, private, individual activity. It's a "team sport."

Most of us are aware of the individual aspects of sanctification. We've heard our traditions speak of mortification and vivification, of the spiritual disciplines, of quiet times and prayer journals and inductive Bible study. We've maybe even sung children's songs about reading our Bible and praying every day so we'll "grow, grow, grow."[16] To be clear, we should be in favor of such things. Just as every team sport involves personal preparation, practice, and commitment, so does sanctification require our personal, voluntary activity and involvement.

But this leads us to the part that's not so familiar for some Christians steeped in our uber-individualistic culture. Even though personal, private elements in sanctification come into play, the overall pattern is team-based. That is, the primary venue for our spiritual growth is the church, where we exhort, encourage, correct, and provoke one another toward Christlikeness.

Even though each individual bears responsibility for his or her growth in holiness (by means of responsible participation with the work of the Holy Spirit), one's growth as an individual *always* occurs in the context of the body of Christ. We train as part of the body. We grow as part of the body. Our life as a Christian reflects on the body.

That's precisely why it's *not* okay to forsake our own assembling together (Hebrews 10:25)—to pursue a "lone ranger sanctification." And that's precisely why it's not okay for churches to abandon either discipleship or church discipline. God intends us to grow together.

Errors to Avoid

In other areas of doctrine, such as the Trinity and salvation, straying from the safe path of clear Scripture and sound doctrine can lead to heresy—or condemnable doctrine. Worshipping the wrong god, denying the right Jesus, trusting in a false gospel . . . such errors bear a skull-and-crossbones warning label because they affect one's eternal life.

When it comes to ecclesiology and sanctification, we're dealing with matters of doctrine for which errors don't really endanger a person's eternal salvation as much as they frustrate their spiritual health and growth. But because we're called "to grow up in all aspects into Him who is the head, even Christ" (Ephesians 4:15 NASB), the following errors should be avoided at all costs.

Error 1: Corporation Over Corpus (Body)

A danger arises from a failure to emphasize the foundational nature of the saving relationship with Jesus Christ. The earmark of a biblical perspective on ecclesiology is maintaining a balance between the invisible and the visible. The invisible church, composed of all who have entered into an eternal saving relationship with God through Christ by the Spirit, is the true church. Every visible church is an expression of the true, invisible church and comprises both true believers (the invisible church) and those who are not.

But when we lose sight of the invisible reality that undergirds the visible church, we can end up focusing on the wrong things. For example, we can begin treating the church on purely visible terms—acting like it's a corporation rather than the body (*corpus*) of Christ. This attitude is destructive to the church, because we all know the rules of business are brutal, cutthroat. A corporation has to thrive to survive. Eliminate the opposition. Get rid of weak team members. Downsize, if necessary, to maximize profitability.

This is *not* the way a body works. When your lungs are congested, you don't fire them and hire a new pair. The whole body works together for healing, and it suffers until that healing comes. The very idea that the church is the body of Christ has honest implications for how we view the church and how we treat the church.

One *possible* danger sign is this: when the only books church leaders read are from the corporate world. This means there may be a problem. Of course, learning about leadership is a positive thing, especially for those who hold leadership positions in ministry. But are church leaders reading books that speak of shepherding? Of body life? Of healing broken relationships? The pattern of Jesus is *not* the pattern of the corporate CEO. As a result, should we really tolerate a situation where the primary paradigm for a church pastor is taken *in toto* from the concept of a CEO?

Leadership in the church isn't *simply* business acumen, nor is it "getting things done." It may involve those things at times, but leadership in the church *absolutely must* focus—again and again—on the spiritual relationship between the Redeemer and the redeemed. It's a *spiritual leadership*, and whenever we as church leaders or as church members tolerate an attitude toward the church that views it as some kind of corporation, we've lost sight of what's most important.

Error 2: Growth over Health

By focusing on visible aspects of the church, we begin measuring the church—and even success in ministry—by looking at visible things. This error is epidemic especially in the western, developed, modern, "first-world" church. Many get duped by the deception that bigger is necessarily better, that a great number of members must mean a church is doing everything right. Oh, and that small church down the street? They must be unhealthy, or maybe even "dead."

It seems many churches equate church growth with the number of attendees, the size of the physical campus, or the dollars in the budget. No matter how we do it, if we prioritize *any* kind of physical growth over spiritual development, we've confused "growth" and "health." Perhaps our Lord intended more by the metaphor of the church as Christ's body than we typically assume. How does a body grow? Certainly not by focusing on physical stature or the quantification of its parts. Instead, a body grows by pursuing health. That ought to be our focus as well.

This principle—that church growth ought to be considered spiritual—seems to be supported by a reading of 1 Corinthians 3. In that chapter, the apostle Paul speaks of "building the church"

(3:10). But in this passage, the kind of building to which Paul refers is apparently not numerical growth of any kind—it's growth in the truth, or growth in spiritual maturity. It's the kind of growth that lays aside divisions and schisms. By the time Paul reaches the end of chapter 4, the issue has become crystal clear. He isn't urging the Corinthian church to grow in size, number, or budget. Rather, he wants them to grow by imitating those who imitate Christ. It's a spiritual growth.

Error 3: Sectarianism's Siren Song

Watching sports is a thousand percent more exciting when you have a team in the game and you're cheering them on. You wear their jersey, you know their players, and you're sure they're the best team in the league or division. Right? Why else would you cheer for them?

While this kind of fandom makes sports fun, it can destroy the church.

Pride can sometimes lead us to conclude that our church—and our church alone—is worthy of the name "Christian." Only *our* church knows the truth, lives the truth, teaches the truth. Such pride encourages us to view other churches as the "competition," which leads to envy at their successes and frustration at our failures.

True Christians rightly value the truth of God's Word. But we can become so convinced of the certainty of our own interpretations of the Bible that those idiosyncratic perspectives end up singing us to our destruction. Like sailors entranced by the song of the sirens, we become enchanted by the sound of our own voices. And we come to the conclusion that only we can adequately represent the body of Christ or true Christianity. We write off other churches as hopelessly misguided or only nominally Christian.

This kind of sectarianism puts asunder the broader body of Christ. We elevate inconsequential issues to the status of essentials. Then on the basis of disagreement on these newly defined "essentials," we refuse to fellowship with or even cooperate with brothers and sisters in Christ with whom we actually have much in common. And in so doing, we reinforce stereotypes about the strange, mythical creatures that inhabit that church down the street.

Sectarianism's siren song destroys the beauty of a unity that could be based upon our common confession of the central truths of the Christian faith. As the fifth-century Vincentian Canon puts it, we share in common truths that have been believed "everywhere, always, by all." The danger of sectarianism's siren song is the danger of sacrificing that unity on the altar of our own church's doctrinal distinctives.

Error 4: Lone Ranger Sanctification

We already referred to a lone ranger sanctification, and maybe you're old enough to have watched first-run episodes of the old TV show *The Lone Ranger*. Or maybe you've run across them or the 2013 film by the same name on a streaming service. Either way, have you ever wondered why they called him the lone ranger? Didn't he always have his partner Tonto around? He was hardly "alone." Nevertheless, the phrase *lone ranger* has come to describe anyone who separates from others and attempts to "go it alone."

In such a case, then, one of the errors we need to confront is the danger of "lone ranger sanctification." This is an all-too-common view that says "My growth in holiness is a matter in which I 'go it alone.'" In other words, "lone ranger Christians" tend to think of the local church as a nonessential part of spiritual growth—or even a distraction from their personal, individual pursuit of godliness.

Why is lone ranger sanctification dangerous?

First, the very baptism that identified us with Christ—the baptism that initiated our spiritual relationship with the Redeemer—is also the baptism that made us part of His body, the church. In other words, we were baptized by the Holy Spirit *into*, not *out from*, the church. And water baptism is a visible expression of that invisible reality, which also aligns us with the visible church.

How can a relationship that started by being made part of His body continue by ignoring that truth? How can any part of the body function well if it's separated from the body?

Certainly, there must be a balance between the corporate aspects of sanctification and the individual aspects of sanctification. As individuals, we pursue intimacy with the Lord, and we practice spiritual disciplines. But that pursuit and practice are not *in denial* of our place in the body. Rather, they *enhance* our place in the body. In fact, they're *aimed* at serving the body of Christ. This is, after all, the exact flow of thought we find in one of the most famous of the "individual sanctification" passages in Scripture: Romans 12:1–2.

To listen to many explanations of that passage, one would think the whole point is to individually present our bodies to God as a living sacrifice, a spiritual service of worship. And that truly is one of the elements affirmed in this passage. But that's not the whole point. Rather, that individual sacrifice, or submission to God, is designed to benefit the body. This is the point of Romans 12:3–13. So, it seems, even individual sanctification is body-oriented. And as a result, lone ranger sanctification is damaging to the body of Christ.

Error 5: Evangelical Antinomianism

Antinomianism is an idea that erupted in the context of Reformation-era Lutheranism. Precisely because Lutheran thought placed such a strong emphasis on the completed work of justification, questions began to circulate about the consequent attitude toward holy living. To say it another way, if justification is a done deal for the believer, and that right standing before God is found by faith alone, apart from any works, then why does one need works after being justified by faith?

This is an honest question, and one the Lutheran tradition quickly sorted out. Their answer was essentially this: Justification *is* complete, and based only on faith, apart from works. But that justification has implications, and one of them is that every believer is expected to live a life befitting justification. So yes, Christians are called and equipped to lead a life of holiness. And no, that life of holiness never *earns* justification. Those in Lutheran circles who denied the necessity of a life of holiness were called *antinomians*, which means "those against law."

Unfortunately, antinomianism didn't disappear five hundred years ago; it keeps rearing its ugly head. Some who sincerely believe in Christ and spout an orthodox doctrine of justification by faith nevertheless fail to see that justification has implications. Christians living in what might be called a Christ-less culture have failed to live *Christ-shaped* lives. Instead, they live *completely cultural* lives. The statistics are everywhere: Christians too often look, think, and act just like the culture around them. We display the same weaknesses, spend our money the same way, and exhibit the same values on life, marriage, and divorce.

Where is the tide of Christian conscience, wrestling seriously with the biblical command "You shall be holy, for I am holy" (1 Peter 1:16)? It seems to have been overcome by antinomianism, and it's high time to take a stand and call the people of God to holy living.

Error 6: Sanctimonious Self-Improvement

If antinomianism represents one extreme of the sanctification spectrum, sanctimonious self-improvement stands on the other extreme. Antinomianism involves a misunderstanding of the proper connection between justification and sanctification, while its opposite error involves a misunderstanding of the Holy Spirit's role in sanctification.

Unfortunately, sanctimonious self-improvement leaves out a vital part of sanctification—the role of the Holy Spirit. If an auto mechanic leaves out the engine when reassembling a vehicle, the car or truck won't run. Similarly, if a Christian leaves out the Holy Spirit in sanctification, the Christian life simply won't work.

Earlier, in wrestling with Romans 6, we encountered the suggestion that sanctification is illustrated by Thing One and Thing

Two in Dr. Seuss's famous book *The Cat in the Hat*. At that time, we observed that one of the earmarks of a proper view of sanctification is the recognition that both Thing One (a divine element) and Thing Two (a human element) are involved in sanctification. The error of sanctimonious self-improvement is a denial of the biblical truth that sanctification is the work of the Holy Spirit with the believer's responsible participation.

The world often distracts us from the fact that growth in holiness must come in a right relationship with the Holy Spirit of God. At every turn we're told to be the masters of our own fate, the captains of our soul. But this is just the cultural voice of sanctimonious self-improvement. It's a lie. The truth is this: Sanctification is part of that invisible relationship between Redeemer and redeemed. And as such, it's entirely dependent upon the ministry of the Holy Spirit.

Don't leave that part out!

Lessons to Live

Alfred, Lord Tennyson's poem "The Charge of the Light Brigade" contains the following heroic but haunting stanza:

> "Forward, the Light Brigade!"
> Was there a man dismayed?
> Not though the soldier knew
> Someone had blundered.
> Theirs not to make reply,
> Theirs not to reason why,
> Theirs but to do and die.
> Into the valley of Death
> Rode the six hundred.[17]

Those noble soldiers, forever immortalized in Tennyson's words, found themselves in the moment of battle with nothing to do but "do and die," to ride gallantly into battle despite the fact that their commanding officer had blundered in giving the order.

Unlike those soldiers doomed to die because they were following the orders of a fallible commander, we can move out with confidence, knowing that our Divine Lord would never err, never mislead us, and never order us into disaster. But in what direction do we ride? In light of the essential truths regarding the church and the spiritual life, what actions should we take as we ride boldly forth, not to "do and die" but to "do and thrive"? Consider the following lessons to live by.

Lesson 1: Pursue the unity of the faith.

As you survey the various churches, denominations, or traditions that make up the Christian landscape today, how do you view them? Are they "the competition" fishing out of the same pond your own church is for the same customers? Are they enemies of the truth—your own church's narrow definition of "truth"—that need to be defeated? Are they strange groups that think, speak, and act in ways so foreign to you it's not worth getting to know them?

Or do you see them as extended families to your own church's "nuclear family"—fellow Christians who, like you, are part of the family of God much, much bigger than yourself? People for whom you are obligated to pray, with whom you should strive to cooperate, and from whom you can learn?

How we answer these questions should be obvious. But hearing and doing are two different things.

The doctrinal statement of Dallas Theological Seminary says "All believers . . . are under solemn duty to keep the unity of the Spirit in the bond of peace, rising above all sectarian differences, and loving one another with a pure heart fervently."[18]

What a great place to start!

Rising above sectarian differences—the differences between Independent Bible Church and Presbyterian, between Baptist and Anglican—we fervently love one another with a pure heart. Why? Because we're all brothers and sisters in Christ! Our family relationship *in Christ* far outweighs the denominational labels we wear.

But as you regard unity with others outside your local church worthy of pursuit, don't forget about unity between you and the fellow members of your own local church. Seek peace with your own brothers and sisters and with your church leaders. Nip gossip in the bud. Put an end to backbiting before it turns into back breaking. Shun faction-forming. Resolve conflicts. Emphasize the weighty, essential truths of the faith and tolerate the light, minor differences of opinion that so often distract us from the most important things.

Lesson 2: Get involved.

If you are a believer in Jesus Christ—spiritually united with the risen and ascended Son of God by the Holy Spirit—then you should get involved in a local church. Your spiritual union with Christ and your consequent incorporation into His body, the church, demand your participation in the local, visible expression of that body. Get involved.

Wrapped up in this principle are several ideas. First among them is the admonishment found in the letter to the Hebrews: "Not neglecting to meet together, as is the habit of some, but encouraging one another, and all the more as you see the Day drawing near" (10:25). Quite simply, honest participation in a local church is mandatory for the believer.

We previously saw the danger involved in "lone ranger sanctification." There's a twin danger in "lone ranger ecclesiology," when you might even join that most popular of all churches, "Bedside Baptist Church," preferring to lie in bed a little longer rather than getting up to participate in a church service. So when we suggest that the first principle is to "get involved," the first part of that principle is to be an active part of a local assembly. That means more than just logging in to a live-streamed service. That's fine if you're stuck sick at home or traveling and can't make it to the gathered, in-the-flesh service. But it's not good for the health of the body. Be present.

But because simply *attending* isn't enough, getting involved has a second part too. According to Scripture, the Holy Spirit has equipped every believer with gifts, talents, abilities, convictions, sensitivities, and the like. These are all intended for the health and growth of the church. So merely "darkening the door of the church" isn't sufficient. No, strive to use your gifts for the benefit of the body. Perhaps this idea is seen in the verse immediately prior to the one we just encountered. Hebrews 10:24 says, "Let us consider how to stir up one another to love and good works."

Lesson 3: Practice obedience to those in authority.

Has anyone in authority over you ever instructed you to do something you knew wasn't right—something morally unacceptable? That kind of situation can be extremely uncomfortable, especially if it looks like your job might be on the line if you refuse. But in this messed-up world filled with crooked people in places of authority, this can happen. And then it's the believer's responsibility to do what's right, come what may.

But those (usually) rare occasions when corrupt bosses try to coax us to sin shouldn't distract us from the fact that, as a general rule and barring any moral compromises, we're expected to practice obedience to those in spiritual authority over us.

Many of us have a difficult time with this principle. From day one we're trained to admire those who, with true grit and a pioneer's spirit, overcome all odds and by sheer force of their independent will achieve success. But the sad thing is this independence isn't the right way—not in the church. According to God's plan, the people of God have spiritual shepherds to help guide them. Pastors. Elders. Overseers. Bishops. Whatever term your particular church, denomination, or tradition uses for its duly appointed leaders, someone in your church is responsible for your spiritual care and feeding.

Based on their convictions regarding the teaching of Scripture and the role of history and tradition, various denominations and churches have adopted different approaches to organization and leadership structures. The major positions regarding authority in the church can be broken into three historical models: episcopal, presbyterian, and congregational.

THREE HISTORICAL MODELS OF CHURCH ORDER

Episcopal	Presbyterian	Congregational
• Church authority and decision-making ultimately rest with the "bishop" (*episkopos*).	• Church authority and decision-making ultimately rest among a plurality of "elders" (*presbyteroi*).	• Church authority and decision-making ultimately rest in the congregation of voting members.
• Roman Catholicism, Eastern Orthodoxy, Anglicanism, Episcopalian, Methodism, some Lutherans, and some local churches led by a single pastor.	• Presbyterianism, Reformed churches, and many local independent churches that often describe themselves as "elder-led."	• Anabaptists, Puritan, Congregational churches, and many "low" or free churches (including most Baptist churches).

Maybe you're thinking, *The word* obey *is too strong. That gives those leaders too much power! I'll respect them, and I'll even support them (within reason), but obey them? Nah.* It's hard to square that response with Scripture, though. Hebrews 13:17 deserves our attention: "Obey your leaders and submit to them, for they are keeping watch over your souls, as those who will have to give an account. Let them do this with joy and not with groaning, for that would be of no advantage to you."

No, those in authority do not have *absolute* authority, for they've been placed in *spiritual* authority. You most certainly don't have to shortchange your moral principles in the interests of obeying your spiritual authorities. But in issues of spiritual development and church order, we need to learn a little old-fashioned *obedience* and *submission*. Church leaders will make morally neutral decisions about ministry priorities, personnel matters, order and content and style of worship—things on which Scripture is silent. In those cases, despite our own personal preferences, we're called to humbly defer to them, knowing they'll give an account to God, as will we.

Lesson 4: Develop the spiritual disciplines.

High school sports programs always have a category of partici-
pants known as benchwarmers. Maybe you were one of them. It's
not a fun position to "play." Sometimes kids are benchwarmers
because, frankly, they just lack the physical ability to play at a
competitive level. But much of the time they're on the bench because they've never put in the effort necessary to improve. They
didn't want to spend the time and energy nor experience the pain
necessary to develop their skills.

But their teammates who got a lot of playing time? They displayed the opposite. They showed up early to practice and stayed
late. They worked on their skills during evenings and weekends.
They practiced and practiced and practiced some more. And their
effort paid off. Because getting better at the game was important
to them. They didn't want to be a benchwarmer.

The price we pay to accomplish various things in life brings
us to another lesson to live: Develop the spiritual disciplines.
These are the spiritual equivalent of push-ups, sit-ups, and laps.
The importance of these disciplines is revealed in Scripture and
emphasized by generation upon generation of faithful Christians.

We don't want to get all wrapped up in any discussion of
"which spiritual disciplines are the best spiritual disciplines," so
why don't we just stick with the ones that have stood the test of
time: Prayer. Studying God's Word. Meditating on God's Word.
Fasting. Memorizing God's Word. Silence.

If these ideas sound odd to you, or faintly "cult-like," you may
have lost touch with the rich heritage of the Christian faith. So
here's the challenge: Read up a bit on these disciplines, and then
start trying them. Don't expect to do a thousand "sit-ups" the
very first time, but practice. Slowly. Consistently.

One word of warning: There's nothing "magical" in any of
these disciplines. Just like doing lots of sit-ups won't automati-
cally make you a great athlete, fasting won't make you a great

Christian. The whole point of each of these disciplines is to help you focus on your relationship with the living God first and with the body of Christ second. Don't let them isolate you from the body of Christ, but rather develop them for the glory of God and the benefit of the body of Christ.

Lesson 5: Encourage accountability.

If you're to "get involved" and "practice the spiritual disciplines," then you're necessarily going to be developing spiritual relationships characterized by transparency. And that transparency will lead to vulnerability, which is reflected in humility. And that humility will allow for accountability.

This kind of accountability—the kind that benefits both individuals and the body of Christ—happens in at least two places. The first place is in personal relationships. Everyone should have at least one person with whom they can share their deep struggles, cry, express their fears and doubts, and seek advice, counsel, and comfort. A mentor. A friend. Someone who loves Jesus, has your best interests in view, and won't be afraid to shoot straight with you even if it means hurting your feelings a little.

The second place is in the life of the local church. Listen to the sermon not to be entertained but to be challenged and changed. Pray that through the worship and preaching you'll be more than informed—you'll be transformed. And listen for what the Lord is saying to *you* through the singing, teaching, and sharing, not what you think He should be saying to others in the church.

This is a huge part of spiritual growth. Every Christian and every local church needs to commit to accountability—holding every member accountable for behavior that befits the body of Christ. Remember the words of the author of Hebrews: "Let us consider how to stimulate one another to love and good deeds, not forsaking our own assembling together, as is the habit of some, but encouraging one another; and all the more as you see the day drawing near" (Hebrews 10:24–25 NASB).

When that "day" draws near, and the Lord returns to reward us for the lives we lived in obedience to Him, we'll know it was all worth it.

Snapshot of History

The doctrines of the church and the Christian life have gone through many changes and developments throughout the Patristic (100–500), Medieval (500–1500), Protestant (1500–1700), and Modern (1700–Present) eras. The following chart summarizes these developments.[19]

THE CHURCH AND THE SPIRITUAL LIFE THROUGH THE AGES

Patristic Period (100–500)	Medieval Period (500–1500)	Protestant Period (1500–1700)	Modern Period (1700–Present)
• Church regarded as spiritual (invisible) and physical (visible), though the visible gradually was emphasized (100–500) • Ignatius of Antioch first uses "catholic" to describe the worldwide church (c. 110) • Threat of heresy leads to strengthening the role of the single bishop (100–500) • Baptism gradually regarded as the means of saving grace (200–400) • Council of Constantinople (381) defines orthodox ecclesiology as "one, holy, catholic, and apostolic" • Gradual rise of Roman claims of worldwide papal authority (250–500)	• Roman Catholic Church exerts authority in the West, pushing for uniformity in doctrine, practice, and organization (500–1500) • The Eastern Orthodox and Roman Catholic Churches officially split, partly over Rome's claims of papal supremacy (1050) • Church organization and power increase with greater role for the church in secular matters (500–1500) • Transubstantiation becomes the official dogma of Roman Catholicism (1215) • System of seven sacraments becomes dogma (1439) • Dissenting voices (e.g., Wycliffe and Hus) are silenced (1300–1500)	• Martin Luther challenges papal authority and sparks the Reformation against illegitimate developments in theology and practice (1517) • The Protestant Reformation results in governance changes, leading to episcopal, presbyterian, and congregational church traditions (1550–1700) • The church fragments into numerous competing denominations, each with its own governance and with some unique doctrines and practices (1500–1700) • Council of Trent solidifies Roman Catholic dogma against Protestant ecclesiology (1545–1563)	• The rise of modern evangelicalism leads to expansion of missions and evangelism (1700–Present) • Controversy over liberal developments in doctrine lead to mainline denominational splits and new denominations and independent churches (1850–1950) • The modern ecumenical movement seeks to establish doctrinal, liturgical, and even organizational unity among diverse churches and denominations (1900–Present) • Diverse and competing models of sanctification proliferate (1700–Present)

SIX

The World to Come—
Future Things and Eternal Hope

But when this present fashion of things passes away, and man has been renewed, and flourishes in an incorruptible state, so as to preclude the possibility of becoming old, then there shall be the new heaven and the new earth, in which the new man shall remain continually, always holding fresh converse with God.[1]

—Irenaeus of Lyons (c. 180)

Can all the saints put together fully measure the greatness of the promise of the Second Advent? This means infinite felicity for saints. What else has he promised? Why, that because he lives we shall live also. We shall possess an immortality of bliss for our souls; we shall enjoy also a resurrection for our bodies; we shall reign with Christ; we shall be glorified at his right hand.[2]

—Charles H. Spurgeon (c. 1890)

In Short . . .

With a few memorable exceptions, many Christians aren't all that concerned about the details of the end times (aka "eschatology").

Yes, they believe Jesus is coming back. All our churches proclaim this truth from the pulpit, write it in their doctrinal statements, or confess it in their songs, hymns, or liturgies! But beyond that major affirmation of Christ's return, most Christians aren't quite sure how details of what will happen in the future actually affect how they think about God, themselves, salvation, or the world around them. And many make little or no connection between coming events and their own lives.

But if we can climb out of the nooks and crannies of eschatology to a vantage point that allows us a bird's-eye view, we'll get a different perspective. Instead of being tangled in the twisted underbrush of confusing controversies and tripping over the strewn debris of centuries-old doctrinal battles, we'll observe a beautiful panoramic vista. This new point of view reveals one major theme that puts all the details in their proper place: *hope*.

Eschatology: It's All About Hope

Shakespeare wrote, "The miserable have no other medicine // But only hope."[3] Had he lived in the twenty-first century, he would not have penned these words. Today we have numerous medicines to treat misery—from antidepressants to herbal remedies. In many respects, the "treatment" of human hopelessness has been removed from the Christian faith and placed in the realm of secular science.

As Christians have neglected future hope as a major theme of their faith story, they've also lost the healing power of hope. Simply put, hope in the future has real value in the present. Not merely a general hope that things will be better "in the sweet by and by" (a reference to heaven in an old hymn), but the authentic Christian hope that has therapeutic value because its hope is *concrete*. Specific promises. Particular expectations. Detailed descriptions. These things paint a picture that looks more like the sharp lines of a Rembrandt than the blurry impressions of a Monet.

FALSE SOURCES OF HOPE	TRUE SOURCES OF HOPE
1. Human Means of Success (Psalm 33:17)	1. God the Father (Psalm 62:5)
2. Personal Strength (Proverbs 11:7)	2. God the Son (1 Timothy 1:1)
3. The Uncertainty of Riches (1 Timothy 6:17)	3. God the Spirit (Romans 5:5)
4. False Revelations (Ezekiel 13:6)	4. Remembrance of God's Faithfulness (Lamentations 3:21–23)
5. Wrong Interpretations (John 5:45)	5. Perseverance in Suffering (Romans 5:3–4)
	6. The Encouragement of Scripture (Romans 15:4)

Why does knowledge of the details of God's coming future have healing and motivating power for us today? Because hope lifts our hearts and minds from our present difficult circumstances. It gives us a glimpse of a glorious future. It helps us look upward and outward at a better life rather than drawing us downward and inward to obsess over our painful and pitiful experiences. The more we recognize here and now the brevity and uncertainty of the present time compared to the eternal weight of glory in the future, the more our attitudes and actions in the present will be permanently affected.

Think back to your brief days in grade school, on what you worried about and obsessed over: the petty squabbles among friends whose names you don't even remember, the problems that seemed so insurmountable at the time, and the fears that now seem so foolish. If you had only known then that most of those "huge problems" were foolish child's play! The same is true when we compare our present earthly lives and the life of the world to come.

The great thing is that God actually *does* inform us of the future realities in a way that can transform our minds today, lifting our heads from the temporal darkness and letting us catch an energizing glimpse of eternity's never-ending light.

Despite the numerous debates about details of end-times events, all Christians are united in the clear, unambiguous content of Christian hope. Scripture describes some key promises to which all believers have looked forward for generations.

The Promise of Christ's Return

After His resurrection and giving the disciples a forty-day crash course on the kingdom of God (Acts 1:3), Jesus ascended into heaven as the disciples watched (1:9). While they kept staring into the clouds, two angels appeared to them and said, "Men of Galilee, why do you stand looking into the sky? This Jesus, who has been taken up from you into heaven, will come in just the same way as you have watched Him go into heaven" (1:11 NASB). With those words, the Christian hope of Christ's return was secure.

At the end of his life of preaching that faith and hope of the person and work of Christ, the apostle Peter still clung to the promise of his Lord's return. He urged his own disciples, "Fix your hope completely on the grace to be brought to you at the revelation of Jesus Christ" (1 Peter 1:13 NASB). And Paul too exhorted his younger understudy Titus to spend his life "looking for the blessed hope and the appearing of the glory of our great God and Savior, Christ Jesus" (Titus 2:13 NASB).

The promise of Jesus' future, physical, bodily return stands at the center of several interconnected promises woven into the coming of the King. Though these promises relate to earthshaking events and revolutionary experiences for God's people, we must never lose sight of the fact that without the central promise of Christ's return, none of them would be possible. Just as a river of fresh water nourishes parched land when the floodgates of a dam are opened, the return of Christ will unleash a deluge of promised blessings that will transform this world and everything in it.

The Promise of Resurrection and Glory

The yearning for the resurrection of the body flies like a banner over Christian hope. Yet a clear understanding of resurrection hope has waned over the course of Christian history. It's often replaced by an undefinable notion of just dying and going to some ethereal place of white light and bright clouds. Yet the biblical hope is a *physical* hope as much as it's a spiritual hope. It involves bodily resurrection, not just spiritual release to heaven.

So crucial is the bodily resurrection to the content of Christian faith that Paul cited it as the reason for his suffering persecution at the hands of his opponents (Acts 26:6–9). In fact, all creation itself longs for the day when the saints will be resurrected, because the resurrection of believers ushers in the "resurrection" of creation from bondage to corruption (Romans 8:20–25).

When we speak of bodily resurrection, we mean much more than a return to these same mortal, weak, decrepit bodies. Rather, we look forward to both resurrection *and glorification*. Our bodies will be upgraded to an immortal, incorruptible, glorious state (1 Corinthians 15:53–54). Paul wrote that believers have Christ within them,

> "We shall therefore rise again, our souls being once more united with our bodies, now made incorruptible and having put off corruption. . . . Those who have done good will shine forth as the sun with the angels into life eternal, with our Lord Jesus Christ, ever seeing Him and being in His sight and deriving unceasing joy from Him, praising Him with the Father and the Holy Spirit throughout the limitless ages of ages."[4]
>
> John of Damascus (c. 740)

who is "the hope of glory" (Colossians 1:27). In fact, when Christ returns, He'll "transform the body of our humble state into conformity with the body of His glory" (Philippians 3:21 NASB). And the Spirit of God, through His empowering presence, has already begun His work of transformation in the life of the believer. Paul wrote, "We all, with unveiled face, beholding as in a mirror the glory of the Lord, are being transformed into the same image from glory to glory, just as from the Lord, the Spirit" (2 Corinthians 3:18 NASB).

In this present mortal life, even the saintliest Christian struggles against sin. Our victories in the spiritual battle against temptation can turn in a brief moment of weakness. Like the apostle Paul himself, many of us have cried out in agony over our conflict with sin: "Wretched man [or woman] that I am! Who will deliver me from this body of death?" (Romans 7:24). But with the coming of Christ, the resurrection of our bodies, and our glorification, God will finally grant us permanent triumph over temptation and sin.

Galatians 5:5 says, "For through the Spirit, by faith, we ourselves eagerly wait for the hope of righteousness." In the glorious future mapped out for us, we won't find even a smudge or speck of unrighteousness, for we ourselves will be conformed to the righteousness of Christ (Philippians 3:21). So in the moment-by-moment conflict against wickedness in our lives, we must continue to persevere as we look up in hope for the heavenly "air support" that will one day provide decisive victory on behalf of the righteousness of God.

The Promise of the Eternal Kingdom

The coming of Christ and the resurrection of the body will coincide with the advent of the fullness of God's eternal kingdom. The kingdom of God has always been a subject of believers' prayers (Matthew 6:10). Though the sin, injustice, and suffering of this present world can be eased somewhat when believers live out the values and virtues of the kingdom in this life, the ultimate triumph of good over evil, peace over calamity, and righteousness over wickedness awaits the coming of the promised Messiah and King, Jesus (Isaiah 9:7; Daniel 6:26). By preaching the "kingdom" of God, the church preaches not merely its own testimony of living lives worthy of our King in the present age but also our hope in the certain fact of God's universal and eternal reign through Jesus Christ (Acts 28:20–31).

What a bold hope in the midst of corrupt politicians, bankrupt political philosophies, failed nations, tyrannical dictators, military coups, and unstable governments! None of these earthly instruments has ever or could ever satisfy the deep inner longings of all nations, societies, cultures, and peoples: peace, justice, security, prosperity. Only the kingdom of God breaking into this world can establish heaven's virtues and values on earth (Daniel 7:27). And with that coming eternal kingdom, we will realize fully the gift of eternal life that has only begun to be experienced in this life.

Yes, in a real sense eternal life began the moment we believed in Jesus Christ. The apostle John wrote, "God has given us eternal life, and this life is in his Son" (1 John 5:11 NIV). Therefore, eternal life is something we presently *have* (5:13). When Christ returns, however, establishing His righteous kingdom and resurrecting believers in their glorious bodies, He will bestow upon us that for which we have been eagerly hoping: *eternal life*. Titus 1:2 describes "the hope of eternal life, which God, who cannot lie, promised long ages ago" (NASB).

Having been justified in the past when we believed, we now look forward to eternal life with unwavering hope (Titus 3:7). Though this eternal life will be fully experienced "in the age to come" (Luke 18:30), believers in Christ can already experience life "abundantly" in this age through the power of the Holy Spirit (John 10:10).

Eschatology: It's All About Him

All these promises of hope center on the Lord Jesus Christ, specifically in relation to His second coming. In fact, 1 Timothy 1:1 says Christ Jesus *is* our hope. He is, as it were, "hope incarnate." When we despair, we look to Him. When we grieve, we find strength in Him. When we lose heart, we long for His coming. In the final analysis, standing at the center of Christian hope is not a promise, a principle, or even a prophecy but a *Person*—the Lord Jesus Christ.

The book of Revelation, written explicitly to reveal to God's people "the things which must soon take place" (1:1) confirms the truth that Jesus Christ himself is the great theme of the Bible's prophecies and therefore of eschatology itself. The angel who showed the prophetic visions to John said, "The testimony of Jesus is the spirit of prophecy" (19:10). Like a master key that can be used to unlock any door of a building, the teaching about Jesus Christ in His person and work in His first and second coming unlocks the deepest mysteries of the Bible.

The Scriptures not only point to Christ's first coming as the suffering servant (Luke 24:27; Acts 17:2–3; Romans 1:1–4; 1 Corinthians 15:1–5), but they point beyond our own age to the endless era of righteousness that will accompany Christ's restoration of all things. In *the past* Christ fulfilled the sufferings declared beforehand by the prophets of the Old Testament (for example, Psalm 22; Isaiah 53; Zechariah 12:10). The same holy prophets of old spoke about *the future* restoration of all things that will come when He returns (Acts 3:18–21).

In light of both the predicted past and future, during the *present* we are to continue proclaiming God's call to salvation by grace through faith in the person and work of Jesus Christ (Ephesians 2:8–9). Therefore, past, present, and future all center on the Lord

"In the consummation of the world, Christ shall appear to judge, and shall raise up all the dead, and shall give unto the godly and elect eternal life and everlasting joys; but ungodly men and the devils shall he condemn unto endless torments."[5]

The Augsburg Confession (1530)

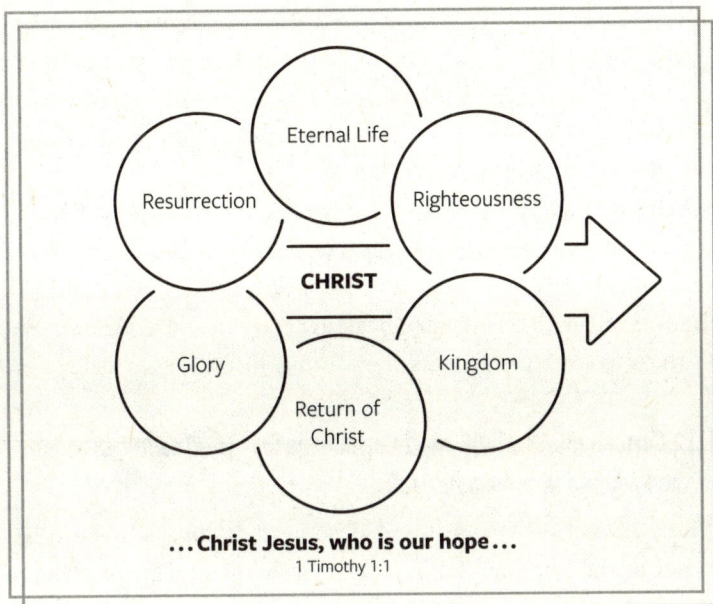

...Christ Jesus, who is our hope...
1 Timothy 1:1

Jesus Christ. Eschatology is all about hope, but it's also all about Him. The attitude-altering, life-changing hope of the Christian faith finds its center and source in none other than "Christ Jesus, who is our hope" (1 Timothy 1:1 NASB). In light of this truth, we must always keep Christ, our true hope, close to our hearts and at the forefront of our minds.

Passages to Ponder

In Isaiah 46:9–10, God declared:

> I am God, and there is no other;
> I am God, and there is no one like Me,
> Declaring the end from the beginning,
> And from ancient times things which have not been done,
> Saying, "My purpose will be established,
> And I will accomplish all My good pleasure." (NASB)

The Scriptures—all God-inspired—have a lot to say about the future (Isaiah 46:9–10). Yet many of the biblical prophecies about coming events have already been fulfilled, in the past, leaving us a permanent record not only of God's ability to *foresee* the future but His willingness to *foretell* it.

The following passages of Scripture—some from the Old Testament, some from the New—represent some of the most central texts that touch on a variety of eschatological issues. By familiarizing yourself with them, you'll be better equipped to navigate some of the often turbulent waters of end-times discussions and debates.

(1) 1 Corinthians 15:12–58 and 2 Corinthians 5:1–10—The Resurrection of the Body and Intermediate State

The resurrection of our physical bodies has always been a core belief of the Christian faith. In 1 Corinthians 15, Paul challenges those who would deny, downplay, spiritualize, or marginalize the doctrine of our bodily resurrection. Regardless of the different ways readers have understood the *number* and *order* of stages of resurrection in 1 Corinthians 15:20–28, all believe in the *reality* of bodily resurrection at Christ's return, leading to the ultimate defeat of death itself.

After highlighting practical arguments in support of the resurrection hope (15:29–35), Paul gives us a general picture of the nature of our resurrection bodies (15:36–49). Like a seed, our present "natural body" will be planted in the ground (or turned to ash if cremated). But the "spiritual body" will be raised immortal and imperishable.

The contrasts between "natural" and "spiritual" highlight the superior *quality* and *power* of the new resurrection bodies, not the substance from which our bodies will be composed. We won't be floating ghosts or see-through spirits. Instead, we'll be like Jesus. As we shared in the mortal, weak, and corruptible body inherited from Adam, we will also share in the immortal, powerful, and incorruptible body inherited through Christ (15:46–49). Just as Christ's body came forth from the tomb in a glorified state, believers' resurrected bodies will be material bodies uniquely designed for existence in both the spiritual and physical realms.

Commentator F. F. Bruce points out that "the present body is animated by 'soul' and is therefore mortal; the resurrection body is animated entirely by immortal and life-giving spirit, and is therefore called a spiritual body."[6]

One of the most frequently asked questions regarding future things is *What if we die prior to Christ's return?* This is the basic question answered in the realm of "personal eschatology"—that is, what happens to us after our physical death but prior to our bodily resurrection?

In 2 Corinthians 5:1–5, Paul turns our attention away from the "light momentary affliction" of the present life toward the "eternal weight of glory" that awaits us in the next (2 Corinthians 4:17). Though the *timing* of this transition is unknown, the *fact* is certain. Paul says in 2 Corinthians 5:1, "For we know [*certainty!*] that if the tent that is our earthly home is destroyed, we have [*certainty!*] a building from God." Because our resurrection is guaranteed by the indwelling Holy Spirit (5:5), Paul can speak of our resurrection body as *already* in our possession.

Surely, Paul hoped Christ would return in his own day and he wouldn't have to experience physical death before putting on his new heavenly body (1 Corinthians 15:51–53). But he knew that even if he were to die before the resurrection of believers, the promise of future resurrection was secure. He also knew that during the intervening period between death and resurrection, he'd be "away from the body" but "at home with the Lord" (2 Corinthians 5:8). In fact, the moment he departed this world by physical death, his soul would "be with Christ" until his bodily resurrection (Philippians 1:23).

We shouldn't be misled about Paul's primary hope, however. He wasn't teaching that the ultimate goal of Christian salvation

PRESENT REALITY VERSUS FUTURE HOPE
IN 2 CORINTHIANS 5

Verse	Present Reality	Future Hope
5:1	Our earthly tent is being destroyed.	We are certain of our eternal building.
5:2	We groan in our present tent.	We long for our heavenly home.
5:3	We don't want to be naked.	We want to be clothed with our eternal dwelling.
5:4	We groan in our mortality.	We long to be, and will be, clothed with life.
5:6	We are at home in the body.	We want to be with the Lord.
5:7	We now walk by faith.	We will one day walk by sight.

is simply to die and go to heaven—that is, to escape the physical body and dwell as a disembodied spirit eternally with Christ in some bright, misty spiritual realm. We don't want to be "unclothed," that is, left without a body, but "further clothed" with our new resurrection body (2 Corinthians 5:4). Even better would be to have our mortal bodies "swallowed up by life" without ever having to experience the temporary separation of physical death (5:4).

Most believers will experience physical death and an intermediate spiritual sojourn with Christ prior to their physical resurrection. Those believers alive at the time of the resurrection won't undergo physical death but a sudden transformation from their mortal bodies to immortal bodies. Regardless of which group we'll be in as believers in Christ, we are to strive to please Him, walking always by faith, not by sight (5:7–9).

(2) Romans 8:18–25—The Restoration of All Creation

Chances are Romans 8 wouldn't appear on most Christians' list of "Top Ten Important End-Times Passages." One could argue, however, that the handful of verses we read in Romans 8:18–25 present the crux of the Bible's teaching on creation, the fall, redemption, and ultimate personal and cosmic restoration.

Paul begins this passage by turning our attention away from the sufferings of this present world to the hope of the coming restoration (8:18). This ultimate Christian hope is much bigger than just dying and going to heaven. Rather, our hope involves a complete restoration of all creation (8:19). The whole created realm—things visible and invisible, physical and spiritual—has been subjected to the bondage of corruption since the day of the fall of Adam and Eve (Genesis 3). And just as our physical bodies will one day be resurrected and glorified, the whole cosmos will be restored and renewed (Romans 8:21–23). Peter called this coming restoration "times of refreshing" that will accompany the return of Christ (Acts 3:20). Jesus himself called it "the new world, when the Son of Man will sit on his glorious throne" (Matthew 19:28).

Romans 8:18–25 is vital for our understanding of the future because it conjoins the physical resurrection of believers and the restoration of creation. But it also expresses the important truth that we are presently stuck in the middle between God's promise of a better world and the fulfillment of that promise. This means the frustration we feel with the "thorns and thistles" of this fallen world is normal (Genesis 3:17–19). Believers especially know things aren't supposed to be like this. We long for a time when the weeds will be pulled, the thorns crushed, and the thistles clipped. We groan inwardly for our redemption, the resurrection of our bodies, and the renewal of creation (Romans 8).

While we try to keep our balance in this time between the fall and the redemption, mediocre to poor is sometimes all we can expect from this life. But don't get cynical. Don't become jaded. Through His death and resurrection, Jesus has overcome the world. And when He returns to reign, His blessings will drive out the curse, and the thorns and thistles will be no more.

PASSAGES TO MASTER AND MEMORIZE

Isaiah 65:17	Romans 8:18–23
Jeremiah 31:33–34	1 Corinthians 15:51–53
Ezekiel 37:26–27	2 Corinthians 5:10
Daniel 12:2–3	1 Thessalonians 4:13–18
Joel 2:30–32	2 Thessalonians 2:7–8
Zechariah 12:10	2 Peter 3:13–14
Matthew 24:36	Revelation 21:1–5
Acts 1:7–9	

Note: Not all of these passages are discussed in the text, but they'll all help you master the doctrine of the end times.

(3) Joel 1–3—The Day of the Lord

When God entered into a covenant with Israel at Mount Sinai, He didn't leave the Israelites with a vague warning of abstract judgment for their unfaithfulness to the covenant. Rather, He spelled out the kinds of disciplinary judgments that would come for their disobedience (Deuteronomy 28:15–68). Among these details, He warned of an invading army that would conquer them and carry them off into exile (28:49–51).

The promises of blessing and cursing set the stage for the vivid imagery of the book of Joel, written perhaps five hundred years before the birth of Christ. In the seventy-five verses packed into this short prophecy of imminent judgment, God calls the people of Judah and Jerusalem to repent because the "day of the Lord" is near (Joel 1:15). He begins by pointing out a devastating plague of locusts—a sure sign that the nation was beginning to experience the curses for covenant unfaithfulness (Deuteronomy 28:38).

Without repentance, even greater judgments would come: an invasion of a massive foreign army and the dreaded day of the Lord (Joel 2:1–11).

Yet in the midst of this harsh prophecy of literal doom and gloom, the Lord God reminds the people of His love, mercy, and grace (2:12–13). If they will return to the Lord, He will instantly turn away the judgment poised against His people and judge their enemies instead (2:20). With this promise of restoration in response to their repentance, the Lord also promises to send His Holy Spirit in a new way, ushering in a new era of blessing unparalleled in their history (2:28–29).

The basic message of Joel is simple: With repentance, judgment gives way to blessing. And in the future, *ultimate* judgment will usher in *ultimate* blessing. Yet when was that prophecy of judgment, repentance, and blessing supposed to be fulfilled? Does it refer to events in the past? To repeated events throughout history? Have some parts of the book of Joel been fulfilled (or partly fulfilled) while other parts await future fulfillment? Or is the entire prophecy reserved for a future tribulation associated with the return of Christ?

Much debate centers on when the pouring out of the Spirit described in Joel 2:28–32 did or will occur. Many see the pouring out of the Spirit at Pentecost (Acts 2) as a direct and complete fulfillment of this prophecy, while others see it as a partial fulfillment or at least foreshadowing of a future end-times fulfillment.[7] Peter's quotation of the Joel 2 passage in his first evangelistic message at Pentecost demonstrates some kind of connection between the two, and most commentators—regardless of their disagreements on other matters related to eschatology—agree that since the pouring out of the Spirit at Pentecost, we're living in what the Bible considers "the last days."[8] The final judgments associated with the return of Christ and the ultimate day of the Lord could begin to unfold in our own generation.

(4) Daniel 2, 7, 9–12—The End of the Wicked Rulers

You've probably never seen a child's Bible story book that didn't include the story of "Daniel in the Lions' Den," right beside the story of "Jonah and the Big Fish." Besides providing one of the best-known Bible stories, the book of Daniel also supplies us with the popular saying "He saw the writing on the wall" (see Daniel 5:5). And many churchgoers have some recollection of Daniel's three friends Shadrach, Meshach and Abednego surviving a trial of faith in a fiery furnace (Daniel 3:1–30).

Beyond these well-known stories, the book of Daniel contains numerous pillars that support a biblical doctrine of the end times. In fact, it would be impossible to exaggerate its role in the study of eschatology. Those who have studied end-times prophecy throughout history have drawn extensively on this book as a key to understanding the Bible's timetable for future events. This is what we might expect when it comes to interpreting stunning symbolic visions that left even their original witnesses dazed and confused (Daniel 8:15, 27).

In Daniel 2, the Babylonian king Nebuchadnezzar (who reigned about 605 to 562 BC) dreams of a giant statue with a head of gold, arms and torso of silver, midsection and thighs of bronze, legs of iron, and feet of iron mixed with clay (2:31–33). This entire statue was broken to pieces by a great stone, demolishing it once and for all (2:34–35). After this, the stone grew in greatness to fill the whole earth (2:35).

Daniel interpreted the dream as indicating four successive Gentile kingdoms, beginning with the Babylonians—the head of gold (2:36–38). Though the rest of the dream was yet future in Daniel's day, the other four parts of the statue were fulfilled throughout history: the empire of Medo-Persia, which succeeded Babylon (about 539–331 BC); the empire of Greece under Alexander the Great (331–63 BC); and then the Roman Empire, which lasted from 63 BC to about AD 476, well into the Christian era. The feet and ten toes of partly iron and partly clay have been understood as either the weakened nature of the Roman Empire in its closing centuries prior to the victory of Christendom or as a future condition of a revived "Roman Empire" composed of a fragile alliance of very different nations—some weak, some strong.

Though this identification of the four empires has been pretty well established among Christian interpreters, the exact meaning of the great stone that destroys the statue has been variously understood (2:44). Does it refer primarily to a yet future second coming of Christ as Judge and King to establish an earthly kingdom (a premillennial view)? Or is it mainly pointing to the establishment of the eternal kingdom of Christ when He took His throne at the ascension and established His spiritual kingdom, reigning through His church (an amillennial view)?

Or perhaps the image of the progressive growth of the stone from a small rock to a great mountain (2:35) indicates a post-millennial fulfillment, in which the kingdom of God will slowly but surely be established on earth as the gospel is proclaimed and the wicked kingdoms of this world are converted.[9] (These three different views of the millennium are explained under the following Passages to Ponder, number 9 on pages 265–269.)

The Four Beasts (Daniel 7)

Several years after Daniel interpreted Nebuchadnezzar's dream of the statue, the prophet had his own night vision portraying a succession of world empires that would end with the establishment of God's kingdom. Those interpreters who understood the four metals of the statue in Daniel 2 as the empires of Babylon,

Kingdoms	Daniel 2	Daniel 7
Babylonian Empire	Head of Gold	Lion
Media-Persian Empire	Torso and Arms of Silver	Bear
Greek Empire	Midriff and Thighs of Bronze	Leopard
Roman Empire	Legs of Iron	Monstrosity

Medo-Persia, Greece, and Rome almost always understood Daniel's vision of four beasts (Daniel 7) in the same way.

But Daniel's vision adds more detail regarding the final destruction of worldly rule and the establishment of the kingdom. Two end-times figures play a particularly prominent role—the "little horn" (Daniel 7:8) and the "son of man" (7:13). The first figure, represented by a little horn on the head of the fourth beast, had "eyes like the eyes of a man, and a mouth speaking great things" (Daniel 7:8). This is interpreted as a world ruler, growing out of the final empire, who will wage a war against the saints for a short time. But ultimately the coming kingdom of God will destroy this world ruler (7:21–22).

The second figure, represented as coming "with the clouds of heaven" to be presented before the throne of God, is called "one like a son of man" (Daniel 7:13). In Jesus' earthly ministry, He frequently identified himself as the "son of man" expected to come and receive the kingdom from God in the end times (Matthew 8:20; 9:6; 12:32, 40; 13:41; 16:27; 19:28; 24:30; 25:31; 26:64). This same title and image appear again in Revelation 1:13 and 14:14. So in Daniel 7, not only do we watch the unfolding drama of the nations of the world in their futile attempt at global domination without God, but we see the final outcome of this conflict: the defeat of ultimate wickedness by the power of the Son of Man.

The End of the Days (Daniel 9–12)

You could probably spend the rest of your life studying the details of Daniel 9–12 and still have countless unanswered questions. These chapters combine startling visions, meticulous prophecies, cryptic interpretations, and confusing details regarding things that will apparently come to full fruition "at the end of the days" (Daniel 12:13). Does this refer to the centuries leading up to the coming of the Messiah? Or to the end of the age before Christ's second coming? Or to both? Scholars are divided on the matter.

Regardless of how we understand these visions, the prophetic portions of Daniel point us to much more central truths. As mortal men and women tossed to and fro by the epochal events of human history, we can rest in the fact that God has all events—past, present, and future—in His hands. Perhaps instead of obsessing about when these things will be and how they will be accomplished, wise people should live hopeful lives because of the promise of the coming of Christ and our own future resurrection, trusting that God will take care of the details leading up to these climactic events according to His all-encompassing plan.

(5) Matthew 24–25 (Mark 13; Luke 21:5–38)—The Great Tribulation

In this speech—known as the Olivet Discourse because of the setting of His teaching on the slope of the Mount of Olives—Jesus answered His disciples' inquiry regarding the destruction of Jerusalem, the signs of the Messiah's coming in judgment, and the end of the age. The details of this prophecy have led to a number of interpretations among Bible-believing Christians.

Some see the elements of Matthew 24 as already (mostly) fulfilled (aka "partial preterism"). Christ's prophecy occurred during the Roman destruction of Jerusalem in the first century. Others believe most of the details await fulfillment in the years leading up to Christ's second coming (aka "futurism."). Still others understand that some of Jesus' prophetic words in the Olivet Discourse have a double referent to both first-century events and future events—some things already fulfilled while others await a future fulfillment. The "both/and" or "partial fulfillment" views appear to be the most common among Christians.

But this leads to a question: Why would Jesus provide information for both the first century and the end times? Advocates of the partial fulfillment perspective would point out that the disciples asked three questions that related both to events of their own lifetime and events that would be fulfilled in the distant future:

(1) the destruction of the temple, which occurred in AD 70; (2) the signs of Christ's second coming, which has not yet occurred; and (3) the end of the "age," which could refer to the end of the Old Testament age or the end of the New Testament age, with which the disciples were likely unfamiliar.

Further New Testament revelation would sort these things out as distinct events that would each be fulfilled on their own. Thus, "partial fulfillment" advocates attempt to sort them out in retrospect in the Olivet Discourse.

(6) 2 Thessalonians 2:1–12—The Man of Sin and the Day of the Lord

Makers of horror films aren't alone in their special interest in the antichrist figure, the number 666, and the end-times plot of some satanic dictator who tries to take over the world. These themes have formed a fabric of "pop theology" for nearly two thousand years, influencing art, poetry, literature, song, and theater—and filling the minds of ill-informed people with less-than-accurate ideas about the end times.

Though the title "Antichrist" doesn't appear in 2 Thessalonians 2, since the second century the "man of lawlessness" (2:3) has been identified with the "beast rising out of the sea" (Revelation 13:1–10); the "antichrist [who] is coming" of 1 John 2:18 and 4:3; and a future great apostasy—rebellion or abandonment of the faith—just preceding the second coming.[10]

This expectation of a future Antichrist, great apostasy, and deceiving signs and wonders has been a common view for much of the church's history. Some Christians, however, believe the events described in 2 Thessalonians 2 were already fulfilled in the years surrounding the destruction of the temple and the end of the age of Israel between the years AD 66 and 73. That is, though the prophecy was still future when Paul wrote 2 Thessalonians around the year AD 50, some today don't believe the passage points ahead to a future reign of an antichrist figure on this earth but to the events of the Roman destruction of the temple in the first century.

But if this refers to a yet future coming of an antichrist, as futurists believe, we see some basic characteristics of this ultimate enemy of God and His people:

- He will arrive prior to the coming of Christ and the day of the Lord (2 Thessalonians 2:1–2).
- He will be associated with a great apostasy or "rebellion" (2:3).
- He will be revealed as a man of sin or lawlessness (2:3).
- He will exalt himself against all religions and God himself (2:4).
- He will sit in the temple of God, claiming to be God (2:4).
- His coming is presently restrained by a mysterious restraining power (2:6–7).
- He will be destroyed by Jesus at His coming (2:8).
- He will be empowered by Satan to perform false signs and wonders (2:9).
- He will deceive the unsaved who rejected the truth (2:10).

(7) 1 Thessalonians 4:13–5:11—Resurrection and Rapture

The word *rapture* comes from the Latin word *rapere*, which means "to snatch." In the Latin translation of the New Testament, *rapere* translates the Greek word *harpazo*. This is the word used in 1 Thessalonians 4:17 for the end-times "catching up" to heaven of those who will have experienced bodily resurrection and transformation from a mortal to an immortal condition (see 1 Corinthians 15:51–52).

For Bible-believing Christians, the question shouldn't be *whether* the saved will be resurrected and caught up to meet the Lord in the air, because this is the straightforward teaching of the passage.

Disagreement really centers on *when* this will happen in relationship to a future "day of the Lord" or "tribulation" period. Some Christians don't believe in a prolonged future period of judgment on the earth prior to the coming of Christ. For them, then, the resurrection and rapture will obviously occur at the very moment Christ comes to judge the living and the dead.

Yet those who expect a distinct period of tribulation in the future leading up to the return of Christ have asked and answered the question of the timing of the rapture in several ways. In fact, there are five basic approaches to the timing of the rapture in relation to the future tribulation period:

Pretribulation Rapture ("pre-trib"): This view of the timing of the rapture described in 1 Thessalonians 4:17 teaches that before the future seven-year tribulation, true believers from the church age will be "caught up" from the earth to heaven and therefore be saved from God's wrath during the tribulation.

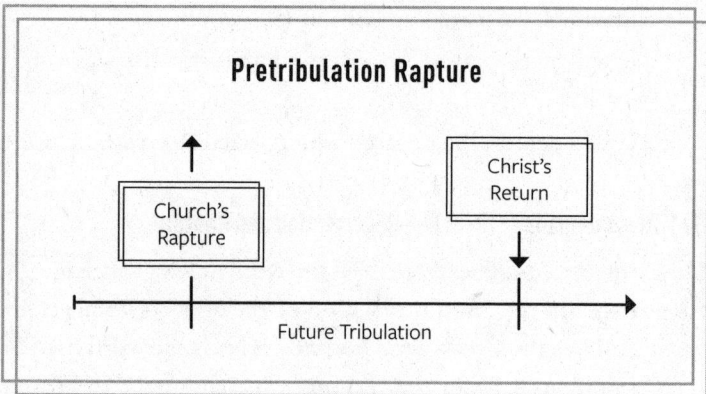

Pretribulation Rapture

Church's Rapture

Christ's Return

Future Tribulation

Midtribulation Rapture ("mid-trib"): This view of the timing of the rapture described in 1 Thessalonians 4:17 teaches that in the middle of the future seven-year tribulation, true believers will be "caught up" from the earth to heaven, saved from the direct wrath of God that comes during the last half of the tribulation.

Midtribulation Rapture

Church's Rapture

Christ's Return

Future Tribulation

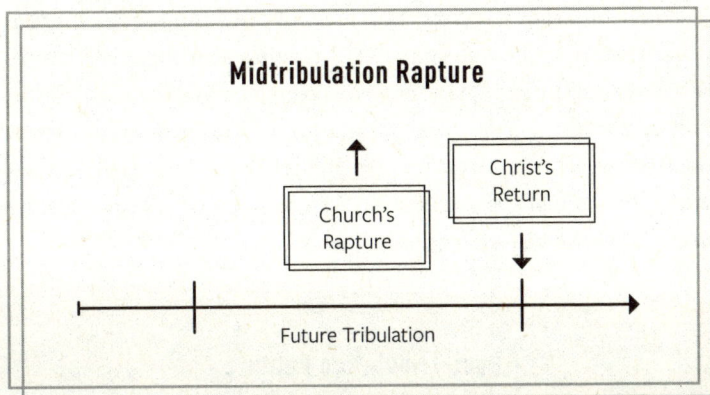

Pre-wrath Rapture: This view of the timing of the rapture described in 1 Thessalonians 4:17 teaches that before God pours out His direct wrath upon the earth, He will rescue His faithful saints. Supporters of this view sometimes limit the period of God's wrath to the seven "bowls of wrath" described in Revelation 15–16, but sometimes they include all events following the six seals in Revelation 6. Therefore, the Pre-wrath position places the rapture somewhere between the Midtribulation and Posttribulation perspectives.

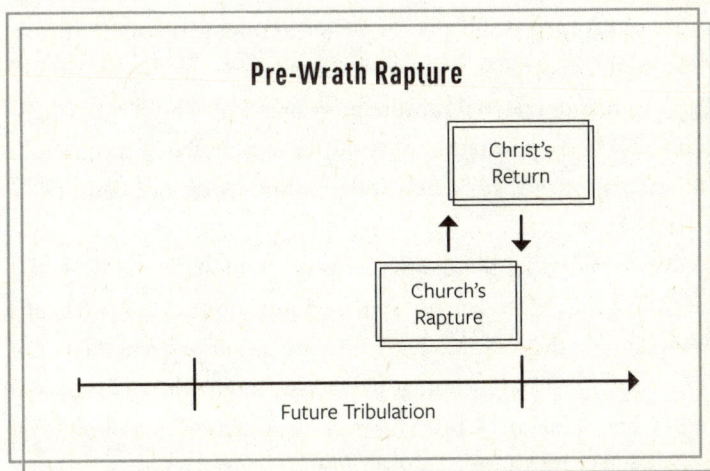

Pre-Wrath Rapture

Christ's Return

Church's Rapture

Future Tribulation

Posttribulation Rapture: This view of the timing of the rapture described in 1 Thessalonians 4:17 teaches that after the future seven-year tribulation, true believers who survived the persecution and martyrdom of the great tribulation will be "caught up" from the earth to heaven, to either immediately return to earth to reign with Christ during the millennium or to reign with Him over the earth from the heavenly sphere.

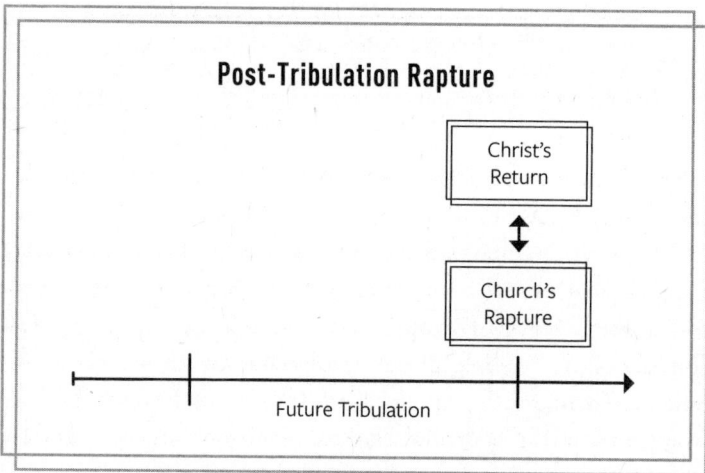

Post-Tribulation Rapture

Christ's Return

↕

Church's Rapture

Future Tribulation

Partial Rapture: This is the belief among futurists that only "spiritual Christians" will be raptured before the future tribulation. Sometimes partial rapture proponents also hold that Christians will have repeated opportunities to be rescued throughout the tribulation as they demonstrate faithfulness or overcome trials to their faith.

We shouldn't let these differences of opinion on just when the rapture of the church will occur in the future distract us from Paul's main point in the passage. The truths are meant to strengthen us in the face of death and encourage us when we mourn the loss of a loved one (1 Thessalonians 4:14). This passage assures us that our mortal bodies will be transformed into glorious immortal bodies—and that

Partial Rapture

```
        ↑              ↑         ┌──────────┐
                                 │ Christ's │
                                 │  Return  │
   ┌──────────┐  ┌──────────┐    └──────────┘
   │   Some   │  │   More   │         ↓
   │ Raptured │  │Raptured? │
   └──────────┘  └──────────┘
├──────────┼──────────────────────────┼──────────────▶
            Future Tribulation
```

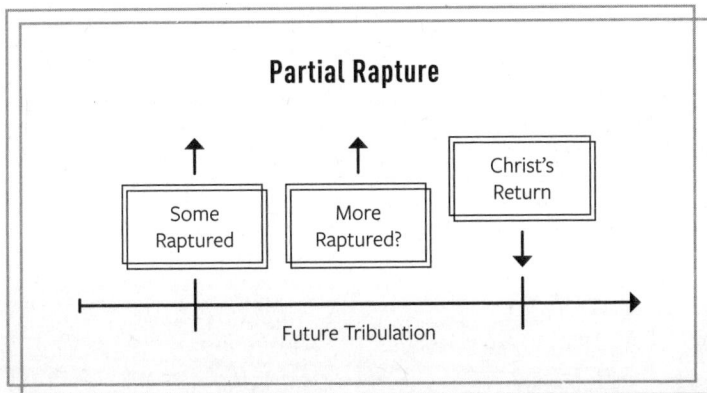

those alive at that moment won't even experience death (1 Thessalonians 4:16–17; 1 Corinthians 15:51–53; 2 Corinthians 5:4).

This amazing truth of our resurrection and transformation is to bring hope, encouragement, and sober living (1 Thessalonians 4:18; 5:4–8, 11). Scripture may not give us as many details about the resurrection and rapture as we'd like, or even enough to answer all our questions. Yet the Bible gives us enough for God's purposes—that we may be "equipped for every good work" (2 Timothy 3:17). Our hope of resurrection and eternal life with all the saints of every age should encourage us to look beyond death and see the glorious light in the coming age. And we should live sober lives as citizens of that coming kingdom rather than letting the wickedness of this age intoxicate us with its appealing but destructive power.

(8) 2 Peter 3:1–18—The Day of the Lord and the New Creation

Scoffers will come (2 Peter 3:3). This is a fact we need to get straight from the start. Motivated by their own sinful desires and not wanting to be held accountable to anyone but themselves, they will reject the idea that someday in the future they will be judged for their sins (3:4). In sharp contrast, the believer knows the same God who made the world and judged it with the flood in the past (3:5–6) will one day unleash judgment on the world in the future (3:8–10).

263

Genesis 1–8	Genesis 8– Revelation 20	Revelation 21–22
Original Heavens and earth	Current Heavens and earth	Future Heavens and earth

Judged by Flood	Judged by Fire
"The world at that time was destroyed, being flooded with water." (2 Peter 3:6 NASB)	"The present heavens and earth are being reserved for fire." (2 Peter 3:7 NASB)

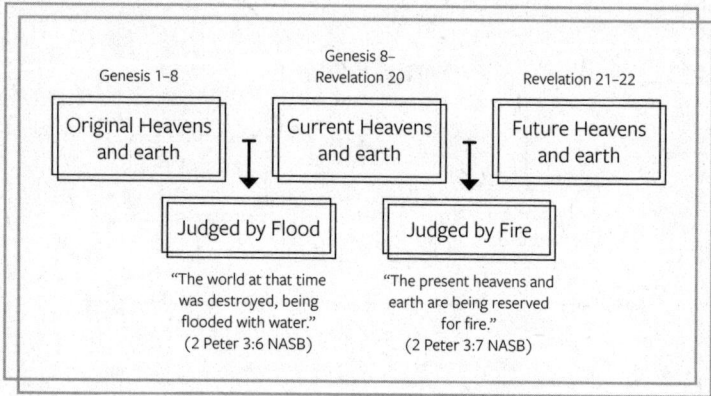

The coming judgment will destroy the present system, including all evil and sin. It will also include the destruction of demons and a razing of the world's geography. In fact, the fires pictured in 2 Peter 3, verses 10, 12, and 13 are best interpreted as purifying fires, likely drawing on metallurgical imagery of heating for purifying and strengthening (Malachi 3:2–4; 4:1–3).

Peter describes the new world established after the return of Christ and His judgment as "new heavens and a new earth, in which righteousness dwells" (2 Peter 3:13). Most commentators throughout history have believed the destruction envisioned in the language and imagery of 2 Peter 3 anticipates a destruction of the world system, its wickedness, and its godless religions and institutions, but not an annihilation of the universe itself. The "new heavens and new earth" would then refer to a completely new condition of this created realm, not a new creation out of nothing.[11] Just as the waters of the flood did not entirely destroy the earth but wiped the world clean and prepared the way for a new world for Noah and his family, the coming fire will purge and purify the present world, preparing the way for a creation liberated from wickedness (2 Peter 3:5–7; Romans 8:20–22).

Regardless of which view one takes, though, Peter's purpose in warning of coming judgment is not to thoroughly address the "where," "what," and "when" of the end times. Rather, his primary purpose is to encourage believers to live lives in holiness and godliness (2 Peter 3:11). We ought to wait eagerly for the coming of the new heavens and new earth, preaching the gospel and living exemplary lives for others (3:11–13). We should be found "without spot or blemish, and at peace" (3:14), avoiding the scoffing, ignorance, and unstable lives of false teachers (3:15–16). Instead of falling from a sure, stable faith and life, we must "grow in the grace and knowledge of our Lord and Savior Jesus Christ" (3:18).

(9) Revelation 19–22—The Return of Christ, the Millennium, and the New Creation

If the book of Revelation presents the dramatic climax of God's plan of redemption, then chapters 19–22 represent the *climax* of the climax. Orchestrated to call the wicked to repentance and punish those who persist in cursing their Creator, God's intensifying judgments remind us that one day He will vanquish all wickedness, and righteousness will enjoy ultimate victory.

The images of Revelation 19–22 stunningly portray this victory over God's enemies at the second coming of Christ (19:11–21). We also witness the binding of Satan (20:1–3), the reign of Christ with His faithful saints and martyrs (20:4–6), the final defeat of Satan, sinners, and death itself (20:7–15), and the ushering in of "a new heaven and a new earth" in which God will dwell among His people and from which all death, mourning, crying, pain, and sinfulness will be banished (21:1–8).

Finally, after an astounding tour of the magnificent destiny and breathtaking destination of redeemed humanity (21:9–22:5), the book ends with oaths, warnings, and a bold invitation: "The Spirit and the bride say, 'Come.' And let the one who hears say, 'Come.' And let the one who is thirsty come; let the one who wishes take the water of life without cost" (22:17 NASB).

Though Bible-believing Christians have understood the details of Revelation 19–22 in different ways, the big picture of God's final intervention in human history can be summed up in two simple words: *God wins*. All agree that Christ will one day return as Judge and King, but one of the most significant disagreements among Christians over end-times events is whether this second coming will occur *before* or *after* the thousand-year reign described in Revelation 20:1–6. The variety of viewpoints on this specific issue can be divided into three tendencies.

Some believe the events or conditions symbolized in Revelation 20:1–6 (the "millennium" or "thousand years") refer to the time between Christ's first and second coming and are therefore already being fulfilled either in heaven or through the church. This view is often called "amillennialism" because it doesn't involve the expectation of a literal one-thousand-year earthly reign in the future, the prefix "a-" meaning "no" or "not." According to the amillennial view, the "first resurrection" mentioned in Revelation 20:5 doesn't refer to the bodily resurrection of both the righteous and the wicked at the return of Christ (Daniel 12:2; John 5:28–29; Revelation 20:11–15). Rather, it refers to the spiritual resurrection of believers saved during the present age of the church's mission (Ephesians 2:5). They reign spiritually with Christ as members of the kingdom of God today—either the church here on earth or the reigning saints already victorious in heaven (Ephesians 2:6; Colossians 1:13).

In contrast to amillennialism, others believe the events described in Revelation 20:1–6 won't occur until after Christ physically returns to earth (Revelation 19:11–21). This view is often called "premillennialism" because Christ is expected to return prior to ("pre-") the fulfillment of an actual thousand-year ("millennial") reign on this earth. They generally understand the period of one thousand years to be a literal number—or at least close enough to one thousand years for the number to be an accurate approximation.

For premillennial readers, the events of Revelation 20 chronologically follow the vision of Christ's earthly return in Revelation.

Amillennialism

Christ's Ascension

General Resurrection

Present Age = Spiritual Kingdom

Spiritual Resurrection of Believers

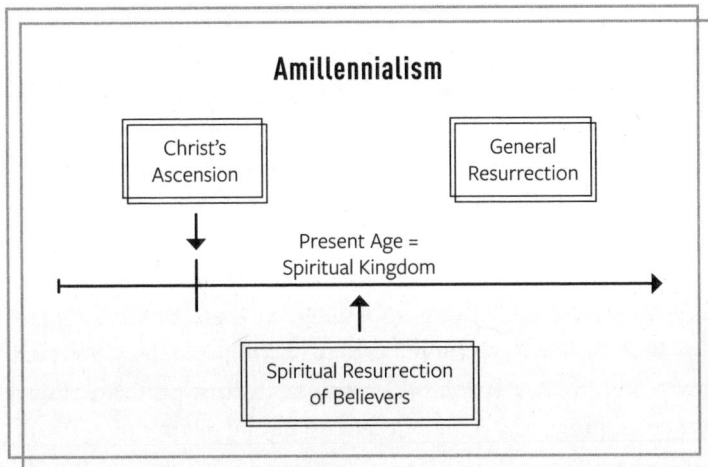

They believe that after the thousand-year reign of Christ over the earth, Satan will be released, a final rebellion will occur, and then the great white throne of judgment of the resurrected wicked from all of history will usher in the eternal state (Revelation 21–22).

A third group of Christians suggests the conditions described in Revelation 20:1–6 are capable of gradual realization in this

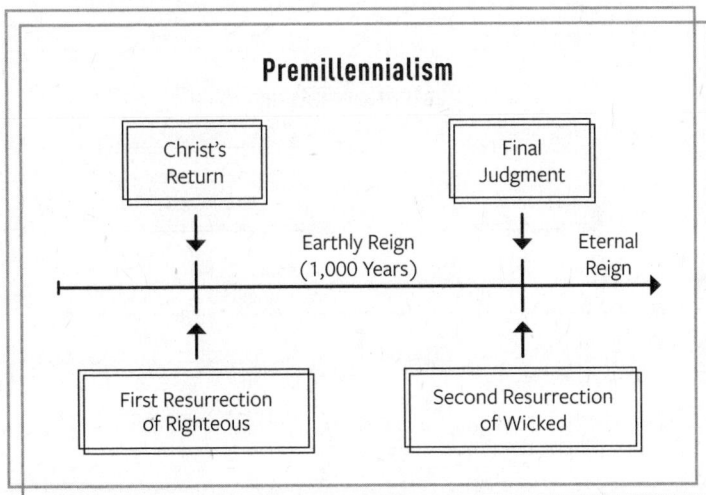

Premillennialism

Christ's Return

Final Judgment

Earthly Reign (1,000 Years)

Eternal Reign

First Resurrection of Righteous

Second Resurrection of Wicked

world through the efforts of God's people but prior to the return of Christ as Judge and King. This view is often called "postmillennialism" because it expects Christ to return after ("post") the world has enjoyed a long period of relative peace, justice, and prosperity through the success of the gospel throughout the world.

Like premillennialists, many postmillennialists see the vision of Christ's return in Revelation 19 and the vision of the binding of Satan and millennial reign in chapter 20 as chronologically sequential, the millennium following the event of Christ's victory described in Revelation. Leading postmillennialists, however, don't interpret Revelation 19 as a vision of Christ's future physical return as Judge and King but as a symbolic picture of spiritual conflict between Christ and His armies on the one side and the God-defying leaders of the earth on the other.

This conflict of spiritual warfare is believed to have begun at Christ's ascension and has been raging for centuries. The actual return of Christ, then, is symbolized by the great white throne (Revelation 20:11), when all humanity is resurrected to stand before God as Judge. After this the eternal state begins, when there will be no death or pain.

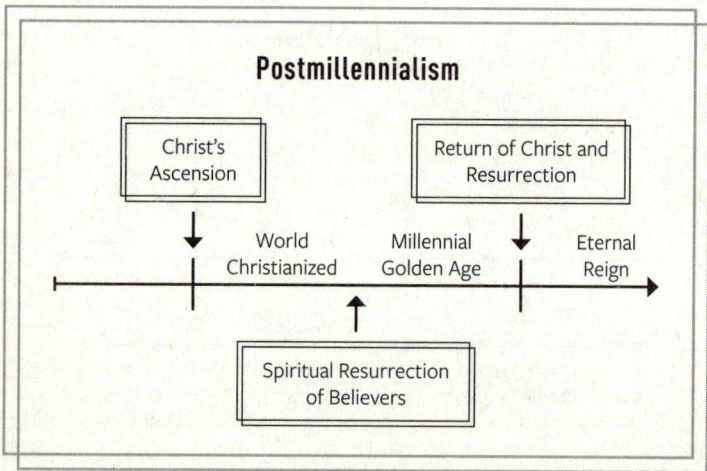

Postmillennialism

Christ's Ascension

Return of Christ and Resurrection

World Christianized — Millennial Golden Age — Eternal Reign

Spiritual Resurrection of Believers

Obviously, several distinctive ways of interpreting the visions of Revelation 19–22 prevail today. Though the differences in reading this section of Scripture are significant, we shouldn't forget the basic message of the book of Revelation. When the dust of our present and future spiritual and worldly warfare settles, Christ and His people will stand victorious forever. Sin, suffering, death, and the devil will all be obliterated. Righteousness and peace will reign forever and ever.

That's the story of Revelation 19–22, and that's an eternal aspect of our ultimate hope in Jesus.

Realities to Remember

Teachers often tell their students, "Even if you retain nothing else from this lesson, remember this." In any field of study, we find essential truths that form the foundation upon which we can build. Without these "first principles" or "axioms" firmly in place, the entire structure will be unstable.

The following realities function like foundational steel piers that hold up the study of the end times, "eschatology." If you commit these realities to memory, keeping them at the front and center of your attention, you'll save both yourself and your future students from distorted teaching.

Reality 1: Jesus Christ will return at an unknown hour.

As the disciples stared into heaven while their resurrected Lord ascended into a cloud, two angels in white robes stood beside them and said, "Men of Galilee, why do you stand looking into heaven? This Jesus, who was taken up from you into heaven, will come in the same way as you saw him go into heaven" (Acts 1:11). Since that moment, faithful followers of Jesus have kept one eye on the skies, so to speak—expecting and longing for the Lord's physical, bodily return. His second coming will bring both judgment and

269

blessing. For the wicked, judgment; for the righteous, a glorious kingdom (2 Thessalonians 1:5–10). His judgment will extend to both the living and the dead (2 Timothy 4:1; 1 Peter 4:5). Yet the kingdom Christ will establish will have no end (Revelation 11:15).

This expectation of the coming of Christ as Judge and King has been a central part of Christian faith from the very beginning. Yet the testimony of Scripture and all well-balanced believers has always been that no one can possibly know when Christ will return. No vision, dream, or clever calculation can change this simple truth. Though His coming is certain, its timing is uncertain (Matthew 24:36; 1 Thessalonians 5:1–2; 2 Peter 3:10; Revelation 3:3; 16:15).

That Christ is coming back one day is a firm, unbreakable promise. *When* He's coming back is completely unknown. False teachers presuming to have somehow figured out when Jesus will come back have always been wrong—and always will be.

Reality 2: God will redeem our bodies through physical resurrection.

For millennia, Jews and Christians have sought to preserve the identity of the remains of their deceased loved ones—burying them in a tomb or grave, marking their names or at least their family name, and memorializing them in some way. Even with cremation, families seek to do the same. Why? Because God has promised to redeem our mortal bodies from death and to crown them with immortality.

Yes, at some point the graves or tombs or urns will burst open, and even ashes will be gathered up. Whatever remains of the dead will be transformed and restored in glorious new bodies that share the characteristics of Jesus' own glorious body. Nothing of the old will remain where it was placed here on earth. All things will be made new. In both Jewish and Christian eschatology, those bits of dust and ashes have a future in God's plan of redemption.

Sadly, far too many Christians believe their bodies are mere shells that contain the "real" them, as if God never intended for us to have a physical presence, a bodily existence, a permanent means of interacting with the creation He fashioned for us. But the Bible's promises of bodily resurrection couldn't be more clear. It's a central hope of the Christian faith (Romans 8:23). When Christ returns, He "will transform our lowly body to be like his glorious body" (Philippians 3:21), no longer subject to mortality and death. Following the example of Jesus' own resurrection, ours will be a *transformation* of our present body, not a re-creation of an entirely different body.

But why would God bother restoring what's been laid to rest? Because by opening the graves and tombs and urns, then transforming our dead bodies into glorious, incorruptible bodies, God will declare once and for all, "O death, where is your victory?" (1 Corinthians 15:55). By snatching our mortal dust and ashes from the grave and transforming them into something eternal and glorious, God will demonstrate that Satan's attempt to destroy humanity failed. Humans, created with body and spirit in the image of God, will not only be rescued from death and restored to life but be crowned with glory and honor (Psalm 8:5).

Reality 3: God will keep His promise to eradicate sin, suffering, death, and the devil.

The majestic Christmas carol "Joy to the World" expresses the glorious hope of ultimate cosmic redemption this way:

> No more let sins and sorrows grow
> Nor thorns infest the ground:
> He comes to make His blessings flow
> Far as the curse is found.[12]

When Christ returns, He'll bring with Him power to liberate all creation from its bondage to corruption (Romans 8:21). As far as the dark stains of sin and death, suffering and pain, evil and tragedy have infected this universe, the cleansing blessings of Christ's life will wash away the darkness forever. Satan himself, that archenemy of humanity, will be ultimately defeated (Revelation 20:10). And though we struggle today with the excruciating pain of a dying world, one day that death will be vanquished by the invincible force of Life itself (21:4). In that restored creation, there will be no more death, mourning, crying, or pain. The terrible things that characterize this present world under the reign of sin and death will be eradicated under the reign of Christ (21:3).

Yet in the meantime it's so easy to let the darkness of this world drag us down, to let it rob our joy, hope, contentment, and patience. In times like that, remember that God isn't flaky, fickle, or feeble. Scripture assures us that all God's promises will be fulfilled (Numbers 23:19; Isaiah 46:10; Romans 11:29). God promised He'll fix what's been broken. The story that began with creation and the fall will be completed when God brings a restoration and renewal of creation. Though at present we don't see all things subject to the sovereign rule of God (Hebrews 2:8), when Christ returns, God will fulfill all His ancient plans and enduring promises through His Son (Acts 3:20–21).

Reality 4: We must all give an account of our lives before God.

Romans 8:1 says, "There is therefore now no condemnation for those who are in Christ Jesus." This truth should shine brightly in the minds of those who are "in Christ," piercing the darkness of doubt and driving out the shadows of despair. Those of us who enter into a relationship with Christ between His first and second coming have received His saving grace (Ephesians 2:8–9). But this doesn't mean God has given us a "license to kill." God warns us of His loving discipline in this life (1 Corinthians 11:32; Hebrews 12:5–11; Revelation 3:19).

Yet Scripture also points to a time in the future—at the return of Christ—when even believers will be subject to the judgment of Christ. Romans 14:10–12 says, "We will all stand before the judgment seat of God . . . So then each of us will give an account of himself to God." And Paul says, "We must all appear before the judgment seat of Christ, so that each one may receive what is due for what he has done in the body, whether good or evil" (2 Corinthians 5:10; compare 1 Corinthians 3:12–15).

Regardless of who we are, when we lived, how much we've had to contribute, or how little we've been given, the Lord expects us to live lives worthy of our calling in Christ (Ephesians 4:1). Though it's not the only motivation to live holy, blameless, and fruitful lives, we must never forget that one day we'll all give an account of our lives before God.

Reality 5: Christ's kingdom will endure forever and ever.

Our King, Jesus, is incorruptible in every sense of that word. Nobody can bribe Him, manipulate Him, or flatter Him. And because He's been raised in glory, never to die again, there will be no end to His kingdom of righteousness and peace (Isaiah 9:6–7). This is great news in a world filled with corrupt politicians, crooked preachers, and cruel parents. When Christ returns, the cycle of despotic rulers, declining societies, and deteriorating cultures will be replaced with a perfect kingdom in which righteousness dwells (2 Peter 3:13).

The Bible paints a picture of the future in which all things will be restored under the reign of Christ, the God-Man. In Him all things hold together (Colossians 1:17). He upholds the entire universe by His powerful word (Hebrews 1:3). And when He returns to reign on earth, this planet will be made the way it was always meant to be. Far from being a temporary reign after which things again fall apart, Christ's reign will be "forever and ever" (Revelation 11:15). His kingdom will have no end (Luke 1:33; compare Daniel 2:44).

Errors to Avoid

The main points of eschatology all Christians have believed for two thousand years function like guardrails on a very wide, multilane road. Though it's difficult to drive off the road with eschatology, it's not impossible. That is, Christians can have differing opinions on a lot of issues related to the end times before getting themselves into deep doctrinal trouble. But in this section, we want to look at several errors to avoid—danger signs warning us travelers when we're approaching hazards on the road.

Error 1: Heinous Heresy

The matters that constitute orthodox eschatology have always been limited to the anticipation of the physical return of Christ as Judge and King, the bodily resurrection of the dead unto either eternal life or eternal condemnation, and the restoration of creation in Christ's eternal kingdom. Even though the shape of orthodox eschatology is painted with such broad strokes, a couple of heresies have developed over the centuries. By "heresy" we mean knowingly, willfully, and persistently believing or teaching doctrines that directly contradict the central, core tenets of the Christian faith.

How could people possibly reject such central doctrines?

First, some believe Christ has already "returned," just in a purely spiritual sense with the coming of the Spirit on Pentecost (John 14:16–20; Matthew 28:20). Others believe Christ "returns" in a personal sense to each individual when they become a believer (Acts 9:3–5; Colossians 1:27). Still others might reinterpret the second coming of Christ as His coming to take each believer to heaven when they die (John 14:3). But from the New Testament onward, Christians have always looked forward to the physical return of Jesus Christ as Judge and King.

Besides presenting untrue teaching concerning the return of Christ, false teachers occasionally challenge the doctrine of the bodily resurrection. Some have said the resurrection is *only spiritual*, referring exclusively to the new birth and eternal life. According to this view, after a saved person dies, they'll immediately receive the full inheritance of salvation apart from a future resurrection of the body. But Christians have always embraced the hope of bodily resurrection at the return of Christ.

Besides these heretical views that can't be held by true Christians, a few erroneous views can also be found among a minority of otherwise orthodox believers. For example, according to the error called "soul sleep," the dead rest in an unconscious state until resurrection and judgment. Another marginal view, annihilationism, sometimes called "conditional immortality," teaches that the wicked will cease to exist rather than endure eternal, conscious punishment, that only those who are saved will have eternal life. And yet another view, universalism, asserts that all people will ultimately be saved, that no one will be eternally condemned.

Soul sleep, annihilationism, and universalism aren't classic Christian views, though they've all been believed by a small minority of Christians.

Error 2: "This-Is-That" Syndrome

Many new Christians cut their teeth on popular-level, end-times books, websites, or podcasts. And lots of those popular teachers and preachers make it sound like we're either definitely in the end times or at the brink. All of them allege that we could (and should) read the Bible alongside our newsfeeds because current events are fulfilling the prophecies of the Bible almost every day!

Some of the more nuanced treatments say things like, "Well, [so-and-so] *could* be the Antichrist," or "[This or that] technology *may* be used as the mark of the beast," or "These events in Europe [or the Middle East, or Russia, or China] *might* set the stage for the rise of the Antichrist." In short, these authors, preachers, pastors, and end-times enthusiasts seek signs in the news that point to the imminent end of the world.

Besides looking foolish, sign-seekers also do damage to people's faith and the cause of Christ. How so? When these "fulfillments" don't pan out, weak believers, unbelievers, skeptics, critics, and scoffers might conclude one of two things: One, that Christianity and the Bible are utterly untrustworthy, legitimately leading to the question *What else does the Bible teach that isn't really true?* Or two—and more likely—that the Bible is hopelessly ambiguous, because if careful interpreters can wrongly read so many different current events into it, then apparently it can be interpreted to say anything people want it to say.

In either case, nothing good has ever come from repeatedly failed sign-seeking. Rather, those who engage in this dangerous sport make authentic, Bible-believing Christians look bad, as they lump us all together, their listeners regarding us as misguided, brainless zealots.

Error 3: The "Dating Game"

For almost two thousand years, misguided Christians have been studying prophecies with a Bible in one hand and a calculator, abacus, or chalk slate in the other, trying to figure out exactly when Jesus will return. And every time they've been wrong. There's a good reason for this: The Bible teaches that whenever anyone tries to play the dating game, *they will lose.*

The New Testament uniformly teaches that nobody knows the hour, day, year, or even season of Christ's return (Matthew 24:36, 42; Mark 13:33, 37). The apostle Paul reiterates this teaching but also teaches that all believers of every generation must remain alert and ready for judgment to come at any moment (1 Thessalonians 5:1–2). Later the apostle Peter echoes this same thought: "The day of the Lord will come like a thief" (2 Peter 3:10), emphasizing the suddenness of the coming of Christ in judgment.

The teaching in the early church as well as in every generation since has been the same as that of Jesus and the apostles: We *do not know* (and we *cannot know*) the time of Christ's return. His second coming could have happened in the apostles' lifetime as well as it can in ours. Therefore, we must be ready for it every day and every moment.

Yet these facts of Christian faith don't stop those high-risk gamblers playing the end-times "dating game." Instead, they suggest that these warnings are for unbelievers. Or they believe God has progressively revealed to them secret knowledge long hidden in Scripture. Or they quote Amos 3:7 out of its specific Old Testament context ("For the Lord God does nothing without revealing his secret to his servants the prophets"), concluding that God would never suddenly judge the world without adequate warning. The truth is the New Testament *is* the prophetic warning that Jesus could come to judge the world at any moment. No additional warning from any date-setters is necessary.

All these people setting dates for Christ's return are simply wrong.

Error 4: End-Times Obsession

One of the greatest things about the advent of the digital music format is that those recordings don't skip. On the other hand, some of us have clear memories of scratched vinyl records playing the same words over and over and over and over again, like this on a Kenny Rogers recording of "The Gambler": "On a train bound for nowhere, I met up with a with a with a . . ." A gentle nudge of the record player might correct the problem, but at "We were both too tired to," the needle might very well jump back to "met up with a with a with a . . ."[13]

Similarly, some well-meaning Christians are obsessed with the subject of the end times. Like a broken record, it seems that every conversation with some people returns to a discussion of eschatology. Every book they read deals with prophecy. They attend conferences on Bible prophecy, devour podcasts on prophecy, and watch current events through the lens of prophecy. If you haven't already encountered such a person, you will. They exhibit a fascination with details, charts, end-times scenarios, and speculations—often in reaction against a perceived lack of interest or attention to eschatology among other Christians or churches.

Though it's unhealthy to avoid eschatology or give the book of Revelation a cold shoulder, it's also unhealthy to neglect all the other vital doctrines of the faith to devote oneself to Bible prophecy. The core convictions of the Christian faith center around the gospel concerning the person and work of Jesus Christ (Romans 1:1–4; 1 Corinthians 15:1–4). This gospel does, in fact, include the second coming of Christ as Judge (Romans 2:16), but we must never exaggerate one element of the gospel message. End-times obsession must be avoided in our own lives—and discouraged as we disciple others in a balanced Christian walk.

Lessons to Live

"How does all this affect how I should live my life today?"

This is a question a lot of Christians ask when they hear pastors or teachers or eschatology enthusiasts talk about details of the end times. And it's the right question. We can make all our end-times charts perfect down to the last arrow and Scripture reference, but if they don't lead us to live in pursuit of Christ and His kingdom, they're pointless.

This doesn't mean we ignore details of eschatology. We've seen that the Bible talks about them. But these details have to be put in their proper place, balanced with other vital areas of Christian belief and practice. We must never forget that God has given us a glimpse into the future for a reason: to change our minds, our hearts, our priorities, our attitudes, and our actions. The promises and prophecies of the future are intended to *transform us*, not merely *inform us*.

The following lessons must be put into practice—not on the eve of Christ's return, not in the perfect world that will accompany His reign, but *right now . . . today . . . and for the rest of our lives*.

278

Lesson 1: Wait eagerly for Christ's return with a life lived in holiness.

The main purpose of all Scripture is to equip believers for "every good work" (2 Timothy 3:16–17). This is no less true for prophetic Scripture. In fact, in one of the most intense apocalyptic passages, where the apostle Peter contrasts the destruction of this world and the establishment of the world to come, he turns our attention from the prophetic to the practical.

On the negative side, as we anticipate the certain judgment of this world, we ought to align ourselves with the side of holiness and godliness rather than the side of wickedness and faithlessness. On the positive side, as we contemplate the glorious blessings of the world to come, we ought to live pure and peaceful lives rather than dirty and disagreeable lives. When you read a passage of Scripture that refers to the future, or as you study themes of biblical prophecy, don't forget to ask yourself, *What sort of person should I be in light of this truth?*

Lesson 2: Invest in eternity, not in temporalities.

We live in a world obsessed with economics, finances, investments, dividends, profits, and interest. People hire debt counselors, financial advisors, and investment strategists to help them achieve

IN LIGHT OF COMING JUDGMENT	IN LIGHT OF COMING BLESSING
Since all these things are thus to be dissolved, what sort of people ought you to be in lives of holiness and godliness!	Therefore, beloved, since you are waiting for these, be diligent to be found by him without spot or blemish, and at peace.
(2 Peter 3:11)	(2 Peter 3:14)

financial stability and independence. In fact, for many people, economic priorities rather than spiritual or moral concerns drive their everyday decisions.

Yet the Bible emphasizes investment in the eternal rather than the temporal—in the heavenly rather than in the earthly. In a blunt rebuke that comes as a slap in the face for anyone obsessed with material possessions, Jesus corrects our common misappropriation of time, energy, and resources:

> Do not lay up for yourselves treasures on earth, where moth and rust destroy and where thieves break in and steal, but lay up for yourselves treasures in heaven, where neither moth nor rust destroys and where thieves do not break in and steal. For where your treasure is, there your heart will be also. (Matthew 6:19–21)

The next time you review your retirement plan or peruse your investment portfolio, weigh the amount of time, energy, and resources you spend on your present investments in eternal things. These might include:

- supporting your local church's ministry
- giving to alleviate suffering and injustice
- contributing to evangelism and discipleship
- donating to worldwide mission efforts
- spending some of your "off" time on a mission trip
- volunteering your time at a homeless shelter
- giving up your "me" time to share Christ's love with others
- asking your church leaders where they need you most and diving in!

Lesson 3: Focus on foundational facts, not on incidental opinions.

In Hebrews 10:23, the author encourages us to "hold fast the confession of our hope without wavering, for he who promised is faithful." This "confession" refers to the simple truths of the Christian faith related to the person and work of Jesus Christ as the center of the triune God's plan of creation and redemption. It's the "confession of the gospel of Christ" (2 Corinthians 9:13), which Paul describes as "of first importance" (1 Corinthians 15:3–4): "that Christ died for our sins in accordance with the Scriptures, that he was buried, that he was raised on the third day in accordance with the Scriptures." This gospel Paul proclaimed even included the reality of the coming day of judgment (Romans 2:16).

In 1 Timothy 3:16, Paul summarizes some elements of this confession of Christ's saving work of incarnation, proclamation, and ascension: "Great indeed, we confess, is the mystery of godliness: He was manifested in the flesh, vindicated by the Spirit, seen by angels, proclaimed among the nations, believed on in the world, taken up in glory."

In an earlier "trustworthy saying," Paul touches on some elements of eschatology that should form the foundation of our doctrine: "If we have died with him, we will also live with him; If we endure, we will also reign with him" (2 Timothy 2:11–12). This saying, perhaps associated with a charge given to new believers at baptism, emphasizes our belief in the resurrection and eternal reign with Christ.

It's so easy to get carried away by the enthralling details and interesting trivia about the end times—the when, where, and how. But if we're to keep the gospel itself central in our preaching and teaching, we must remain focused on those elements of eschatology that are part of the confession of faith—our future resurrection as a result of Christ's resurrection, our reign with Christ the King, and the reality of Christ's coming judgment.

Lesson 4: Don't be crushed by present suffering; be comforted by future splendor.

The loss of a loved one—a parent, a sibling, a child, or a friend—is a heart-wrenching and life-changing experience. The wound of suffering such a loss never fully heals. But even in the face of such anguish, believers in Christ can confess the following inconceivable truth: *Our present sufferings pale when compared to our future splendor*. We may not be able to fully understand this truth either intellectually or emotionally, but we can fully embrace it.

In Romans 8:18 Paul says, "I consider that the sufferings of this present time are not worth comparing with the glory that is to be revealed to us." When we read these words, we shouldn't imagine a balancing scale holding a glowing treasure chest on one side that outweighs a bin of putrid rubbish on the other. Paul doesn't say our future glory *outweighs* our present suffering; he says the two aren't even worth comparing! It's like comparing the sky with a speck of sand or an ocean with a drop of water. The difference between the two is so vast that they aren't even worthy to compare.

Now, the fact of an immeasurable future glory doesn't change the reality of the present suffering. It doesn't ease the pain, but it does promise a future without pain. It doesn't save our sick children from death, but it does promise to bring them back from the dead. It doesn't lessen the tears of sorrow in this life, but it does promise that God himself will wipe away the tears in the next. When we embrace by faith the assurance of the good things to come, the Lord God himself will give us a hope that helps us survive in our struggle with the real suffering of this world.

Equip yourself now with a concrete hope of future glory, so when the inevitable storms of suffering blow in, you won't be washed away in the flood. As Christ promised, "In the world you will have tribulation. But take heart; I have overcome the world" (John 16:33).

Lesson 5: Gather often to exhort one another to love and good works.

To the question "How can we apply the coming of Christ to our lives today?" very few would respond with, "Go to church often."

In fact, I've never heard a student in either church or seminary answer the question that way. But the Bible does!

In Hebrews, the author urges us to "consider how to stir up one another to love and good works, not neglecting to meet together, as is the habit of some, but encouraging one another" (Hebrews 10:24–25)—then to firm up this exhortation, adds "and all the more as you see the Day drawing near" (10:25). As we anticipate the coming of the day of judgment, we should respond by gathering together frequently, exhorting one another to live in holiness.

Also, as the church gathers for regular participation in the observance of the bread and cup as the body and blood of Christ, they "proclaim the Lord's death until he comes" (1 Corinthians 11:26). This observance represents our oneness in the body of Christ as we partake together of the "one bread" (1 Corinthians 10:17)—not only in memory of Christ and in celebration of His abiding presence but also in anticipation of His return.

Do you want to do something easy and practical in light of the return of Christ? It's as easy as joining together for worship, prayer, praise, accountability, and exhortation as the members of the body live together in anticipation of the coming day of judgment and salvation.

Snapshot of History

Throughout the Patristic (100–500), Medieval (500–1500), Protestant (1500–1700), and Modern (1700–Present) ages, the doctrine of the end times has seen many changes. The following chart highlights some of the most important changes.[14]

THE END TIMES THROUGH THE AGES

Patristic Period (100–500)	Medieval Period (500–1500)	Protestant Period (1500–1700)	Modern Period (1700–Present)
• Expectation of Christ's soon return (30–100)	• Fear of future judgments gives way to fear of fiery judgment in the afterlife	• Reformers label the Pope the Antichrist and the Roman Church his anti-Christian kingdom (1517–1700)	• Classic doctrines (return of Christ, bodily resurrection, and hell) rejected by liberal theologians (1700–2000)
• Persecution and martyrdom seen as signs of the end and Antichrist's coming (100–325)	• Roman Catholic doctrine of purgatory develops and dominates (600–1500)	• Reformers believe they're living in the last days	• New England Puritans advocate a postmillennial eschatology (1700–1800)
• Cessation of persecution (313)	• Rise of Islam (622–700) increases fear of Antichrist's coming	• Most maintain Augustine's amillennial views	• Premillennial theology has resurgence among mainline theologians (1700–1900)
• Premillennialism declines, amillennialism rises (150–500)	• Prevalence of disease, war, and heresy leads many to believe the end times had arrived	• Minority (and often radical) postmillennial views rejected	• Rise of dispensational premillennialism (1850–1900)
• Apologists defend a literal bodily resurrection (150–500)		• Doctrine of purgatory rejected	

CONCLUSION

Where Do You Go from Here?

Now what comes to mind when you hear the word *theology*?

Hopefully, this survey of the essentials of Christian theology has helped you past the all-too-common images of boredom, bickering, and browbeating often attached to "systematic theology." We've laid a firm foundation of passages to ponder, realities to remember, errors to avoid, and lessons to live. We've seen a brief overview of the basics of each area of theology as well as snapshots of historical developments.

With repeated words like *brief, short, surveys, essentials, snapshots, foundations, summaries, and basics,* obviously much, *much* more could be said. The truth is we've just laid the foundation of theology.

Maybe this introduction to Christian theology met your needs, satisfied your curiosity, or answered your questions. Great! Consider reading through the book again as a refresher, consulting it when questions come up, or recommending it to a friend who needs this kind of practical handbook of theology.

But maybe you're ready to build on the foundation established by this little book. You've learned the ABCs of theology, developed a bit of a vocabulary, and understood its grammar, and now you want to try your hand at something more advanced. Where do you go from here? Allow us to suggest a handful of resources for deeper study.

If *Essentials of Christian Theology* is a first step in your further exploration of theology, we want to help you in your journey.

Exploring Christian Theology, Volumes 1–3

The *Exploring Christian Theology* trilogy, on which this single volume is based, presents Christians with so much more: much-needed introductions, overviews, and reviews of key tenets of orthodox protestant theology without getting bogged down in the details or distracted by the debates. These three simple and succinct volumes provide accessible and convenient summaries of major themes of Christian doctrine, reorienting believers to the essential truths of the classic faith while providing vital guidebooks for those who want to grow in their understanding of theology. Think of these volumes as a way to advance from a grade-school to a high-school study of theology.

Each volume includes more extensive treatments of primary biblical texts, a history of each doctrine, a selection of important quotations from Christians throughout history related to the doctrine, relevant charts and graphs, practical implications, and suggestions for literature you might want to have in your own library. They also include glossaries of terms with clear definitions. The series is an ideal next step after reading *Essentials of Christian Theology,* and it's available in both paperback and ebook.

Other Systematic Theologies

If you're ready to dive into the "deep end," the following published systematic theologies—some older, some newer—provide good points of entry. We've also categorized them as "beginner," "intermediate," and "advanced." They approach theology from a variety of different theological traditions and denominations, so be aware of the perspectives you'll encounter as you read.

Beginner (appropriate for church or high-school contexts)

Berkhof, Louis. *A Summary of Christian Doctrine*. Eerdmans, 1938. A succinct, readable guide from the Reformed view.

Frame, John M. *Concise Systematic Theology*. John Hughes, ed. P&R, 2023. A concise summary of Frame's extensive theological books.

Grudem, Wayne A. *Christian Beliefs: Twenty Basics Every Christian Should Know*. Elliot Grudem, ed. Zondervan, 2022. A readable guide to twenty basic Christian beliefs with an emphasis on clarity and application.

Jones, Beth Felker. *Practicing Christian Doctrine: An Introduction to Thinking and Living Theologically*. 2nd ed. Baker Academic, 2023. An introductory text that articulates basic Christian doctrines with a focus on connecting Christian thought to everyday lives of faith.

Little, Paul E. *Know What You Believe*. 5th ed. InterVarsity, 2008. A classic handbook on the orthodox, protestant, evangelical faith's fundamentals, with laypeople in mind.

McGrath, Alister E. *Theology: The Basics*. 4th ed. Wiley Blackwell, 2018. An introduction to central beliefs, key debates, and leading thinkers of Christianity.

Ryrie, Charles C. *Basic Theology*. Moody, 1999. A comprehensive but popular handbook from a Calvinist, premillennial, dispensational perspective.

Thiessen, H. C. *Lectures in Systematic Theology*. Vernon Doersken, ed. Eerdmans, 1979. A comprehensive, popular-level presentation from a moderate Calvinist vantage point.

Intermediate (appropriate for college level)

Akin, Daniel L. ed. *A Theology for the Church*, rev. ed. B&H, 2014. An overview of Christian theology from a Baptist perspective.

Allison, Gregg R. *Historical Theology: An Introduction to Christian Doctrine*. Zondervan, 2011. A comprehensive overview of theological history, accessible for informed readers.

Chafer, Lewis Sperry. *Systematic Theology*. 8 vols. Dallas Seminary, 1947–48. The first complete theology from a dispensational perspective; there's also a revised, abridged edition. John F. Walvoord, ed. Victor, 1988.

Erickson, Millard J. *Introducing Christian Doctrine*. L. Arnold Hustad, ed. 2nd ed. Baker, 2001. An abridged version of his *Christian Theology*, accessible to the average reader.

Grenz, Stanley J. *Theology for the Community of God*. Eerdmans, 2000. From a broadly evangelical Baptist perspective, emphasizes the establishment of community as God's central plan in creation.

Grudem, Wayne. *Bible Doctrines: Essential Teachings of the Christian Faith*. Jeff Purswell, ed. Zondervan, 1999. An abridged version of his *Systematic Theology*, for the average reader.

Kendall, R. T. *Understanding Theology*. 3 vols. Christian Focus, 2001. An outline-based and rather comprehensive approach to systematic theology from a conservative evangelical in the UK.

McGrath, Alister E. *Christian Theology: An Introduction*. 5th ed. Blackwell, 2010. A masterful summary, balanced and well-organized, with a strong historical emphasis.

Swindoll, Charles R. and Roy B. Zuck. *Understanding Christian Theology*. Thomas Nelson Publishers, 2003. An accessible collection of doctrinal treatises from scholars with strong ties to Dallas Theological Seminary.

Advanced (appropriate for seminary level)

Bavinck, Herman. *Reformed Dogmatics*. 4 vols. John Bolt, ed., John Vriend, trans. Baker Academic, 2003–2008. An English translation of an influential Dutch Reformed theology originally published around 1900.

Beeke, Joel R. and Paul M. Smalley. *Reformed Systematic Theology*. 4 volumes. Crossway, 2019–2024. An extensive treatment of theology from a Reformed perspective.

Berkhof, Louis. *Systematic Theology*. Eerdmans, 1996. By an authoritative voice in the conservative Dutch Reformed tradition, this edition combines two volumes into one.

Bird, Michael. *Evangelical Theology: A Biblical and Systematic Introduction.* Zondervan, 2013. A thorough work by an evangelical New Testament scholar.

Bray, Gerald. *God Is Love: A Biblical and Systematic Theology.* Crossway, 2012. A conservative, Anglican, evangelical perspective.

Erickson, Millard J. *Christian Theology.* 3rd ed. Baker, 2013. A thorough and balanced conservative evangelical theology from a moderately Calvinist Baptist perspective.

Grenz, Stanley J. *Theology for the Community of God.* Reprint ed. Eerdmans, 2020. A baptistic and pietistic evangelical theology.

Grudem, Wayne. *Systematic Theology: An Introduction to Biblical Doctrine.* 2nd ed. Zondervan, 2020. Popular and thorough, from a uniquely Calvinistic, non-cessationist, historic premillennial vantage point; fair and inclusive of other legitimate perspectives.

Hodge, Charles. *Systematic Theology.* 3 vols. Scribner's, 1877. A thorough treatment from a nineteenth-century Calvinist at Princeton.

Horton, Michael. *The Christian Faith: A Systematic Theology for Pilgrims on the Way.* Zondervan, 2011. A thorough Reformed Covenant presentation.

Lewis, Gordon and Bruce A. Demarest. *Integrative Theology.* 3 vols. in 1. Zondervan, 1996. A thorough evangelical effort to integrate the perspectives of biblical, historical, systematic, apologetic, and practical theology.

MacArthur, John and Richard Mayhue. *Biblical Doctrine: A Systematic Summary of Bible Truth.* Crossway, 2017. A summary of biblical doctrine that undergirds MacArthur's preaching and teaching.

Oden, Thomas C. *Classic Christianity: A Systematic Theology.* HarperOne, 2009. This revised and condensed edition of his three-volume *Systematic Theology* seeks to provide the consensus of the faith, especially seen in the patristic period, as well as to appreciate the diversity of the orthodox protestant evangelical traditions.

Pieper, Francis. *Christian Dogmatics,* 4 vols. Concordia, 1950–1953. A conservative confessional Lutheran classic.

Reymond, Robert L. *A New Systematic Theology of the Christian Faith.* 2nd ed. Zondervan, 2020. A Reformed overview of systematic theology.

Shedd, W. G. T. *Dogmatic Theology*. 3rd ed. 3 vols. Scribner's, 1891. A nineteenth-century classic from a conservative Presbyterian perspective.

Strong, A. H. *Systematic Theology, A Compendium*. 3 vols. Judson, 1962. A thorough treatment from a Northern Baptist view.

Warfield, Benjamin B. *Biblical and Theological Studies*. P&R, 1952. A collection of essays on various topics by a conservative Presbyterian.

Wellum, Stephen J. *Systematic Theology*. B&H Academic, 2024–. A projected multi-volume systematic theology from a Baptist Reformed view.

Williams, J. Rodman. *Renewal Theology: Systematic Theology from a Charismatic Perspective*. One-volume edition. Zondervan, 1996. Systematic theology from a charismatic perspective.

Free Online Courses and Resources

If you're interested in a more formal, classroom-like learning experience, consider taking one of many free online courses through the Dallas Theological Seminary Global Institute (courses.dts.edu). For more than a hundred years, Dallas Seminary has been teaching theology from a conservative, Bible-believing perspective, having trained thousands of pastors and teachers serving worldwide.

The free online DTS Global Institute is designed to provide accessible, quality courses on a variety of topics relevant for Christian life and ministry. Topics include books of the Bible, theological issues, and current trends in doctrine and application.

Besides the free online courses, you can access a host of additional resources at voice.dts.edu, including sermons, podcasts, articles, book reviews, interviews, and more. You'll even find several resources from the editors of *Essentials of Christian Theology*.

ACKNOWLEDGMENTS

We want to recognize the helpful contributions of several individuals who were directly or indirectly involved in the *Essentials of Christian Theology* project. First, we express appreciation to our past and present colleagues in the Department of Theological Studies at Dallas Theological Seminary who were part of the original *Exploring Christian Theology* team and served as contributing writers and consulting editors for that project, which is the springboard for this single-volume work. These include John Adair, Douglas K. Blount, J. Lanier Burns, J. Scott Horrell, and Glenn R. Kreider. Though several of that team have moved on since the original trilogy, two of these, John Adair and Glenn Kreider, were able to join us as consulting editors for *Essentials of Christian Theology*. This book is incalculably better because of the voices and perspectives that helped us craft the final product.

We also want to acknowledge some of our own teachers who influenced us in so many ways in our formative years—academically, spiritually, professionally, and personally. Charles C. Ryrie taught us that theology didn't need to be so complicated; Craig A. Blaising made us think and rethink how to do what we do; D. Jeffrey Bingham urged excellence in scholarship and fortitude in conviction; John D. Hannah showed us that history, too, can be fun.

On the technical side of things, we want to thank, once again, Steve Laube, who ably handles the professional side of projects like this; Tim Peterson, formerly of Bethany House, for having a bigger vision for the original trilogy from the beginning; Andy McGuire, for giving us a chance to revisit this fertile field to cultivate something new; Hannah Ahlfield for shepherding this project efficiently through The Process; and Jean Bloom, of Bloom in Words Editorial Services, for her attention to detail and obvious love for the art of wordsmithing. Of course, countless editors, proofreaders, artists, and designers at Bethany House Publishers labored behind the scenes to take our rough gem and make it shine. Thank you!

Finally, the general editors of this volume wish to thank their families for their years of constant support and encouragement:

I (Mike) want to thank my loving wife, Stephanie, and my now-adult children, Sophie, Lucas, and Nathan, who journey joyfully with me through this life of faith. You are all gifts from God.

I (Nathan) would like to express my gratitude to Janice. Your *joie de vivre* has made our life journey better than I could ever have imagined! And to my children: Watching you fly inspires me!

Nathan D. Holsteen
Michael J. Svigel
General Editors

NOTES

Introduction

1. See Glenn R. Kreider and Michael J. Svigel, *A Practical Primer on Theological Method: Table Manners for Discussing God, His Works, and His Ways* (Zondervan, 2019), 25–26.

Prelude

1. For a classic discussion of ancient hero myths, see Joseph Campbell, *The Hero with a Thousand Faces*, 3rd rev. ed. (New World Library, 2008).

2. See, for example, James Bonnet, *Stealing Fire from the Gods: The Complete Guide to Story for Writers and Filmmakers*, 2nd ed. (Michael Wiese Productions, 2006) and Christopher Vogler, *The Writer's Journey: Mythic Structure for Writers,* 3rd ed. (Michael Wiese Productions, 2007).

Chapter 1 A Firm Foundation—God's Revealed Truth

1. "Clement of Rome, First Epistle of Clement to the Corinthians," 45.2–3, in Michael W. Holmes, ed., *The Apostolic Fathers: Greek Texts and English Translations*, 3rd ed. (Baker Academic, 2007), 105.

2. John Calvin, "Commentary on Second Timothy 3:16–17," in Joseph Haroutunian and Louise Pettibone Smith, eds. and trans., *Calvin: Commentaries*, The Library of Christian Classics (Westminster Press, 1958), 85.

3. Charles C. Ryrie, *Basic Theology: A Popular Systematic Guide to Understanding Biblical Truth* (Moody, 1999), 81.

4. Paul D. Feinberg, under "Bible, Inerrancy and Infallibility of . . ." in Walter A. Elwell, ed., *Evangelical Dictionary of Theology*, 2d ed. (Baker Academic, 2001), 156.

5. See the original articulation and full discussion in Paul D. Feinberg, "The Meaning of Inerrancy," in Norman L. Geisler, ed., *Inerrancy* (Zondervan, 1980), 298–302.

6. Carl F. H. Henry, under "Bible, Inspiration of" in Walter A. Elwell, ed., *Evangelical Dictionary of Theology*, 2d ed. (Baker Academic, 2001), 160.

7. See Michael Svigel and John Adair, *Urban Legends of Church History: 40 Common Misconceptions* (B&H Academic, 2020), 237–42.

8. Bernard, Sermon 84 on the Song of Songs 7 in Ray C. Petry, ed., *Late Medieval Mysticism*, The Library of Christian Classics (Westminster John Knox, 1957), 78.

9. Doctrinal Statement, Article I, "The Scriptures," Dallas Theological Seminary, https://www.dts.edu/about/doctrinal-statement/. Accessed March 17, 2025.

10. Frederick W. Robertson, *Sermons Preached at Trinity Chapel, Brighton*, vol. 1 (Ticker & Fields, 1857), 335.

11. For a more detailed explanation of "Holy Scripture in Retrospect," see Nathan D. Holsteen and Michael J. Svigel, eds., *Exploring Christian Theology*, vol. 1, *Revelation, Scripture, and the Triune God* (Bethany House, 2014), 57–71.

Chapter 2 God in Three Persons—The Trinity: Father, Son, and Holy Spirit

1. *Creed of Constantinople* (NPNF 2.14:163).

2. Benjamin B. Warfield, "Trinity," in *The International Standard Bible Encyclopedia*, vol. 5, James Orr, ed. (Eerdmans, 1930), 3,012.

3. Thomas Aquinas, Summa Contra Gentiles 4.26 in Joseph Rickaby, ed. and trans., *Of God and His Creatures: An Annotated Translation (with Some Abridgement) of the Summa Contra Gentiles of Saint Thomas Aquinas* (Burns & Oates, 1905), 358.

4. You can explore each of these more deeply in Nathan D. Holsteen and Michael J. Svigel, eds., *Exploring Christian Theology*, vol. 1, *Revelation, Scripture, and the Triune God* (Bethany House, 2014), 145–53.

5. Wording from International Consultation on English Texts (ICET, 1969), adaptation by Thomas C. Oden, gen. ed., *Ancient Christian Doctrine*, 5 vols. (InterVarsity Press, 2009), 1. xviii.

6. The Westminster Confession of Faith 2.1, in Philip Schaff, *Creeds of Christendom*, vol. 3, *The Evangelical Protestant Creeds*, 4th enl. ed. (Baker, 1977), 607–608.

7. Joseph Smith, *Teachings of the Prophet Joseph Smith*, 4th ed., Joseph Fielding Smith, ed. (Deseret News Press, 1943), 370.

8. W. J. Hollenweger, *The Pentecostals: The Charismatic Movement in the Churches* (Augsburg, 1972), 31–32.

9. David K. Bernard, *Oneness and the Trinity, A.D. 100–300: The Doctrine of God in Ancient Christian Writings* (Word Aflame Press, 1991), 66, 127–28, 131.

10. For a more detailed explanation of "The Father, Son, and Holy Spirit in Retrospect," see Nathan D. Holsteen and Michael J. Svigel, eds., *Exploring Christian Theology*, vol. 1, *Revelation, Scripture, and the Triune God* (Bethany House, 2014), 168–85.

Chapter 3 Fashioned and Fallen—Humanity and Sin

1. Theophilus, *To Autolycus* 2.17 (*ANF* 2:101).

2. *The New Hampshire Baptist Confession* 3 in Philip Schaff, ed., *The Creeds of Christendom*, vol. 3, 4th ed. (Harper & Row, 1877), 743.

3. See Michael J. Behe, "Scientific Orthodoxies," *First Things*, December 1, 2005, https://www.firstthings.com/article/2005/12/scientific-orthodoxies. Accessed January 28, 2014 and March 17, 2025.

4. *The Augsburg Confession*, 2 in Philip Schaff, ed., *The Creeds of Christendom*, vol. 3, 4th ed. (New York: Harper & Row, 1877), 8.

5. Thomas à Kempis, *The Imitation of Christ*, 5, Aloysius Croft and Harold Bolton, trans. (Bruce, 1940), 195–196.

6. A helpful survey and critique of *imago dei* theories is found in Marc Cortez, *Theological Anthropology: A Guide for the Perplexed* (T & T Clark, 2010), 14–40.

7. Charles C. Ryrie, *Basic Theology: A Popular Systematic Guide to Understanding Biblical Truth* (Moody, 1999), 252.

8. Anyone over forty knows what these "dums" signify. If you're under forty, see https://www.youtube.com/watch?v=nx5GwULPU90.

9. Actually, Joe Friday never said "Just the facts, ma'am" until Dan Aykroyd played the character in a 1987 tongue-in-cheek film version of *Dragnet*.

10. James W. Sire, *Naming the Elephant: Worldview as a Concept* (InterVarsity, 2004), 122.

11. Thomas C. Oden, *Classic Christianity: A Systematic Theology* (HarperOne, 2009), 150.

12. See Antony Flew, *There Is a God: How the World's Most Notorious Atheist Changed His Mind* (HarperOne, 2007).

13. Flew, *There Is a God*, xix. Roy Abraham Varghese (Flew's coauthor) cites Richard Dawkins, *What We Believe but Cannot Prove*, John Brockman, ed. (Pocket Books, 2005), 9.

14. Thomas A. Harris, *I'm OK—You're OK* (Harper and Row, 1969).

15. Dorothy L. Sayers, "The Image of God," in *Letters to a Diminished Church: Passionate Arguments for the Relevance of Christian Doctrine* (Thomas Nelson, 2004), 25.

16. For a more detailed explanation of "Humanity and Sin in Retrospect," see Nathan D. Holsteen and Michael J. Svigel, eds., *Exploring Christian Theology*, vol. 2, *Creation, Fall, and Salvation* (Bethany House, 2015), 51–67.

Chapter 4 Saved by Grace Through Faith—God's Rescue of Sinners

1. Clement of Rome, *1 Clement* 32 (*ANF* 1:13).

2. Martin Luther, *Lectures on Romans*, Wilhelm Pauck, ed., Library of Christian Classics (Westminster, 1961), 18.

3. Van. Mahasi Sayadaw, "The Theory of Karma," Buddhanet, https://www.buddhanet.net/e-learning/karma/. Accessed June 17, 2014, and March 17, 2025. Karma, "the law of moral causation," is "a fundamental doctrine in Buddhism" and other Asian religions. It's being used here not in the technical sense but as shorthand for the view of causation.

4. John of Damascus, *An Exact Exposition of the Orthodox Faith* 27 (NPNF 2.9:72).

5. To say this does not deny God's concern for His glory. God's glory is the ultimate goal of His work of redemption. See Charles C. Ryrie, *Dispensationalism*, revised and expanded edition (Moody, 2007), 22.

6. Doctrinal Statement, Article IV, "Humanity, Created and Fallen," Dallas Theological Seminary, https://www.dts.edu/about/doctrinal-statement/. Accessed June 18, 2014, and March 17, 2025.

7. Herman Bavinck, *Sin and Salvation in Christ* in *Reformed Dogmatics*, ed. John Bolt, trans. John Vriend (Baker Academic, 2006), 3:376–377.

8. Jerram Barrs, *Echoes of Eden: Reflections on Christianity, Literature, and the Arts* (Crossway, 2013).

9. Philip Yancey, *Rumors of Another World: What on Earth Are We Missing?* (Zondervan, 2003), 29.

10. John Newton, "Amazing Grace," 1779. Public domain.

11. Charles C. Ryrie, *Basic Theology: A Popular Systematic Guide to Understanding Biblical Truth* (Victor Books, 1986), 277.

12. Ryrie, *Basic Theology*, 277.

13. Ryrie, *Basic Theology*, 277.

14. Ray Pritchard, *In the Shadow of the Cross: The Deeper Meaning of Calvary* (B&H Publishers, 2001).

15. "The Nicene Creed," http://www.creeds.net/ancient/nicene.htm. Accessed June 17, 2014, and March 18, 2025.

16. Harper G. Smyth, "Make Me a Channel of Blessing," 1903. Public domain.

17. Doctrinal Statement, Article IV, "Humanity, Created and Fallen," Dallas Theological Seminary, https://www.dts.edu/about/doctrinal-statement/. Accessed June 18, 2014, and March 17, 2025.

18. John Calvin, *Institutes of the Christian Religion*, 3.2.7, Henry Beveridge, ed. and trans. (Eerdmans, 1989).

19. Calvin, *Institutes of the Christian Religion*, 3.2.17.

20. Calvin, *Institutes of the Christian Religion*, 3.2.18.

21. Derek Webb, *She Must and Shall Go Free*, INO Records, 2003. Liner notes.

22. Robert Robinson, "Come, Thou Fount of Every Blessing," 1758. Public domain.

23. For a more detailed explanation of "Salvation in Retrospect," see Nathan D. Holsteen and Michael J. Svigel, eds., *Exploring Christian Theology,* vol. 2, *Creation, Fall, and Salvation* (Bethany House, 2015), 168–86.

Chapter 5 The Communion of Saints—The Church as the Growing Family of God

1. Theophilus of Antioch, *To Autolocus* 2.14 (*ANF* 2:100).

2. John Calvin, *Institutes of the Christian Religion*, 4.1.9.

3. Wim Balke, "Calvin and the Anabaptists," trans. Henry J. Baron, in *The Calvin Handbook,* ed. Herman J. Selderhuis (Eerdmans, 2009), 151.

4. John Wycliffe, *The Church and Her Members*, 2.

5. Thomas Oden, *Systematic Theology*, vol. 3, "Life in the Spirit" (HarperCollins, 1992), 303.

6. R. B. Kuiper, *The Glorious Body of Christ* (Eerdmans, 1966), 21–22.

7. D. Douglas Bannerman, *The Scripture Doctrine of the Church* (Edinburgh: T&T Clark, 1887), 5.

8. Millard Erickson, *Christian Theology* (Baker, 1983), 1047–49.

9. Dr. Seuss, *The Cat in the Hat* (Random House, 1957).

10. Compare Anthony A. Hoekema, "The Reformed Perspective" in *Five Views on Sanctification,* Melvin Dieter, ed. (Zondervan, 1987), 61.

11. See C. E. B. Cranfield, *A Critical and Exegetical Commentary on the Epistle to the Romans,* vol. 1, *Introduction and Commentary on Romans I–VIII,* The International Critical Commentary on the Holy Scriptures of the Old and New Testaments, J. A. Emerton et al. eds., (T&T Clark, 1975), 347.

12. For a representative defense of this view, see C. K. Barrett, *A Commentary on the Epistle to the Romans,* Black's New Testament Commentaries (Black, 1957), 146–48.

13. For a more complete list of views, see Cranfield, *A Critical and Exegetical Commentary on the Epistle to the Romans*, 2:344.

14. Dr. Seuss, *The Sneetches and Other Stories* (Random House, 1961).

15. Hoekema, "The Reformed Perspective" in *Five Views on Sanctification*, 70.

16. "Grow, Grow, Grow" is a song from the Livin' LOUD for You CD and DVD, lyrics and music by Jana Alayra, copyright 2014. Produced by Ron Alayra. Film editing by Ken Robertson. www.youtube.com/watch?v=HqmwCWUiI8A.

17. Alfred, Lord Tennyson, "The Charge of the Light Brigade," Poetry Foundation, https://www.poetryfoundation.org/poems/45319/the-charge-of-the-light -brigade. Public domain.

18. Doctrinal Statement, Article XIII, "The Church, A Unity of Believers," Dallas Theological Seminary, https://www.dts.edu/about/doctrinal-statement/. Accessed December 20, 2012, and March 17, 2025.

19. For a more detailed explanation of "The Church and the Christian Life in Retrospect," see Nathan D. Holsteen and Michael J. Svigel, eds., *Exploring Christian Theology*, vol. 3, *The Church, Spiritual Growth, and the End Times* (Bethany House, 2014), 55–76.

Chapter 6 The World to Come—Future Things and Eternal Hope

1. Irenaeus of Lyons, *Against Heresies* 5.36.1 (*ANF* 1:566).

2. Charles Haddon Spurgeon, *According to Promise: The Lord's Method of Dealing with His Chosen People* (Funk & Wagnalls, 1887), 66–67.

3. William Shakespeare, *Measure for Measure*, Act III, Scene 1.

4. John of Damascus, *An Exact Exposition of the Orthodox Faith* 4.27 (*NPNF* 2.9:101).

5. *Augsburg Confession of Faith* 17 in Philip Schaff, ed., *The Creeds of Christendom*, vol. 3, *The Evangelical Protestant Creeds*, 4th ed. (New York: Harper & Row, 1877), 17.

6. F. F. Bruce, *1 & 2 Corinthians*, The New Century Bible Commentary (Eerdmans, 1971), 152.

7. H. W. Wolff, *Joel and Amos,* Hermeneia (Fortress, 1977), 66; Duane A. Garrett, Vol. 19A, *Hosea, Joel*, The New American Commentary (Broadman & Holman Publishers, 1997).

8. Keith A. Mathison, *Postmillennialism: An Eschatology of Hope* (P&R Publishing, 1999), 97–98.

9. Mathison, *Postmillennialism*, 93–94.

10. Irenaeus of Lyons, *Against Heresies*, 5.25.2.

11. Wayne Grudem, *Bible Doctrine: Essential Teachings of the Christian Faith*, First Edition, Jeff Purswell ed. (Zondervan, 1999), 467.

12. Isaac Watts, "Joy to the World," 1878. Public domain.

13. "The Gambler," written by Don Schlitz, copyright Lyrics © Sony/ATV Music Publishing.

14. For a more detailed explanation of "The End Times in Retrospect," see Nathan D. Holsteen and Michael J. Svigel, eds., *Exploring Christian Theology*, vol. 3, *The Church, Spiritual Growth, and the End Times* (Bethany House, 2014), 180–91.

MICHAEL J. SVIGEL (ThM, PhD) is Chair and Professor of Theological Studies at Dallas Theological Seminary. He has written numerous popular-level Bible study guides, articles, and papers, and is the author of *RetroChristianity: Reclaiming the Forgotten Faith* (Crossway, 2012). He is also the coeditor (with Nathan D. Holsteen) of the *Exploring Christian Theology* trilogy (Bethany House, 2014–2015) and coauthor (with Glenn Kreider) of *A Practical Primer on Theological Method* (2019) and *Urban Legends of Church History* (B&H Academic, 2020).

Connect with Michael:

- FathersOnTheFuture.com
- @svigel
- @michaelsvigel
- @svigel
- @svigel.bsky.social

NATHAN D. HOLSTEEN (ThM, Dallas Theological Seminary; PhD, University of Aberdeen) has taught full time at Dallas Theological Seminary and Southwestern Baptist Theological Seminary, and has served as Adjunct Professor at Criswell College and Dallas Theological Seminary. Besides being co-editor (with Michael J. Svigel) of the *Exploring Christian Theology* trilogy (Bethany House, 2014–2015), he has contributed chapters to edited works, including *Eschatology: Biblical, Historical, and Practical Approaches* (Kregel Academic, 2016) and *Evidence for the Rapture* (Moody, 2015).

Connect with Nathan:

✖ @nholsteen